Essays and Studies 2012

Series Editor: Elaine Treharne

The English Association

The objects of the English Association are to promote the knowledge and appreciation of the English language and its literature, and to foster good practice in its teaching and learning at all levels.

The Association pursues these aims by creating opportunities of co-operation among all those interested in English; by furthering the recognition of English as essential in education; by discussing methods of English teaching; by holding lectures, conferences, and other meetings; by publishing journals, books, and leaflets; and by forming local branches.

Publications

The Year's Work in English Studies. An annual bibliography. Published by Blackwell.

The Year's Work in Critical and Cultural Theory. An annual bibliography. Published by Blackwell.

Essays and Studies. An annual volume of essays by various scholars assembled by the collector covering usually a wide range of subjects and authors from the medieval to the modern. Published by D.S. Brewer.

English. A journal of the Association, English is published three times a year by the Association.

The Use of English. A journal of the Association, The Use of English is published three times a year by the Association.

Newsletter. A *Newsletter* is published three times a year giving information about forthcoming publications, conferences, and other matters of interest.

Benefits of Membership

Institutional Membership

Full members receive copies of *The Year's Work in English Studies*, *Essays and Studies*, *English* (3 issues) and three *Newsletters*.

Ordinary Membership covers *English* (3 issues) and three *Newsletters*.

Schools Membership includes copies of each issue of *English* and *The Use of English*, one copy of *Essays and Studies*, three *Newsletters*, and preferential booking and rates for various conferences held by the Association.

Individual Membership

Individuals take out Basic Membership, which entitles them to buy all regular publications of the English Association at a discounted price, and attend Association gatherings.

For further details write to The Secretary, The English Association, The University of Leicester, University Road, Leicester, LE1 7RH.

Essays and Studies 2012

Dickens and Modernity

Edited by
Juliet John

for the English Association

D. S. BREWER

ESSAYS AND STUDIES 2012
IS VOLUME SIXTY-FIVE IN THE NEW SERIES
OF ESSAYS AND STUDIES COLLECTED ON BEHALF OF
THE ENGLISH ASSOCIATION
ISSN 0071-1357

First published 2012
D. S. Brewer, Cambridge

D. S. Brewer is an imprint of Boydell & Brewer Ltd
PO Box 9, Woodbridge, Suffolk IP12 3DF, UK
and of Boydell & Brewer Inc.
668 Mt Hope Avenue, Rochester, NY 14620–2731 USA
website: www.boydellandbrewer.com

ISBN 978-1-84384-326-9

A CIP catalogue record for this book is available
from the British Library

The publisher has no responsibility for the continued existence or accuracy of
URLs for external or third-party internet websites referred to in this book, and
does not guarantee that any content on such websites is, or will remain, accurate
or appropriate

Papers used by Boydell & Brewer Ltd are natural, recyclable products
made from wood grown in sustainable forests

MIX
Paper from
responsible sources
FSC
www.fsc.org   FSC® C013604

Typeset by Word and Page, Chester, UK

Printed and bound by
CPI Group (UK) Ltd, Croydon, CR0 4YY

Contents

Illustrations

Acknowledgements

I am grateful to Elaine Treharne for inviting me to edit this volume, to my husband Calum and my children Iona, Hamish and Seren, for tolerating the time it took up in the run-up to Christmas 2011, and to Holly Furneaux, for commenting on a draft of my essay. My own contributions to this book are published here for the first time but at times revisit textual examples used in my book *Dickens and Mass Culture* (2010) in order to expand, evolve and reframe earlier analyses.

Web addresses referred to in the volume were current as of April 2012.

Notes on the Contributors

Jay Clayton, William R. Kenan Jr Professor of English at Vanderbilt University, is author of *Charles Dickens in Cyberspace: The Afterlife of the Nineteenth Century in Postmodern Culture* (2003) and other books on nineteenth-century literature.

John Drew is Professor of English Literature at the University of Buckingham, where he has taught since 1998. His publications include extensive work on the *Oxford Reader's Companion to Dickens* (1999), the co-editing (with Michael Slater) of volume 4 of the *Dent Uniform Edition of Dickens' Journalism* (2000), and an edition of Oscar Wilde's *The Picture of Dorian Gray* (2001). He is author of the first full-length study of Dickens as a journalist, *Dickens the Journalist* (2003), and of numerous articles and reviews on aspects of Victorian periodical culture. He is currently directing the *Dickens Journals Online* project, due to be launched in 2012, which is based around an open-access digital edition of *Household Words* and *All the Year Round*, the phenomenally popular Victorian magazines edited by Dickens between 1850 and 1870. The work has been funded in large measure by the Leverhulme Trust, and also involves a large-scale public/community collaboration.

Holly Furneaux is a Reader in Victorian Literature at the University of Leicester. She is author of *Queer Dickens: Erotics, Families, Masculinities* (2009), editor of John Forster's *Life of Charles Dickens* (2011), and, with Professor Sally Ledger, *Dickens in Context* (2011). She has also co-edited special editions of the journals *19: Interdisciplinary Studies in the Long Nineteenth Century* and *Critical Survey*, and has published articles about various aspects of Victorian literature and culture and the histories of sexuality and gender. Her current research is focused on Victorian military men of feeling.

Michael Hollington is a retired professor of English living in Italy. He has taught in every continent, most particularly in Britain, France and Australia. He was Professor of English at the University of New South Wales until 2002 and at the University of Toulouse-Le Mirail until 2007. He is still active as a researcher and speaker at various universities, on Dickens and other subjects. He has published several books on Dickens, as well as on Katherine Mansfield and Gunter Grass, and is currently editing the two-volume *Reception of Dickens in Europe* for Continuum Press.

Juliet John holds the Hildred Carlile Chair of English at Royal Holloway College, University of London. She has published widely on Victorian literature and culture and is author of *Dickens's Villains: Melodrama, Character, Popular Culture* (2001; paperback 2002) and *Dickens and Mass Culture* (2010). She is editor-in-chief of *Oxford Bibliographies: Victorian Literature*.

Kim Edwards Keates is a doctoral candidate at the University of Liverpool, completing research on the representation of inter-female intimacy in the writings of Charles Dickens. She has delivered papers on Dickens in Britain, Europe and the United States and is currently working on a co-edited essay collection on the economies of desire in the literature and culture of the *fin de siècle*. She has taught undergraduates at the University of Liverpool and currently teaches at Liverpool John Moores University.

Michaela Mahlberg is Associate Professor in English Language and Applied Linguistics at the University of Nottingham, where she is also the Director of the Centre for Research in Applied Linguistics (CRAL). She is the editor of the *International Journal of Corpus Linguistics* (John Benjamins), and co-editor of the series Corpus and Discourse (Continuum).

Joss Marsh is an archival scholar whose work is driven by two broad interests – the intersections of 'high' and 'popular' culture (especially film), and the history of the imagination. Her most recent book was *Word Crimes: Blasphemy, Culture, and Literature in 19th-Century England* (1998); she has begun work on a related project, *Heretica: Impossible Women, Impious Lives, 1819–1898*. She is currently also involved in a book project about Dickens, cinema and all the popular culture that intervened between, including Victorian melodrama, the late Victorian theatrical star system, celebrity photography, Victorian virtual tourism, and the relationship between performativity and anti-Semitism in Britain. She has lectured and published most recently on Victorian film, Chaplin, the imperial reprocessing of Sydney Carton, and the filming of Murnau's 1922 Nosferatu. With her partner, David Francis, she has also recently both lectured on the Victorian magic lantern and early cinema and recreated actual lantern performances at a range of archives and venues, including the Cinemateca Portuguesa, the Dickens Universe and the Academy of Motion Pictures.

Dominic Rainsford is Professor of Literatures in English at Aarhus University. His main research interests lie in the relationships between literature and moral philosophy. He has published on Dickens in journals such as *Victorian Newsletter* and *Dickens Quarterly*, in various edited collections, and in his books *Authorship, Ethics and the Reader: Blake, Dickens, Joyce* (1997) and *Literature, Identity and the English Channel* (2002). His current projects include several more essays on Dickens, *Studying Literature in English* (forthcoming from Routledge) and a book on literature, ethics and quantification.

Florian Schweizer is Director of the Charles Dickens Museum in London and Project Director of the international Dickens 2012 campaign. His research focuses on authorship and the status of writers in the nineteenth century, the history of the book and the concept of material culture and celebrity. He has curated numerous exhibitions since 2002 and is responsible for the £3.2m redevelopment of the Charles Dickens Museum for the bicentenary. He has lectured and published widely on Dickens and the heritage industry and is currently engaged in leading a number of innovative technology projects such as smartphone apps and social media applications.

Carrie Sickmann is a doctoral candidate and associate instructor at Indiana University. Her dissertation project, 'Continual Reading: Modern Adaptations and Victorian Reading Practices', examines the similarities between Victorian reading practices and current methods of consuming Victorian novels via film, television, theatre and neo-Victorian novels. Recently, she has presented her work on J. M. Barrie's *Peter Pan* at the Victorian Futures conference hosted by the Dickens Project and her study of continuations of *The Mystery of Edwin Drood* at the North American Victorian Studies Association conference.

For my mother, Jackie John, and my daughter, Seren Forsyth, with love

Introduction

ON THE CENTENARY in 1970 of Dickens's death, his image appeared on the postage stamps of thirteen British Commonwealth countries. For over a decade (1992–2003), Dickens was the face of the British ten-pound note and the image of a cricket match at Dingley Dell from *The Pickwick Papers* formed its background. As I write this Introduction in 2011 on the eve of the bicentenary of Dickens's birth, new Dickens adaptations, biographies, press stories, events, conferences and exhibitions are already announcing themselves all over the world. Dickens's continued cultural prominence and the 'brand recognition' achieved by his image and images seem to suggest that his vision has a certain consonance in the post-Victorian world. But how modern was Dickens? This question gives rise to no simple answer but to a myriad of paradoxes and contradictions. To the general public, Dickens has come to represent all that is not modern; he has become synonymous with a Victorian age defined in opposition to the present. It is notable that though Dickens is the most adapted author of all time for the screen, whereas it is a familiar experience to view 'modern' Shakespeare adaptations, there are relatively few Dickens adaptations that eschew costume for contemporary dress and settings; significantly, those that do so are often set and directed abroad.[1] The viewing public likes to fix Dickens in a particular vision of a Victorian period which it associates with 'the past' as well as with a distinctive brand of Englishness or Britishness. The decision of the organisers of the Dickens bicentenary to promote an image of a young, unbearded Dickens instead of the more familiar, 'Victorian' image of the author betrays, as the bicentenary Director Florian Schweizer argues in this volume, a conscious determination to revive associations between Dickens, youth

---

[1]   For example, *Twisted* (diected by Donsky 1996), *Twist* (diected by Tierney 2003) and *Boy Called Twist* (directed by Greene, 2004), set in New York, Toronto and Cape Town respectively. See p. 7 below for Akbar (2011a) on the reluctance to modernise Dickens among adapters.

and modernity. The bicentenary indeed foregrounds the central paradox underlying Dickens's cultural status: in the year of the Olympics and Queen Elizabeth's diamond jubilee, why is Dickens popular enough to merit a large-scale, global programme of events and celebrations if he has come to symbolise modernity's antithesis?

The answer is partly, of course, because the heritage industry thrives on marketing the past as past, as 'Other', and as salve to the complex problems of the present. Dominic Rainsford's essay, 'Out of Place: *David Copperfield*'s Irresolvable Geographies', and Regenia Gagnier's Global Circulation project both attest to Dickens's status as a global cultural icon and recent critical interest in it.[2] If the evidence of the tourist industry is anything to go by, 'fans' of Dickens from beyond the British Isles do not value Dickens primarily for his modernity. Visitors to the Charles Dickens Museum in London, which is Dickens's former Doughty Street home, come from all over the globe, though Americans comprise the largest constituency of visitors. The Museum does some of its best business at Christmas time and indeed on Christmas Day, American visitors in particular wanting to experience a 'genuine' Dickensian, English Christmas in Dickens's former home. The sense of the home as a religious shrine is made explicit in some of the comments in the Museum's visitors' book: one tourist from Illinois claimed that the visit had been 'worth the 3,500 mile pilgrimage' (12 October 2005), the word 'pilgrimage' making explicit the almost spiritual investment in this view of Dickens and the past. The idea of Dickens as a saintly reformer able to offer succour in the face of even the most extreme of modern disasters is strikingly articulated by a couple from New Orleans, Louisiana, who commented in the wake of the devastating hurricane that destroyed their city: 'We could use Dickens in post-Katrina relief efforts' (23 December 2005). Local visitors are not immune to this tendency of cultural tourists to sublimate and 'Other' the past: a London visitor commented, 'charmingly old-fashioned museum. Very pleased to note that there is little in the way of modern touches' (27 November 2005).

---

[2]   <http://literature-compass.com/global-circulation-project/>. 'Global Dickens' is a pilot for the general project, which describes itself as 'a global map and dialogue on how key Anglophone works, authors, genres, and literary movements have been translated, received, imitated/mimicked, adapted, or syncretised outside Britain, Europe, and North America, and, conversely, how key works from outside these areas have been translated, received, imitated/mimicked, adapted, or syncretised within Anglophone literary traditions'.

The truth is, however, that Dickens and Shakespeare would not be regularly cited as the most popular authors in the English language if they functioned only as antidote to the ills of the present. The ability of both authors to transcend their historical moment and geographical place, to become cultural icons, is testimony to their attunement to that state of uncertainty and instability we associate with the nebulous but resonant concept of modernity. Literary criticism of Dickens has recognised his modernity for quite some time, though inevitably, attempts to define its nature are as mobile as the topic itself. There is some sense of agreement about the literary history of criticism of the 'modern' Dickens, however. Philip Collins argued persuasively in 1970 that 'the modern reinterpretation of Dickens [. . .] dates from around 1940-1' (153), positioning critics of the 'macabre' and/or more complex Dickens, Edmund Wilson, Humphrey House and George Orwell, as its originators. The 1940s was also the decade that saw Sergei Eisenstein identify Dickens as the most influential 'father' of film; though the screen has undoubtedly functioned as the most potent means by which Dickens has been able to permeate the post-Victorian cultural consciousness, Eisenstein ironically used Dickens to argue that 'our cinema is not entirely without an ancestry and a pedigree, a past and traditions, or a rich cultural heritage from other epochs' (222). Eisenstein's association between Dickens and 'rich cultural heritage' ran counter to the ambivalence in literary criticism at this time about Dickens, influenced no doubt by the modernist distaste for Dickens and by F. R. Leavis's 1948 omission of him from his 'great tradition' of English novelists on the grounds that he was more 'great entertainer' than serious novelist (Leavis 29). Yet even Leavis's ambivalence about Dickens was in no small part a response to his modernity, to his associations and indeed engagement with the new mass market for culture which emerged during the Victorian period. It is perhaps for this reason that the Leavis who excluded Dickens from *The Great Tradition* was also able to claim: 'if any one writer can be said to have created the modern novel, it is Dickens' (quoted by Gardiner 174).[3] In recent years, John Gardiner has reconfirmed Collins's sense that 'The more complex Dickens that we know today can

---

[3]   Gardiner quotes from a 1983 version of *The Great Tradition* (1948; Harmondsworth: [Penguin], 1983), p. 30, adding, 'I have not been able to trace when Leavis changed his mind, but the note appears to have been added some time in the 1960s' (Gardiner 250).

[. . .] be traced to the years around the Second World War' (Gardiner 178). Indeed, Gardiner has gone so far as to claim:

> That is why the life of Dickens remains important as well as interesting: for it is in his 'use' of the Victorian age, and in our subsequent 'use' of Dickens, that we can trace his contribution to modernity and the nature of our response to it. (179)

Though the critics I have cited are a highly selective sample of the many voices that have attested to Dickens's modernity, there has not been universal agreement that Dickens is indeed 'modern', even since the 1940s. Philip Collins, for example, though pinpointing the emergence of the emphasis on Dickens's modernity very precisely to 1940–1, is equally exact in the enunciation of his view that this new Dickens is a critical fiction and that 'Dickens is consistently mis-read to make him more modern, and radical than he was' (157). Collins rightly points out that what we could call the 'modern turn' in Dickens studies, at least in its early days, tended to suppress the 'Chestertonian', 'Christmassy' Dickens (148). The main representative of this distorting reinvention of Dickens, to Collins, is J. Hillis Miller, whose work (1958) had become significantly influential by 1970 for its post-structuralist insistence on Dickens's texts as autonomous works of art, displaced from what Collins views as their rightful Victorian context. Whatever we think of the value judgements informing the respective views of Miller and Collins, it is true that Miller omits *A Christmas Carol* from his groundbreaking assessment of Dickens (though the reason for this is also clear: his focus is on the novels). *A Christmas Carol* has overtaken *Oliver Twist* since the 1940s as the most adapted Dickens text for the screen (largely because of the difficulty of knowing how to represent Fagin in the wake of the Holocaust), but as a literary text, its critical heyday was before the 1940s, when its spirit of optimism and community was more closely associated with Dickens than the darker mood of the late novels.

The critical emphasis on Dickens's modernity has, then, tended to marginalise earlier texts like *A Christmas Carol*, *The Pickwick Papers* and *The Old Curiosity Shop*, in which idealism and sentimentality occlude anxieties about alienation and change. Scanning through the extensive collection of Dickens press cuttings held in the basement of the Charles Dickens Museum, for example, the emphasis at key commemorative moments that pre-date the Second World War – Dickens's death and the centenary of his birth – is on the 'cheery' Dickens who broke down class barriers, united families and made people smile. An article by A. Austen in *Temple Bar* on Dickens's death, for example, describes him simply as 'the Happy Author' (556). A poem 'To His Memory' in *The Argosy* the same year, asked

> [. . .] who, like him, the barrier high 'twixt rich
>   and poor removing,
> Has led the differing classes all, to be together
>   loving?
>
> Charles Dickens! Oh, so free from pomp, from
>   undue exaltation:
> The poor man was his brother still – while
>   worshipped by the nation.
>
> [. . .]
>
> Charles Dickens! He is with us yet, our lives
>   shall gladness borrow
> From the cheery tale, that sparkles – o'er the
>   dull, dark cloud of sorrow;
> Often our weary hearts shall be to laughter
>   gently stirred,
> And our children's children keep his name, –
>   a happy Household Word!
>
> ([Anon.] 1870b: 114)

In August 1870, *Harper's New Monthly Magazine* echoed the sentiments of Trollope's better-known obituary, emphasising that Dickens 'was the most popular author of a time when reading was universal, and popular without a hint of impurity [. . .] he left no man living whose death would be so sore a personal grief to the English-speaking race as his has been' ([Anon.] 1870a: 453).[4]

In 1912, the image of a benign, popular Dickens was still very much in evidence, along with an emphasis on the serious and beneficial social

---

4   Thackeray wrote in his obituary of Dickens, 'he has accomplished that which must be the desire of every author, – he has spoken to men and women who have opened their ears to his words, and have listened to them. [. . .] In this respect Dickens was, probably, more fortunate during his own life than any writer that ever lived. The English-speaking public may be counted, perhaps, as a hundred millions, and wherever English is read these books are popular from the highest to the lowest, – among all classes that read' (371–2).

and political uses to which Dickens put his benevolent compassion. An article on 'Dickens the Reformer' in *The Observer* (10 February 1912), for instance, claimed that he 'did more than any man in England to establish Democracy on a firm and lasting basis', adding that

> It was Dickens's compassionate love for the masses of the people, his sympathy with their simple lives and apparently unimportant doings and sayings, which revealed Democracy to itself, and made it believe in itself and in its power. He awoke the average man to a sense of his dignity, and if the Democracy of England were to think of choosing a patron saint, they could not discover a more deserving candidate for that honour [than Dickens]. ([Anon.] 1912)

An interesting clipping in the uncatalogued collection of Dickensiana in the Charles Dickens Museum records a centenary lecture by J. Cuming Walters, ex-President of the Dickens Fellowship, at Knutsford, entitled 'Dickens the Patriot', in which Dickens is celebrated as a particularly modern lover of his country:

> It is as a patriot that I present him to you tonight, the patriot who dreamt of a better England, the patriot who stirred the pulses of a progressive people, the patriot who crushed wrong and error underfoot, and the patriot who laboured for the ushering in of the brighter day, the nobler era, the time of greater and worthier deeds. He believed in British capacity to understand higher ideas, and he therefore appealed steadfastly and confidently British capacity to achieve them.

There is thus some truth in Collins's assertion that attempts to 'modernise' Dickens since the 1940s have rather marginalised the 'Happy Dickens' who used humour and sympathy to achieve a unique bond with an audience which spanned beyond what we could call the 'known', literate, cultured public to an 'unknown public', to use Wilkie Collins's phrase (1858). However, it is also true that the idea of the darker, more modern Dickens was itself downplayed before the 1940s, partly because of his own determination to foster a 'happy' public image of himself and partly because Dickens's cultural prominence in the years between his death and the Second World War was maintained by his popularity with the reading public and film-goers rather than with modernist arbiters of taste. Indeed, as Modernism defined itself in contradistinction to what had gone before, it is perhaps inevitable that the most popular author of the previous generation would not be seen as laying claims to the modernity with which it identified itself. After the Second

World War, the emphasis on Dickens's modernity has been therefore partly driven by a desire to recover marked tendencies in Dickens's writing which his public image had worked to marginalise, and also, significantly, by a desire to raise Dickens's reputation from that of great entertainer to that of great literary author. Hillis Miller's work was in this respect crucial; he was the first in several generations of theorists of different denominations to draw attention to Dickens's sophistication and self-consciousness as an artist and a thinker.

Theory has done wonders for Dickens's reputation in the academy: post-structuralist and Foucauldian criticism in particular, but there is also an increasingly deep fund of psychoanalytic, feminist and postcolonial work. Theory has in general worked to reveal layers and nuances of philo-sophical, psychic or political meaning not immediately apparent to a child reading Dickens or to a non-reader viewing a Dickens adaptation. In place of a simple, Victorian Dickens, it has presented a complex, modern Dickens. For many years, however, even theory gave Dickens's commercialism a wide berth, side-stepping his immersion in the newly emerging mass culture of the Victorian period. Commemoration counter-intuitively makes such commercialism visible, even as it attempts to hide it. In a 1913 file of uncatalogued centenary Dickensiana at the Charles Dickens Museum, for example, press articles about Dickens the reformer or Dickens the patriot sit alongside articles celebrating 'Dickens "Doultonised"', or the availability of Dickens characters as Doulton pottery figurines ([Anon.] 1913a]). The release of Dickens centenary stamps to give financial assist-ance to the Dickens family caused a stir in the press but objections were not strong enough to stop their successful sale ([Anon.] 1913a]). On the eve of the bicentenary, Arifa Akbar's lead Arts article for the *Independent* (2 December 2011), 'Great expectations for brand Dickens' is sub-titled 'Charles Dickens' bicentenary next year is set to make a fortune' (Akbar 2011b). Money generated does not come through Dickens commodities like china figurines or stamps, but through tourism, the film, heritage and publishing industries. Several new Dickens screen adaptations are in the pipeline, for example (which Akbar criticises in another article for not rejecting costume (Akbar 2011a)) and the British press is currently awash with articles on Dickens. On 3 December 2011, Dickens made an appearance on five pages of *The Times*, and some of these pages (14–15) promoted a selection of recent Dickens books, including a carefully timed spate of recent biographies (a reissue of Forster's original biography of

Dickens, edited by Holly Furneaux, Claire Tomalin's *Charles Dickens: A Life*, Anne Isba's *Dickens and Women*, and Miriam Margolyes's transcript of her show *Dickens' Women*).[5] Radio 4's Book of the Week in the first week of December 2011 was Tomalin's biography and the Museum of London launched its Dickens and London conference on 7 December the same year. All this before the bicentenary had officially started.

There is a certain irony about the fact that Collins's hostility to the critical modernisation of Dickens is expressed in *Dickens and Fame, 1870–1970* (Slater 1970), an outstanding and now largely neglected special double edition of the *Dickensian*, published on the centenary of Dickens's death to reflect on one hundred years of Dickens criticism. Edited by Michael Slater, *Dickens and Fame* is ahead of its time in the sense that it reflects seriously on Dickens's fame and his shifting relationship to both literary and popular culture. It anticipates the material and cultural turn in nineteenth-century studies in the last twenty years that has allowed critics to see Dickens as both a literary writer and a cultural icon, to analyse both his works and his cultural legacy. *Dickens and Fame* acknowledges both the 'happy Dickens' and a modern Dickens whose modernity inhered as much in his vision of literature as both art and popular cultural medium as it did in the content of the novels themselves. Slater's editorial announces of the essays in the collection that they

> do not confine themselves solely to the history of Dickens scholar-ship and criticism but seek also to indicate, in their respective periods, the extent and nature of Dickens's impact on the general public, the development of his 'image' (to borrow a word from the world of con-temporary advertising). (Slater 1970: 80)

Because the volume pre-dates the large majority of theoretical work on Dickens and focuses mainly on the critical reception and status of Dickens, it is a scholarly volume with a textual bias, acknowledging the material culture Dickens inhabited whilst largely avoiding non-print texts. Dilys Powell's very short postscript on 'Dickens on Film' is tellingly different from the other contributions, briefer and lacking in their rigour,

---

[5]   Other Dickens books listed are Dickens's *Life of Our Lord*, Jenny Hartley's *Selected Letters of Charles Dickens*, Lucinda Dickens Hawksley's *Charles Dickens*, the online manuscript of *Great Expectations*, Michael Slater's *The Genius of Dickens*, Ebury Press's *Dickens's Victorian London* and Quentin Blake's illustrations to *A Christmas Carol*.

as if, despite the good intentions signalled by including an essay on film, the essay's author is not quite sure how to treat the subject seriously.

The current volume has benefited from the absorption of cultural studies into Victorian studies in the years since Slater's edition was published but it has been fashioned as a development of Slater's vision of Dickens as both a literary and a cultural icon, rather than a radical departure from it. There is still a great deal of work to be done on Dickens's cultural lives in the Victorian period and after, but what *Dickens and Modernity* demonstrates is that oppositions which have pervaded Dickens studies – Victorian vs modern, artist vs entertainer, culture vs commerce – are false oppositions. Dickens's legacy survived his passing in part because of the quality of his writings, but in part because he embraced the emerging mass market for culture. He appreciated that he was writing in 'the age of mechanical reproduction', to quote Walter Benjamin, but also that this age created a need for emotional community, for moral and spiritual values, for roots and for belonging.[6] A *Christmas Carol* perfectly captures this dialectic in Dickens, its 'Victorian' emphasis on family, sympathy, community, growing out of the emotional needs of urban, capitalist 'modern' society for an affective sense of roots and history – for heritage, if we want to use that term, or a sense of the past channelled by emotional will.

While *Dickens and Fame* offers a linear, chronological sense of Dickens's literary and cultural trajectory, *Dickens and Modernity* works laterally, aiming to capture the diversity and multiplicity of Dickens's textual and extra-textual lives. Like all such commemorative volumes, this one will inevitably be of its time, its emphasis on inclusivity, cross-fertilisation and expansiveness in approaches to Dickens necessarily avoids any claims to be definitive. In enlisting contributors, I have sought writers whose work is new, interesting and different, suggesting innovative directions for further study. The volume is characterised by an eclecticism, by a 'porousness', to take a word that Grahame Smith borrowed from Walter Benjamin (Smith 51), characteristic of Dickens's own imagination. Many of the essays make unexpected connections and turn apparent conceptual oppositions into thresholds in a spirit we could call Dickensian.

[6] This phrase is taken from the familiar translation of the title of Benjamin's essay 'The Work of Art in the Age of Mechanical Reproduction' (1935), more recently translated by Eiland and Jennings (2002) as 'The Work of Art in the Age of its Technological Reproducibility'.

Several draw attention to the fertile relationship between Dickens and machines or the mechanical in his own day and since, undermining the misconception that is sometimes derived from a cursory reading of *Hard Times* that Dickens's work is hostile to machines and technology. Thus, in 'The Dickens Tape: Affect and Sound Reproduction in *The Chimes*', Jay Clayton demonstrates the affective use of machines in Dickens's Christmas tale *The Chimes* and in music as an art form, investigating sound-reproduction technologies before the advent of recordings. He discusses bells alongside barrel organs, clock chimes, factory whistles, theatrical sound effects, telegraphs and other acoustic devices as ways to re-produce, in the sense of repeating, sound. He argues that prior to recording technology, this kind of reproduction was the only way in which remembered sounds could be heard again. Every performance of the sound was a singular event, even if the auditory experience evoked all the sensory effects, emotional resonances and public meanings of its previous iterations. The capacity of an oft-heard bell to evoke both personal associations and civic meanings – holidays, religious occasions, deaths, anniversaries – anticipates, to Clayton, the distinction between emotion and affect proposed by recent affect theorists. If, as a number of theorists have proposed, emotion requires a subject and affect does not, he reasons that Dickens's account of the power of sound to shatter the subject – in the person of poor Toby Veck – takes the analysis a step further. In the process, he argues that Dickens's story captures the way a physiological state can be deeply social and collective in character and can motivate a politics of reform. For it is not, to Clayton, the sentimental feelings or the satire of the heartless rich that most effectively communicate Dickens's social message but the affect that sound-reproducing technology produces in the body of both the individual and the community.

Holly Furneaux's essay, 'Dickens, Sexuality and the Body or, Clock Loving: Master Humphrey's Queer Objects of Desire' also features clocks and works to break down Carlylean oppositions between mechanism and human emotion. Her essay on 'Dickens's fascination with stuff' brings together lines of enquiry inspired by thing theory, queer theory and gender studies to explore Dickens's investment in the imaginative, emotional and erotic appeal of objects, specifically his interrelated interests in strange bodies and strange things. In conjunction, her chosen approaches reveal the centrality of the material to Dickens's queer imagination, as his thinking on human/object relations participates in his wider scrutiny of the naturalness and inevitability of gender roles, heterosexuality and, indeed, the human. She is inspired by William Cohen's recent treatment of queer, which is not (just) about 'sexual counterorthodoxy' but about a presentation of 'the openness of the body to the world by the senses as a type of permeability, or penetrability, that is not reducible to heterosexuality, nor is it even limited to the realm of the sexual'. Queer theory here meets posthuman and cyborgian approaches, offering a 'critique of the human – with its phantasmatic completeness and integrity' (Cohen 134). For Furneaux, *Master Humphrey's Clock* is Dickens's most explicit meditation on the joys of object-loving.

John Drew and Michaela Mahlberg both offer fascinating insights into the ways in which machines today are furthering access to, and understanding of, Dickens's art. Drew first explores some of the ways in which the texts Dickens handled as a magazine editor in the 1850s and 1860s were imaged, presented, published and distributed by him. On the one hand, their framing in different formats and modes of presentation constitutes a set of significant 'paratexts' which can be investigated; on the other, the series of transformations worked in order to bring the material to its destination invests the writing with characteristics foreshadowing the modern concept of the e-text. Drew suggests that Dickens's sense of enthusiasm about, and desire to celebrate, the sheer power of the connection between writers and readers that new technological and industrial processes were forging, marks out something important about his work as a journalist, that occurs within a definable Anglo-American Romantic tradition. Taken together with the contribution of the other writers Dickens collaborated with to 'conduct' his weekly magazine to its readers, this can be considered, Drew argues, as a kind of inchoate poetics of communication, worked out through the columns first of *Household Words* (1850-9), then *All the Year Round* (edited by Dickens 1859-70). In developing these ideas, he draws on the experience of setting up *Dickens Journals Online*, an open access online edition of Dickens's weekly journals – now under construction at <http://www.djo.org.uk> – and some of the curious parallels which seem to obtain between the dynamism of modern web publishing and that of the Victorian periodical press. The commodification of literature and the reproducibility of art are necessarily bound up with these processes, now as then, so the essay concludes by considering the authenticity (or otherwise) of such enterprises.

In her essay, Mahlberg proposes an innovative text-driven approach, taken from corpus linguistics, to the study of characters in Dickens's fictional worlds. Employing computer-assisted methods, she introduces five-word clusters, i.e. repeatedly occurring sequences of five words such as *and his nose came down*, as textual cues for the creation of characters. In addition to clusters, the essay also considers suspensions, i.e. spans of (narrator) text that interrupt quoted speech, as places in the text that can potentially provide character information. Mahlberg uses corpus methods to study these linguistic patterns, but her text-driven approach does not stop with the retrieval of linguistic examples. The language patterns are interpreted in terms of building blocks of fictional worlds, described along a continuum of highlighting and contextualising functions, and discussed within a wider context of literary criticism. Patterns of body language are shown to relate to the externalised techniques of characterisation that John highlights as being key to Dickens's narrative prose. At the same time, the corpus approach addresses questions of characterisation that are raised by Rosenberg when he focuses on readers' reactions to Dickens's language of 'doubt'. The essay emphasises that the patterns under investigation only form part of the range of linguistic devices that build Dickens's fictional worlds, but it already becomes clear how a text-driven approach can provide the linguistic detail for the study of characterisation in Dickens.

The relationship between words and the material world is also the focus of my own essay, 'Things, Words, and the Meanings of Art'. Like Furneaux's essay, mine engages with 'thing theory', but I explore the implications of the basic fact, often ignored by thing theory, that things in print culture are not things but words representing things. I share Trotter's urge to reinstate proportion and a renewed attention to representational texture in our analysis of objects in nineteenth-century writing; as Trotter argues, some things are symbolic in literature, others are just 'stuff', and art creates meaning by framing or differentiation. However, I argue that as a popular, mass-cultural artist, Dickens did not define material and literary or aesthetic culture oppositionally but used self-reflexive analysis of the relationship between words and things – highlighting the dependency of each on the other to forge meaning – to explore, represent and promote a new kind of understanding of art. Dickens's 'thing art' understands 'literature' and fiction as part of a nuanced cultural landscape which differentiates laterally as well as hierarchically. Ideas of rhetorical hierarchy, generic difference, aesthetic proportion and temporal change, as Trotter and Pettitt have both argued, are all important and necessary to a complex understanding of the representation of things in nineteenth-century culture. But for Dickens, it is not art as traditionally defined that carries out the work of creating proportion, which in turn creates meaning. I argue that it is rather 'Fancy', imagination, the agent of art but evident for Dickens in all areas of life including the commercial, which creates the proportion which Trotter and Pettitt have emphasised, but also, importantly, connection. Aesthetic categories function as framing mechanisms, but they are unstable products of history, time and indeed fancy. To Dickens, I conclude, modern artists in a world where objects have new power should respond not by objectifying the idea of art, but by animating, extending and rejuvenating the realm of the aesthetic.

Dickens's afterlives have relied on this modern expansion of the realm of the aesthetic and the blurring of the lines between high and low or commercial culture. The essays of Hollington, Edwards Keates and Marsh and Sickmann all look at specific ways in which Dickens has been adapted for new times and new periods. Hollington argues that Dickens had a hand not only in the invention of modern Christmas, but in the formation and development of a cult of the circus in the period of Modernism and modernity. His vision of a circus utopia distinct from, and antagonistic to, the ravages of modern industrialisation in *Hard Times* is echoed, directly or indirectly, in a host of twentieth-century artworks – writings, paintings, films, musical scores – that joyously celebrate the alternative world under the big top. His idea of the circus as a democratic cultural and social phenomenon capable of uniting social classes is echoed in the practical commercial policies pursued by circus companies such as that of Bertram Mills in the twentieth century. He looks at paintings by Picasso and Kees van Dongen, writings by Ramon Gomez de la Serna, Virginia Woolf, Walter Benjamin and Angela Carter, and films by Chaplin, the Marx Brothers and Cecil B. DeMille, to illustrate and support his argument. But, in an era where 'shlock horror' circus movies thrive at the expense of the circus itself, he concludes that the great tradition appears to be at an end.

'The *Oliver!* Phenomenon' – what its authors, Joss Marsh and Carrie Sickmann, call 'a critical', sometimes very critical, 'love song' – takes analysis into new territory, exploring the phenomenal popularity of the 'father' of the modern 'monster' musical, pop composer Lionel Bart's *Oliver!* Brilliantly designed by architect Sean Kenny, the show was a revolution in theatre history, and a sharp spur to the Dickens adaptation industry. It was also an extraordinarily powerful iteration of Dickens's novel – and of Dickens himself, a star-making machine, a prize-winning British export and a populist post-modern tourist experience. *Oliver!* ushered in the era of the fully mechanised (and primarily British-made) large-scale musical which now dominates Broadway and the West End; it is a key part of the economic entertainment juggernaut piloted by Cameron Mackintosh, by whom it is shipped, fully packaged and strictly quality-controlled, to such apparently unlikely venues as Japan, Estonia, Israel and the Czech Republic; its consumerist ideology, written into the libretto ('Who Will Buy – This Beautiful Morning?'), and its pleasure in criminality ('You've Got to Pick a Pocket or Two'), are all too easy to skewer. But *Oliver!*, Marsh and *Sickmann* argue, burst onto the London stage in 1960 with the full force of new freedoms behind it: more sexual independence, liberty from class oppression, and the freedom to say to life and society, 'Please, sir, I want some more'. The show embraced the fashion, the music and the spirit of the 1960s, they explain, but it also paid artistic homage to its Dickensian inheritance and transcended its era and genre, incorporating and redeeming (for example) strong influences from David Lean's flawed and anti-Semitic film masterpiece, *Oliver Twist* (1948), and anticipating its own future as a BBC television talent and reality show. They conclude that at bottom, *Oliver!* survives, and will almost certainly continue to thrive, as a gift of pleasure, to millions, that Dickens himself might have approved.

In 'Re-Reading/Re-Viewing Dickens and Neo-Victorianism on the BBC', Kim Edwards Keates examines how Dickens's representation of inter-female intimacies has been creatively interpreted and translated onto the television screen in Andrew Davies's recently serialised BBC adaptations, *Bleak House* (2005) and *Little Dorrit* (2008). Influenced like Furneaux by queer theory, Keates suggests that Davies engages in a careful but complex negotiation with the source text that simultaneously balances Dickens's vexed rendering of female–female desires with twenty-first-century perceptions of those relationships. In doing so, these neo-Victorian adaptations, Keates argues, utilise multiple cross-textual reference points to present a creative and critical interrogation (Llewellyn 2008: 170) of the radical potentialities of Dickens's fiction.

Dominic Rainsford links anxieties, in Dickens's work, about being, identity and location in the world with Dickens scholarship's recent concern with 'global Dickens'; that is, his awareness of, relations with and posthumous presence in lands beyond his own. Rainsford argues that

Dickens, the would-be 'Manager of the House', was acutely conscious of ways in which the world resisted management, both practically and conceptually, and that this consciousness permeates the concern with psychological grounding, social placement and metaphysical validity that marks his explorations of human character and identity – whether the humans in question be foreigners, locals or even ourselves. His essay concentrates on *David Copperfield*, unpacking that novel's representations of geography, travel, home and away, and arguing that the most persuasive accounts of placement and movement within the physical world depicted in Dickens's writing will also pay attention to his representations of individual characters and narrators, suspended, like David, within an imagined geography that is personal, unstable and incomplete.

The volume ends fittingly with a fascinating insight by Florian Schweizer, Director of the Dickens 2012 celebrations, into the shaping of this year-long public programme of commemoration of Dickens – its vision, rationale, challenges and events. Schweizer asks us to consider the nature of our connection with 'this quintessentially Victorian writer' and what it is about Dickens that still appeals to people around the world. Why Dickens?, in other words. The answer, for the bicentenary organisers, is culture, learning and charity. Despite the use of the young Dickens as the image of the bicentenary, values with which Dickens has been traditionally associated have been chosen to represent all that is 'Dickensian' during the bicentenary year – 'uncommercial' values that serve the not-for-profit aims of Dickens 2012 well (whilst no doubt having knock-on benefits for the economy). The range of events and activities planned for the bicentenary on the whole combines the familiar with the new, however, innovative adaptations, 'hip hop happenings' and smartphone apps appearing alongside more traditional forms of commemoration. *Dickens and Modernity* provides answers to the questions Schweizer poses about why Dickens still matters today which admirers of a more familiar, Victorian, 'Christmassy' Dickens may at first find surprising. But this volume seeks to complement rather than subvert the 'Dickensian' Dickens, recognising that the secret of Dickens's enduring appeal is his ability to bring together not just readers from all over the globe, but ways of seeing and feeling that received logic positions as oppositional. Thus, in Dickens, a communal, nostalgic, organic view of the world co-exists and indeed grows out of a very modern sense of instability, mobility and radical uncertainty. *Dickens and Modernity* foregrounds an unfamiliar, mobile Dickens, taking him to new places through new media. The popularity of the familiar Dickens is, of course, the foundation of this cultural adaptability, while reciprocally, the underlying modernity in Dickens has enabled his portability. *Dickens and Modernity* offers itself as an academic work of commemoration alongside the public festivities. It foregrounds the transformative power of Dickens's texts and the cultural processes that have enabled Dickens to continue to matter.

Juliet John
December 2011

Works cited
(Note that the uncatalogued archives of the Charles Dickens Museum do not always provide full bibliographical information for clippings.)

Akbar, Arifa, 2011a. 'Spare us Another Conventional Take on Dickens', *Independent* (11 October), <http://www.independent.co.uk/arts-entertainment/films/features/spare-us-another-conventional-take-on-dickens-2368449.html?origin=internalSearch>.

Akbar, Arifa, 2011b. 'Great Expectations for Brand Dickens', *Independent* (2 December), <http://www.independent.co.uk/arts-entertainment/books/features/great-expectations-for-brand-dickens-6270459.html?origin=internalSearch>.

[Anon.], 1870a. 'Editor's Easy Chair', *Harper's New Monthly Magazine*, 41 (August): 451–8.

[Anon.], 1870b. 'To his Memory', *The Argosy* (1 August): 114; taken from Charles Dickens Museum, Frederic G. Kitton, *Dickensiana*, 3 [Magazine Articles].

[Anon.], 1912. 'Dickens the Reformer', *Observer* (10 February). From Charles Dickens Museum: The Dickens Newspaper Clipping Archive, File 13.

[Anon.], 1913a. 'Dickens in Pottery', Charles Dickens Museum: The Dickens Newspaper Clipping Archive, File 13.

[Anon.], 1913b. 'The Dickens Stamp Controversy', Charles Dickens Museum: The Dickens Newspaper Clipping Archive, File 13.

Benjamin, Walter, 2002 [1936]. 'The Work of Art in the Age of its Technical Reproducibility', in *Walter Benjamin: Selected Writings*, ed. Howard Eiland and Michael W. Jennings. Cambridge, MA: Belnap Press, pp. 3–92.

Cohen, William, 2008. *Embodied: Victorian Literature and the Senses*. Minnesota: Minnesota University Press.

Collins, Philip, 1970. 'Enter the Professionals', in *Dickens and Fame 1870–1970: Essays on the Author's Reputation*, ed. Michael Slater. Special Centenary edn of *Dickensian*, 66: 143–61.

Collins, Wilkie, 1858. 'The Unknown Public', *Household Words*, 18 (21 August): 217–22.

Cuming Walters, J., 1913 [1912], speech on 'Dickens the Patriot' (Knutsford). From Charles Dickens Museum: The Dickens Newspaper Clipping Archive, File 13.

Dickens, Charles, 2010 [1934]. *The Life of Our Lord*. Richmond: Oneworld Classics.

Dickens, Charles, 2011. *A Christmas Carol*. Ill. Quentin Blake. London: Pavilion.

Dickens, Charles, 2011. *The Manuscript of Great Expectations*. Cambridge: Cambridge University Press.

Dickens Hawksley, Lucinda, 2011. *Charles Dickens*. London: Andre Deutsch.

Eisenstein, Sergei, 1996 [1942]. 'Dickens, Griffith and Ourselves', in *Selected Works*, ed. Richard Taylor and William Powell, 4 vols, vol. III. London: British Film Institute, pp. 193–238.

Forster, John, 2011 [1872]. *The Life of Charles Dickens: The Illustrated Edition*, ed. Holly Furneaux. New York: Sterling Signature.

Gagnier, Regenia, ed., 2009. <http://literature-compass.com/global-circulation-project/>.

Gardiner, John, 2002. *The Victorians: An Age in Retrospect*. London: Hambledon and London.

Hartley, Jenny, 2012. *Selected Letters of Charles Dickens*. Oxford: Oxford University Press.

Isba, Anne, 2011. *Dickens and Women: His Great Expectations*. London: Continuum.

John, Juliet, 2001. *Dickens's Villains: Melodrama, Character, Popular Culture*. Oxford: Oxford University Press.

Leavis, F. R., 1962 [1948]. *The Great Tradition*. Peregrine Books. Harmondsworth: Penguin.

Margolyes, Miriam, and Sonia Fraser, 2011. *Dickens' Women*. London: Hesperus.

Miller, J. Hillis, 1958. *Charles Dickens: The World of his Novels*, Cambridge, MA: Harvard University Press.

Pettitt, Clare, 2009. 'Peggotty's Work-Box: Victorian Souvenirs and Material Memory'. *Romanticism and Victorianism on the Net*, 53: 1–9 <http://www.erudit.org/revue/ravon/2009/v/n53/029896ar.html>.

Powell, Dilys, 1970. 'Dickens on Film', in *Dickens and Fame 1870–1970: Essays on the Author's Reputation*, ed. Michael Slater. Special Centenary edn of *Dickensian*, 66: 183–5.

Rosenberg, Brian, 1996. *Little Dorrit's Shadows: Character and Contradiction in Dickens*. Columbia: University of Missouri Press.

Slater, Michael, ed. 1970. *Dickens and Fame 1870–1970: Essays on the Author's Reputation*. Special Centenary edn of *Dickensian*, 66.

Slater, Michael, 2011. *The Genius of Dickens*. London: Duckworth.

Smith, Grahame, 2003. *Dickens and the Dream of Cinema*. Manchester: Manchester University Press.

Thackeray, William Makepeace, 1870. 'Charles Dickens', *St. Paul's Magazine*, 6 (July): 370–5.

Tomalin, Claire, 2011. *Charles Dickens: A Life*. Viking.

Trotter, David, 2008. 'Household Clearances in Victorian Fiction', *19: Interdisciplinary Studies in the Long Nineteenth Century*, 6: 1–19 <http://19.bbk.ac.uk/index.php/19/article/viewFile/472/332>.

Werner, Alex, and Tony Williams, 2012. *Dickens's Victorian London: The Museum of London*. London: Ebury.

Screenography

Donsky, Seth Michael, dir., 1996. *Twisted*. Water Bearer Films.

Greene, Timothy, dir., 2004. *Boy Called Twist*. Monkey Films and Twisted Pictures.

Tierney, Jacob, dir., 2003. *Twist*. Victorious Films.

The Dickens tape:
affect and sound reproduction in The Chimes

JAY CLAYTON

WHAT WOULD YOU GIVE for a recording of Dickens reading? Who would not treasure a scrap of the Inimitable's voice? Dickens himself wanted people to hear him. He revelled in public readings where his voice brought to life Micawber and Pickwick, the death of Little Nell and the hanging of Sikes. Recordings of other nineteenth-century voices exist – Tennyson, Browning and Whitman, among writers – and the tenuous thread of their words reaches toward us as from another world. The crackle of static is like the noise of time itself. Dickens, who was interested in sound technology, would have been one of the first in line to bury his head in a speaking trumpet and bellow, 'I never will desert Mr Micawber'. But, unless Charles Babbage is right and sound waves leave permanent impressions on the air, we shall never hear the departed voice of one of the pioneers of public readings.[1] Dickens died seven years before the invention of the phonograph, and the sound of his speech has been lost for ever.

Visual recordings of Dickens abound. The novelist lived to see the development of several different forms of photography, and there are memorable drawings, paintings and photographs of the author. In fact, no writer has ever dwelled in a world devoid of visual representation. But until the late nineteenth century, sound was rarely thought of as a suitable medium for recording. There were oral formulaic poets, traditional storytellers, classically trained rhetoricians and actors, who could use

I would like to thank Erin Garcia-Fernandez for her research assistance on this project, Jason Camelot for directing me to the nineteenth-century recording of Big Ben, Jamie Adams for photographing the illustrations, and Juliet John for valuable advice on the revision of this chapter.

[1] See Babbage 108.

remembered words as records of the past. The memory theatre and other mnemonic tricks could become technologies for sound reproduction of a sort – technologies of the self, which disciplined the mind to recall streams of data for oral recitation. That said, sound was not a medium of choice for recording, despite the paradoxical fact that sound was often believed to trigger memories more powerfully even than sight. Sound shared with memory a transitory, evanescent quality, which would soon give the first phonographic recordings some of their power to haunt. Until Edison's wax cylinders changed everything, sound was primarily a medium for communication, not for the preservation of the past.

In the absence of recordings, we must take the measure of Dickens's voice in other terms, find a different kind of tape to tie up the bundle of meanings and memories that sounds in his texts evoke. Different forms of sound reproduction were common before the age of recording. Jonathan Sterne, one of the few scholars of nineteenth-century sound, makes this point: 'One could argue that ancient uses of animal horns to amplify the voice and aid the hard-of-hearing are, in a certain sense, sound-reproduction technologies' (19). Although Sterne goes on to define 'sound reproduction' in more specialised terms, he is right to point out that nineteenth-century speaking automata, for example, or music boxes and player-pianos, could be counted as forms of sound reproduction. To these, I would add Dickens's many barrel organs, bells, clock chimes, train and factory whistles, theatrical sound effects, telegraph sounders, and more. If one stretches out the tape to take the measure of these early sound-reproduction technologies, what does one discover about acoustic experience in the nineteenth century?

First, one defamiliarises the concept of *reproduction*. Each time a bell rings or train whistle blows, it produces a characteristic sound, *re*-producing it only in the sense of repeating it. Prior to recording technology, this kind of reproduction was one of the main ways in which remembered sounds could be heard again. Every performance of the sound was a singular event, even if the auditory experience evoked all the sensory effects and emotional resonances of its previous iterations. Second, instruments that reproduce sound without storing acoustic data challenge a key dogma of contemporary media studies, the belief that information technology contributes to the abstraction and disembodiment of modern experience.[2]

---

[2] Friedrich Kittler's discussion of the typewriter, which 'unlinks hand, eye, and

Attending to sound reproduction as a separate process from recording, however, yields different conclusions. Nineteenth-century communication technologies such as the telegraph and telephone, which reproduced without storing information, appeared to their first auditors to intensify sensory effects, producing embodied rather than abstracted forms of experience. Third, this embodied sensory experience prompts us to attend to the distinctive kinds of affect Dickens and other nineteenth-century authors attributed to sound reproduction. As a sensory phenomenon that causes affective responses in a listener, sound seems like an ideal test case for the ideas emerging in the field of affect studies.

Over the last decade, affect studies have become an important topic in literary and cultural criticism, in part because they provide an opportunity to engage social and material conditions without sacrificing the lessons of deconstruction. After the 'end of theory' (proclaimed and denied in a series of volumes published around the turn of the century),[3] affect studies became one of the places where theory migrated. Affect theory allows critics to attend to emotional states without reinstating a feeling subject, for affect is defined in terms of bodily intensities that are not easily translated into particular meanings or intentions. In this respect, it has affinities with other critical enterprises that attempt to decentre the humanist subject, such as animal studies and 'thing theory' (Brown). Among the senses, sound and scent are especially prone to cause affective responses untethered to the desires of the individual. Building on a distinction common in experimental psychology, literary theorists generally define *affect* as the bodily or physiological dimension of feelings and use the word *emotion* for more psychological aspects. Lawrence Grossberg inaugurated this line of thinking in cultural studies, writing 'unlike emotions, affective states are neither structured narratively nor organised in response to our interpretations of situations' (81). Rei Terada relies on much the same distinction: 'by *emotion* we usually

letter in the moment' of writing and thus disrupts the 'continuous transition from nature to culture' (194–5) is the *locus classicus* of this idea for many subsequent critics. Prominent critics who follow Kittler in emphasising the abstraction and disembodiment brought about by information technology include Crary and Seltzer. For a counterview, see my discussion (2003: 65–70) of the way that Kittler's emphasis on media that record rather than communicate information results in a fundamental misconception of the relationship of technology to the senses.

[3] Butler, Guillory and Thomas; Eagleton; Mitchell; and Elliott.

mean a psychological, at least minimally interpretive experience whose physiological aspect is *affect*' (4). Brian Massumi and Sianne Ngai both oppose the subjective character of emotion to the objective existence of affect, since the latter is something that can be perceived as an 'intensity' even when its meaning is vague (Massumi 27) and is 'as fundamentally "social" as the institutions and collective practices that have been the more traditional objects of historicist criticism' (Ngai 25). For example, Ngai's interest in 'dysphoric feelings' such as anxiety or paranoia, which produce 'situations of suspended agency' (1), illustrates how the social character of affects may stem from their decentring of the individual will. Affect, then, indicates comparatively unstructured, non-narrative and free-floating bodily intensities, unmoored to the subject's desires and intentions.

Dickens dramatises the power of sounds to provoke emotion through-out his career, but he is just as sensitive to the affect of sounds. His fiction frequently registers the physical impact of sounds – not just on the ears, but on the body and the mind of listeners too. Given the noisy urban environment of much of his fiction, this is hardly surprising. Bells, though, occupy a special place in Dickens's auditory world. Dickens published an article on bells in *All the Year Round* (19 January 1867), and church bells toll throughout Dickens's fiction – notably in *The Old Curiosity Shop* (1841), where Little Nell hears the village bell 'almost as a living voice' (657), and in his second Christmas book, *The Chimes* (1844), where the entire tale revolves around 'the Spirits of the Bells'. This latter work develops a powerful account of the confused affective response caused by the sound of pealing bells.

The Chimes features an old man named Toby Veck (called 'Trotty' by most acquaintances), who tirelessly and cheerfully works for subsistence wages as a courier for the rare customer who asks him to carry a small package or message. One night, after several encounters with rich, self-important men who label Toby and his daughter Meg as surplus popula-tion and prove to them through the unimpeachable precepts of political economy that Meg should never marry and Toby should cease to exist, the old man falls asleep and has a series of disturbing dreams. In these dreams he climbs to the top of the neighbouring church tower, where hang the bells that have been his only source of encouragement through many a long year. There he has a series of visions of what the future entails if the political economists are correct.

THE TOWER OF THE CHIMES,

Figure 1.1 'The Tower of the Chimes'
Reproduced with permission, Vanderbilt University Library

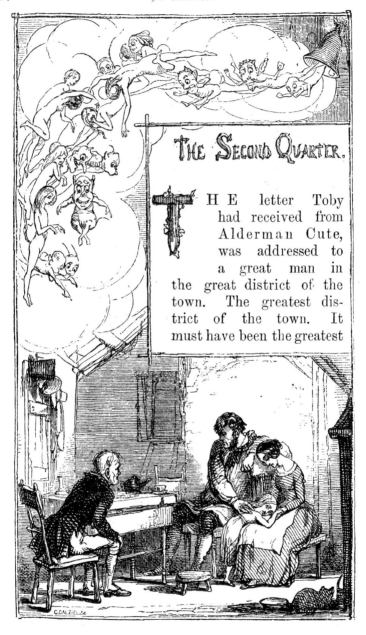

Figure 1.2 'The Second Quarter'

As a sound-reproduction technology, a bell might seem like a one-note affair. But a bell does have the capacity to reproduce a sound for years on end and hence to speak to a listener of vanished days. Moreover, a church bell is an impressive piece of technology, involving metal-casting, acoustic expertise, a rope, tower, beam and pivot. Schiller's immensely popular poem 'The Song of the Bell', which may have been a source for *The Chimes*,[4] alternates passages recounting the arduous process of forging a bell with the sweet and sublime impressions of its peal:

> Now with potash permeating,
> Let us hasten quick the cast.
> And from lather free
> Must the mixture be,
> That from metal pure abounding
> Pure and full the voice be sounding.
> (Schiller, lines 43–8)

In Dickens's tale, Toby's bells have a more articulate voice than any I have ever heard. They speak to Toby continuously, explaining things, telling him what to do, reminding him of his past, and exhorting him for the future. 'Many's the kind things they say to me', Toby tells his daughter; 'how often have I heard them bells say, "'Toby Veck, Toby Veck, keep a good heart, Toby!'"' (161–2). These bells are full of wisdom and good cheer, the most articulate and verbose sound technology one could ever want. The bells

> were company to him; and when he heard their voices, he had an interest in glancing at their lodging-place, and thinking how they were moved, and what hammers beat upon them. Perhaps he was the more curious about these Bells, because there were points of resemblance between themselves and him. They hung there, in all weathers: with the wind and rain driving in upon them: facing only the outsides of all those houses; never getting any nearer to the blazing fires that gleamed and shone upon the windows, or came puffing out of the chimney tops; and incapable of participation in any of the good things that were constantly being handed, through the street doors and the area railings, to prodigious cooks. (155)

---

[4]   See Slater (1970: 526). An anonymous review of *The Chimes*, in the *Christian Remembrancer* in 1845, remarks, 'the influence of the chimes, and the leading idea of the story, is taken from Schiller's Song of the Bell' ([Anon.] 164).

We recognise the distinctive Dickens note in a passage such as this one
– the poor and overlooked denizen of the streets, gazing at the warmth
and food and finery that he will never enjoy, yet not repining. These are
the emotions readers have always counted on Dickens to furnish, the
feelings we especially associate with his early fiction and his Christmas
stories. If such palpable tugging on readers' heartstrings no longer appeals
today, there can be no doubt of its power in Dickens's time. The author
personally witnessed the extraordinary effect of *The Chimes* when he read
it out loud in what has been identified as his first public reading to a group
outside his home (Andrews 128). Dickens's friend John Forster gathered
a circle of the author's friends to hear him read from the manuscript of
The Chimes in early December 1844, shortly before it was published. The
dozen or so grown men who listened alternated between laughter and
sobbing. The artist Daniel Maclise was so impressed that he drew a pencil
sketch of the event that captures the auditors' intense emotions.[5] Maclise
wrote to Dickens's wife, 'there was not a dry eye in the house . . . shrieks of
laughter – there were indeed – and floods of tears as a relief to them – I do
not think there ever was such a triumphant hour for Charles' (*Letters*, IV:
235, n. 6). Dickens added in his own letter: 'If you had seen Macready last
night, undisguisedly sobbing, and crying on the sofa as I read, you would
have felt (as I did) what a thing it is to have power' (Dickens 1977: 235).

Dickens used this power to capture the personal associations that the
bells had for Toby Veck and to translate those associations into emotion.
The personal, however, is augmented by the public associations that a
bell can evoke. For centuries, the sound of church bells has been integral
to complex social networks: systems of time-keeping, religion, mourn-
ing, marriage, community relations, national holidays, civic honours and
emergencies. The historian Alain Corbin charts the persistence of the
communal role of bells from medieval times all the way up to the end of
the nineteenth century. Corbin describes how the 'impact of a bell helped
create a territorial identity' for those who lived in range of its sound, an
'auditory space that corresponded to a particular notion of territoriality,
one obsessed with mutual acquaintance' (184). The sense of 'an enclosed
space structured by the sound emanating from its center' (184) was crucial to the communal associations of bells. 'Bells shaped the habitus of a
community or, if you will, its culture of the senses. They served to anchor

[5]   For a reproduction of Maclise's drawing, see Cohen 168.

localism, imparting depth to the desire for rootedness and offering the peace of near, well-defined horizons' (185). Corbin's history focuses on villages and small townships, but he insists that much of what he says applies to bell towers dotting the cityscape of Paris in the nineteenth century. We know that Dickens felt this way too from his repeated references to the insular Cockney world bounded by the sound of Bow Bells. Toby certainly looks to his bells for a sense of safety and daily reassurance that, even in his infirm old age, he is a valued contributor to his community.

Such are the inarticulate feelings the bells initially convey. They are a part of Toby's *habitus*, the most crucial part, and Dickens is keenly aware that they play this role in Toby's life without his being able to interpret all these vague feelings to himself, to give them a name or identify them clearly. The bells produce the *affect* of belonging, not more crisply defined emotions. Here we see the first glimmering of why affect theory can be of use to our reading of Dickens – it enables us to distinguish two ways sound operates in Dickens, two forms of acoustic feeling in *The Chimes*, and elsewhere in the author's work. One is direct, emotional – we encounter it most clearly in passages where the author's moral or instructive tendencies come to the fore. Sentimental passages, didactic rhetoric, overt satire, and melodramatic moments often exhibit a direct appeal to readers' emotions. The other is more diffuse, affective – we find it most often in the author's resonant world-building, his magical powers to bring the entire environment of a story to life. Only rarely, as in *The Chimes*, do we see the novelist attempt to represent affect, as opposed to emotion, in dramatic scenes directly. The rarity of such direct assaults on unstructured, non-narrative feelings is perhaps for the best, but it is worth observing that they occur with frequency in the author's Christmas tales. In his second Christmas story, Dickens tries to let personification carry the burden of affect – tries, and I am afraid, fails for most readers today. The allegorical personifications of the chimes as goblin Spirits of the Bells strike an odd note, but the oddity becomes more explicable when one grasps them as the author's straining after indefinable affects.

Dickens points directly to the indefinable character of the bells' affect. 'I don't mean to say that when [Toby] began to take to the Bells, and to knit up his first rough acquaintance with them into something of a closer and more delicate woof, he passed through these considerations one by one, or held any formal review or great field-day in his thoughts' (155). Instead of conscious meanings, the bells produce bodily sensations of belonging.

Dickens almost seems to spell out the distinction central to today's affect theory when he contrasts Toby's inability to 'hold any formal review' of his thoughts about the bells with his physical response to their sound:

> But what I mean to say, and do say is, that as the functions of Toby's body, his digestive organs for example, did of their own cunning, and by a great many operations of which he was altogether ignorant, and the knowledge of which would have astonished him very much, arrive at a certain end; so his mental faculties, without his privity or concurrence, set all these wheels and springs in motion, with a thousand others, when they worked to bring about his liking for the Bells. (155-6)

For Dickens, as for recent literary theorists, affect operates physiologically – it alters the very autonomic nervous system of the body, from the digestive organs to other preconscious mental faculties. As Dickens puts it later in the story, Toby understood such things 'not as a reflection but a bodily sensation' (203).

Dickens seems aware of the importance to affect of the somatic dimension of sound. For those who know how capacious Dickens's curiosity was about all manner of technologies and practices, it will come as no surprise that the novelist knew something about the acoustic theory of the day.[6] John Picker (2003) has written the best account to date of Dickens's interest in contemporary theories of sound and sound technology, from the novelist's eager response to acoustic research in the 1830s to the chapter titled 'What the Waves were Always Saying' in *Dombey and Son* (1846-8) to the 'astonishing' powers of auscultation exhibited by Durdles the stonemason in Dickens's last novel, *The Mystery of Edwin Drood* (1870). Picker highlights Dickens's response to a passage in Charles Babbage's *Ninth Bridgewater Treatise* (1837) on the permanence of sound waves, which the novelist twice alludes to in later decades. Babbage maintained that

> The air itself is one vast library, on whose pages are for ever written all that man has ever said or woman whispered. There, in their mutable but unerring characters, mixed with the earliest, as well as with the latest sighs of mortality, stand for ever recorded, vows unredeemed, promises unfulfilled, perpetuating in the united movements of each particle, the testimony of man's changeful will. (Babbage 112)

---

[6] I discuss Dickens's relationship with two prominent acoustical theorists, Wheatstone and Babbage, in 'The Voice in the Machine' (1997) and 'Hacking the Nineteenth Century' (2000) respectively.

In *Dombey and Son* Dickens mentions the 'speculation of an ingenious modern philosopher' (Babbage), that the 'vibration' of 'a sound in air . . . may go on travelling for ever through the interminable fields of space' (quoted in Picker 17).

Dickens knew about acoustic wave theory not just from Babbage but from his acquaintance with Wheatstone. The two probably first met in the early 1840s at a dinner given by the actor William Macready; Dickens refers to Wheatstone in his letters as a friend of Miss Burdett-Coutts; and Dickens may have also known him through George Cruikshank, who was a good friend of the scientist. Sir Charles Wheatstone, who invented the telegraph in the same year as Samuel Morse, began his research career by investigating the properties of acoustic waves. At the age of nineteen, he created a stir in London by exhibiting a musical toy called the 'Enchanted Lyre', in which a replica of an ancient lyre was hung from the ceiling by a thin cord and was made to play tunes for hours on end without any apparent human intervention. This stunt turned out to be a scientific demonstration of the ability of sound waves to travel more efficiently through solids than air. The lyre was connected to the sounding board of a piano in a room above, and the notes propagated down through the wire were reproduced on the strings, but the sound of the piano did not reach the audience's ears through the air. In Wheatstone's publication of his results in 1823, he emphasised that sound waves produced sympathetic vibrations on the strings of the lyre and thus onward to the ears of the listener through physical contact. One vibrating membrane 'communicated' its motion to another via a physical medium, whether wire or air.

Wheatstone's best-known acoustic instrument was a device he named the 'Kaleidophone'. In Wheatstone's 1827 paper on this 'new Philosophical Toy', he explains that if the rods are plucked or tapped with a hammer, the bead on the top will describe elaborate but regular patterns, which vary depending on the angle of vibration. This instrument, like his later wave machine, helped demonstrate the physical presence of sound waves not merely as static patterns but as motion. Wheatstone's experiments also suggested that the motion of the 'vibrating particles' was more complex than researchers had guessed, something Wheatstone confirmed six years later by developing the mathematical formula for the famous patterns created by sound waves on Chladni plates.[7] Historians of science have

[7] For an account of the research of Ernst Chladni, the Father of Acoustics, see

focused on Wheatstone's efforts to make sound visible, and hence, to 'write' sound. But his acoustic experiments actually had a double impulse: (1) to make the feeling of sound accessible through as many senses as possible and (2) to explain the sensory effects of sound mathematically. In both of these ambitions, he sought ways to make apparent the material or embodied presence of the sound wave.

Wheatstone and Babbage's findings challenge the tendency in contemporary media studies to regard information technology as inevitably leading to the disassociation of the senses. Following Friedrich Kittler, critics often assert that technological mediation abstracts the subject, dislocating the senses. According to this line of thinking, reproduced sounds divide the original from its copy, detaching sounds from the context of their utterance. Kittler's point, however, applies more to recording technology, which stores sound for later playback, than to communication technology, which transmits sound from one point to another. Of course, all communication devices such as the telegraph store data (however briefly) in the process of communicating, and recording technologies such as the phonograph communicate as well as store information. But attending to sound reproduction in itself, as a theoretically separate process from sound recording, would alter current approaches to the history of nineteenth-century soundscapes. The imposition of a recording paradigm on all forms of sound technology results in an overemphasis on sound as a form of inscription or writing, with all the modern problems of abstraction and dislocation which that entails, rather than as a form of embodied experience. Jonathan Sterne's research in this area brings him to a similar conclusion. Sterne notes that the tendency to 'fetishize sound recording over other forms of sound reproduction' is what makes many critics emphasise a 'certain disembodiment of sound' (50).

In the first sound-recording device, Edison's phonograph (1877), the function of data storage is paramount, just as it was in many nineteenth-century visual technologies: the typewriter, teletype and early cinema. Edison's device did seem to produce an eerie sense of disassociation.

Sterne (43-5). Chladni demonstrated that sound impinges on matter in physical ways, forming reproducible patterns that can be seen with the eye, under certain circumstances, and preserved in drawings. The vibrations produced beautiful patterns, which have come to be known as 'Chladni figures'. Chladni toured Europe, delighting audiences in lecture halls by producing his figures in sand by drawing a violin bow across a metal plate.

Ivan Kreilkamp has shown how Edison's phonograph provoked uncanny responses in listeners. Hearing a 'human voice re-articulated again and again by a machine' could have the paradoxical effect of seeming to alienate the words from the person who spoke them: they became 'autonomous, detached phonemes, fragments of sound waves given material form on a tape or phonograph cylinder' (Kreilkamp 213, 217). The alienation, however, should be seen as a distinctive feature of recording technology's capacity to store sound, to preserve it as in a wax museum – or rather, wax cylinder. Hence the uncanny effect Kreilkamp notes. Eric Ames observes, 'The late-nineteenth-century discourse on the phonograph revolved around the medium's claim to give voice to the dead' (311). Ames quotes Edison's prediction that 'For the purpose of preserving the sayings, the voices, and *the last words* of the dying member of a family – as of great men – the phonograph will unquestionably outrank the photograph' (Edison 533–54, italics in original; quoted in Ames 312).

One might be tempted to recuperate the affective difference between recording and communication technologies in terms of periodisation, identifying the sense of dislocation produced by Edison's machine with modernity, but that would oversimplify the issues. Nineteenth-century communications such as the telegraph and telephone persisted into the twentieth century, side by side with the recording technologies that Kittler studies. The former devices reinforced rather than severed the connection between signs and the senses. The physical impact of sound and touch in the telegraph's operation contrasts with the disembodiment often identified with the modern encounter with information (Clayton 1997). By consolidating the sensory properties of the signal, communication technologies appeared to intensify rather than abstract. Steven Connor emphasises a similar point about the telephone: 'The telephone offers a quasi-controlled collapse of boundaries, in which the listening self can be pervaded by the vocal body of another while yet remaining at a distance from it' (206). The affective difference was simultaneously social and technological. Nineteenth-century communication devices brought people together and hence were perceived as 'annihilating distance', while storage devices reanimated the dead. The phonograph preserved rather than transmitted sound waves – the voices of the dead seemed uncannily contained inside the phonograph. The physical transmission of sound, by contrast, appeared to enhance life, connecting two distant but equally vital places.

In *The Chimes*, the ringing bells both reproduce sound and communicate messages, but communication is primary. Although the bells continually remind Toby of who he is and where he has come from, they also communicate in visceral terms what he should think about the world and what he owes to himself and his daughter. This medium does not distance sound from body but rather reinforces the sense of material connection. Toby's feeling of being physically battered by sound waves while the bells toll captures this somatic dimension: 'The Chimes came clashing in upon him' and 'made the very air spin' (174); or again, later in the story: 'Bewildered by . . . the uproar of the Bells, which all this while were ringing, [Toby] clung to a wooden pillar for support, and turned his white face here and there, in mute and stunned astonishment' (202).

The assault on Toby's ears shatters his sense of self. The belief in his competence as a porter, which had sustained him through many a frostbitten day while waiting on the streets for work, collapses under this sonic battering. The assault takes the form of reproduced words. Dickens stresses the fact that the bells re-articulate the words Toby had heard earlier in the day. These bells are able to quote the cruel lessons of political economy verbatim. Listen to them repeat the teachings of the three callous rich men that hectored Toby earlier in the day: that the complaining poor should be 'put down', that the present was worse than the 'good old Times', and that charity should be regulated by 'Facts and Figures':

> Still the Bells, pealing forth their changes, made the very air spin. Put'em down, Put'em down! Good old Times, Good old Times! Facts and Figures, Facts and Figures! Put'em down, Put'em down! If they said anything they said this, till the brain of Toby reeled. (174)

This is an example of what sound reproduction was prior to recording. But an unexamined reliance on a recording paradigm limits our ability to hear it as such. Acoustic technologies that reproduce sound without storing data produce distinctive affects. Reproducing sound by producing it anew preserves the listener's relationship to a singular event, even as it repeats the sounds one has heard before. Toby's experience in the bell tower helps recover what it feels like to hear sounds re-articulated not as disembodied echoes but as material presences. The advent of sound recording may have introduced a new relation to acoustic experience, but it did not do away with older modes of responding to sound. Toby's embodied auditory experience would not have vanished with the invention of recording – it persisted alongside characteristically 'modern', fragmented affects such as the eerie sense of dislocation experienced by the first auditors of Edison's phonograph.

Where the bells initially produced feelings of safety and reassurance, confirming Toby's identity as a valued worker and member of the community, at the crisis in the story they carry a terrible affect. The shift takes place because Toby's enclosed auditory space is invaded by the three reformers from the upper classes. Alain Corbin sees the territorial identity of a bell, its habitus, as always vulnerable to potential violation. Auditory space is fragile, 'haunted by the notion of limits as well as the threat of their being transgressed' (Corbin 185). Toby's space is violated in a particularly rude fashion when the three men step out of a fine house onto the doorstep where Toby is eating his meagre lunch and begin berating him for his shiftlessness. One who indicts him for eating the supposedly wasteful meal of tripe – wasteful because the poor should consume less expensive dishes – adds injury to insult by taking the last bite of Toby's tripe and popping it into his own mouth.

Dickens's satire of these three reformers, and a fourth wealthy man, a hypocritical philanthropist that Toby meets later in the story, has attracted most of the critical attention that *The Chimes* has received over the years. Michael Slater calls the story 'the most overtly Radical fiction [Dickens] ever wrote' (2009: 229). Dickens told Forster with glee that he was out 'to shame the cruel and canting' (Dickens 1977: 204), and judging from the accusations of the Tory press that he was 'holding up to ridicule and contempt the efforts of the higher classes' (quoted in Slater 1971: 140), Dickens succeeded. The three wealthy men are Mr Filer, a satirical version of a political economist, who proceeds to prove by mathematics that Toby is helping to starve his neighbours and that Meg and her fiancé are too poor to marry (Dickens 1971: 168); Alderman Cute, who prides himself on being able to talk to the poor in their own lingo, wants to 'put down' all the 'nonsense about Want' and the 'cant in vogue about Starvation', and he vows to punish with especial fury anyone who thinks himself so desperate as to attempt suicide (170); and a melancholy man who is always lamenting 'the good old times', when there was a 'bold peasantry, and all that sort of thing' (168).[8] In the best recent treatment

---

[8] Slater discusses the decision Dickens made at the urging of Forster to delete references to Disraeli's Young England movement in the portrait of the Tory

of *The Chimes*, Sally Ledger discusses the influence of Dickens's Radical friend and fellow journalist, Douglas Jerrold, on these satiric portraits, and relates them to Dickens's renunciation of paternalism as a way to ameliorate the condition of the poor (106–41).

These satirical passages were meant to provoke fierce *emotion*, to goad readers into sharing the novelist's outrage. Dickens wants his Christmas audience to understand the magnitude of the injustice in the world. When the bells give voice to the 'hopes and thoughts of mortals', they only say what all humane people should say, what the very streets should shout to the heavens. They cry out in anger at the wrongs of poverty and starvation, of workers reduced to impotent fury, of little girls driven to prostitution, of old men dying abandoned and friendless in the workhouse. As Toby says, 'What does it matter whether they speak it or not?' (161) – they *should* say such things. They should proclaim in peals of embodied speech the hopes and thoughts of mortals. This 'militant joy and scorn' delighted G. K. Chesterton at the beginning of the twentieth century – 'the cheap advice to live cheaply, the base advice to live basely, above all, the preposterous primary assumption that the rich are to advise the poor and not the poor the rich' (Chesterton 124). The satire seems over-obvious and too topical to readers today. But the blatant emotional claims of such polemics allow us to distinguish this vein in his fiction – the political equivalent of the melodramatic vein in the dream of Meg's suicide and the sentimental vein in the rescue of a poor man's daughter from the dangers of prostitution – as vehicles for emotion, with unmistakable Radical intentions and unambiguous lessons for the reader. This vein stands over against the comparatively unstructured and free-floating affect the bells elsewhere provoke.

We witness the affective power of bells most distinctly in Dickens's fiction when they seem to reproduce the inchoate thoughts and words of a people as a whole. Dickens's bells sound notes belonging to social groups, not just personal emotions, and the collective longing their voice most often conveys is captured by a line from a nursery rhyme, 'Turn again, Whittington, Lord Mayor of London'. Characters in *Barnaby Rudge, Old Curiosity Shop, Martin Chuzzlewit, Dombey and Son, David Copperfield,*

gentleman who misses the good old days (Slater 1970: 511–14), and Slater also identifies Alderman Cute as a satire of Sir Peter Laurie, who had recently gained notoriety for sentencing to hanging an impoverished mother who had attempted to kill herself and her baby (1970: 524).

Bleak House, *Little Dorrit*, and *A Tale of Two Cities*, all hear that same phrase ringing in the bells of London. The rhyme commemorates the legend that Dick Whittington, thrice mayor of London, was running away from home as a boy to seek his fortune elsewhere until the city bells called him back, promising the greatness he ultimately achieved. The rhyme appealed to Dickens, almost as an allegory of his own success (James Joyce noticed this fact in an essay on Dickens),[9] and the allegory conveys more than a single idea. For Dickens, the bells in Dick Whittington are connected with virtues such as hard work, self-help and persistence under adversity that the novelist sees as the hallmarks of his own success. For example, when in *The Old Curiosity Shop*, charming but shiftless Dick Swiveller muses, 'Perhaps the bells might strike up "Turn again Swiveller, Lord Mayor of London"', the comedy comes from the immense improbability, despite the fact that, as Swiveller says, 'Whittington's name was Dick' (466).

Like legends, bells accrue whatever societal meanings they possess through repetition of the same motif. Big Ben, for example, has deep associations with English national identity. It is a symbol of England's majesty and power, the note that spoke most clearly in the nineteenth century of London's place as the capital of world-wide empire. One of the earliest sound recordings made on English soil was a tape of Big Ben (1890), a fact that certainly should not surprise us. This recording was made for Thomas Edison by Mary Helen Ferguson, the governess of Edison's London agent, using one of Edison's brown wax cylinders. Mary Ferguson described herself as 'the first English lady phonographist', and she is thought to have been the person who made the recordings of Florence Nightingale and Robert Browning, among others.[10]

---

[9]   Joyce observes that Dickens's true genius flourished best within earshot of 'the chimes of Bow Bells' and that Dickens may have regarded Dick Whittington's story as a parable for the course of his own life (Berrone 34–5). Joyce's essay on Dickens, 'The Centenary of Charles Dickens', was written in Italian as part of an examination for a teaching appointment in Padua.

[10]   In an e-mail communication, Jason Camlot supplies the following information about Mary Helen Ferguson from an unpublished manuscript by Bennett Maxwell in the British Library: 'Mary Helen Ferguson was governess to the Gouraud children and also worked as Colonel Gouraud's part-time secretary. Shortly after the arrival of the "Perfected Phonograph" she wrote an article for *The Lady* in which she described herself as "the first English lady phonographist", in other words, the first audio typist. Many of Colonel Gouraud's early speech recordings were accompanied by a typed transcript, and these were usually signed with the

The collective character of bells' sonic experience has the advantage for an artist such as Dickens of expanding the range of figurative associations with which the note could be charged. In that respect, sound reproduction before recording functioned a little like fairy tales, legends and literary conventions. Each repetition of a fairy tale or rhyme is a new performance, but it draws upon the accumulated reservoir of associations created by prior performances. This is the deep logic 'Dick Whittington' shares with a bell. Both rhyme and ring mean more by sounding the same. This idea can be taken further. Dickens's view of bells is related to his love of barrel organs, pantomimes, Punch and Judy shows and the popular theatre. All these modes of popular entertainment are so conventional as to be what we call formulaic. They represent a form of folk memory, of reproduction without recording. Yet each performance is unique. It is not merely the associations of the listener that vary. The objective conditions of each rehearing change – the air quality, surrounding noises, time of day, proximity, attention level, social context and more. The effect is of repetition within the context of difference, an effect that allows the imagination – both private and public – room to range.

A similar affect is achieved by allegory in Dickens. At the climax of *The Chimes*, Dickens personifies the bells as goblins. The allegorical personification gives rise to the story's subtitle, 'A Goblin Story of Some Bells that Rang an Old Year Out and a New Year In', and it inspires the copious illustrations, created by no fewer than four of the author's favoured artists. The illustrations carry this personification to extravagant lengths. The frontispiece (Figure 1) shows nude goblins streaming from the mouths of the bells and flowing to all the margins of the page. The story is divided into four quarters, and each begins with an illustration showing the various moods and expressions Toby will hear in the bells during that chapter. In Richard Doyle's opening plate for the 'The Second Quarter' (Figure 2), the goblins grin their approval at Toby comforting a fugitive labourer and his exhausted little girl. During Toby's nightmare, in which he climbs to the top of the church tower, or dreams he does, the goblins angrily reproach him for believing what the political economists have said. The

initials M.H.F. She went on to make recordings of Florence Nightingale, Martin Lanfried, Robert Browning and Cardinal Manning, and was later placed in charge of the "Music Room" at Edison House in Northumberland Avenue, where she supervised all the musical recordings.'

third section begins with another illustration by Doyle. Dickens explains these goblin figures as manifestations of Toby's own thoughts: 'Spirits of the Bells. Their sound upon the air. . . . They take such shapes and occupations as the hopes and thoughts of mortals, and the recollections they have stored up, give them' (208).

This explanation might at first seem to trivialise the sound of the bells. It suggests that their unchanging tones can only express what a listener reads into them, that the meanings they reproduce are only projections of the hearer's own thoughts. But this point – virtually self-evident to the sceptical modern reader – is not what Dickens means to convey. The multitudinous goblins that throng the drawings and texts indicate the collective character of the bells' allegory. It is instructive that Dickens's allegorical bent surfaced in his Christmas books, tales meant to embody the spirit of a shared festival season. At its most basic, allegory functions by invoking communal values. It gives most pleasure when its listeners understand and accept the world view it expresses. This is how allegory escapes being merely subjective, and this is why readers who are used to the multiple meanings of modern texts sometimes find allegory unappealing. Sceptical modern readers do not like a work's meaning being circumscribed. They do not like having to accept a collective understanding rather than their own, private interpretation. But before recording technology made sound into a form of writing, allegory was one of the most effective ways reproduced sounds gave voice to public meanings. A bell such as Big Ben allegorises English national pride, regardless of what personal associations it also has for individuals.

At the end of *The Chimes* Toby awakes from his self-shattering dreams and finds a joyous New Year's day dawning. Meg is beside him, plying her needle to brighten her simple wedding dress with ribbons. While Toby struggles to shake the cobwebs from his head, the circle by the hearth is joined by his daughter's fiancé, and shortly thereafter, what should start ringing in the New Year, but the 'Great Bells', 'melodious, deep-mouthed, noble Bells' (242)? No sooner had the pealing finished than the door was thrown open again to admit the labourer and his little girl, whom Toby had saved from starving the day before, and again, to admit a whole procession of friends and neighbours, beating on drums and playing bells, 'not *the* Bells, but a portable collection, on a frame' (243). And as you might expect, the story ends on this joyous note, closing right there with only a final direct address to You, the reader, to join the celebration.

The ending takes only a few pages, for the restoration of emotion, narrative and New Year's good cheer comes so pat to Dickens that he need spend almost no time on this dénouement. After the indistinct and disordering affects, the allegorical assault of goblin sounds, familiar sentiments perform their expected role in drawing the tale to a close. The ready availability of these emotions for their appointed task cheapens them in our eyes. We have learned to prefer the kind of 'intensities' (Massumi) that lie at the very edge of intelligibility. What we have not learned, or perhaps have forgotten, is how the body listens to remembered sounds.

Works cited

Ames, Eric, 2003. 'The Sound of Evolution', *Modernism / modernity*, 10: 297–325.

Andrews, Malcolm, 2006. *Charles Dickens and his Performing Selves: Dickens and the Public Readings*. New York: Oxford University Press.

[Anon.], 2005. 'From an Unsigned Review of *The Chimes*', *Christian Remembrancer* ((January 1845), ix: 301–4). In *Charles Dickens: The Critical Heritage*, ed. P. Collins. London: Routledge.

Babbage, Charles, 1837. *The Ninth Bridgewater Treatise: A Fragment*. 2nd edn. London: John Murray, 1838.

Berrone, Louis, 1977. *James Joyce in Padua*. New York: Random House.

Brown, Bill, 2001. 'Thing Theory', *Critical Inquiry*, special issue on *Things*, 28: 1–22.

Butler, Judith, John Guillory and Kendall Thomas, eds., 2000. *What's Left of Theory? New Work on the Politics of Literary Theory*. London: Routledge.

Chesterton, G. K., 1942 [1906]. *Charles Dickens, The Last of the Great Men*. New York: The Press of the Readers Club.

Clayton, Jay, 1997. 'The Voice in the Machine: Hazlitt, Hardy, James', in *Language Machines: Technologies of Literary and Cultural Production*, ed. J. Masten, P. Stallybrass and N. J. Vickers. New York: Routledge, pp. 209–32.

Clayton, Jay, 2000. 'Hacking the Nineteenth Century', in *Victorian Afterlife: Postmodern Culture Rewrites the Nineteenth Century*, ed. John R. Kucich and Dianne F. Sadoff. Minneapolis: University of Minnesota Press, pp. 186–210.

Clayton, Jay, 2003. *Charles Dickens in Cyberspace: The Afterlife of the Nineteenth Century in Postmodern Culture*. New York: Oxford University Press.

Cohen, Jane R., 1980. *Charles Dickens and his Original Illustrators*. Columbus: Ohio State University Press.

Connor, Steven,1997. 'The Modern Auditory I', in *Rewriting the Self: Histories from the Renaissance to the Present*, ed. R. Porter. London: Routledge, pp. 203–23.

Corbin, Alain, 2004. 'Identity, Bells and the Nineteenth-Century French Village', in *Hearing History: A Reader*, ed. M. M. Smith. Athens, Georgia: University of Georgia Press, pp. 184–204.

Crary, Jonathan, 1990. *Techniques of the Observer: On Vision and Modernity in the Nineteenth Century*. Cambridge, Massachusetts: MIT Press.

Dickens, Charles, 1965–2002. *Letters of Charles Dickens*, vol. IV (1977), ed. Kathleen Tillotson. Pilgrim Edition. Oxford: Clarendon Press.

Dickens, Charles, 1971 [1844]. *The Chimes*, in The *Christmas Books: Volume One*, ed. Michael Slater. Harmondsworth: Penguin.

Dickens, Charles, 1972 [1840-1]. *The Old Curiosity Shop*, ed. Angus Easson. Harmondsworth: Penguin.

Eagleton, Terry, 2003. *After Theory*. New York: Basic Books.

Edison, Thomas A., 1878. 'The Phonograph and Its Future', *North American Review*, 262: 527–36.

Elliott, Jane, 2011. *Theory after 'Theory'*. London: Routledge.

Grossberg, Lawrence, 1992. *We Gotta Get Out of This Place: Popular Conservatism and Postmodern Culture*. New York: Routledge.

Kittler, Friedrich A., 1990. *Discourse Networks 1800/1900*, ed. Michael Metteer. Stanford, California: Stanford University Press.

Kreilkamp, Ivan, 1997. 'A Voice without a Body: The Phonographic Logic of Heart of Darkness', *Victorian Studies*, 40: 211–44.

Ledger, Sally, 2007. *Dickens and the Popular Radical Imagination*. Cambridge: Cambridge University Press.

Massumi, Brian, 2002. *Parables for the Virtual: Movement, Affect, Sensation*. Durham, North Carolina: Duke University Press.

Mitchell, W. J. T., ed., 2004. *Special Issue of Critical Inquiry on the State of Literary Theory*, 30.

Ngai, Sianne, 2005. *Ugly Feelings*. Cambridge, Massachusetts: Harvard University Press.

Picker, John M., 2003. *Victorian Soundscapes*. New York: Oxford University Press.

Schiller, Friedrich, 'The Song of the Bell', trans. Marianna Wertz. The Schiller Institute, online at <http://www.schillerinstitute.org/transl/trans_schil_1poems.html>.

Seltzer, Mark, 1992. *Bodies and Machines*. New York: Routledge.

Slater, Michael, 1970. 'Carlyle and Jerrold into Dickens: A Study of "The Chimes"', *Nineteenth-Century Fiction*, 24: 506–26.

Slater, Michael, 1971. 'Introduction to *The Chimes*', in *The Christmas Books: Volume One*, ed. Michael Slater. Harmondsworth: Penguin, pp. vii–xxiv.

Slater, Michael, 2009. *Charles Dickens*. New Haven: Yale University Press.

Sterne, Jonathan, 2003. *The Audible Past: Cultural Origins of Sound Reproduction*. Durham, North Carolina: Duke University Press.

Terada, Rei, 2001. *Feeling in Theory: Emotion after the 'Death of the Subject'*. Cambridge, Massachusetts: Harvard University Press.

Dickens, sexuality and the body; or, clock loving: Master Humphrey's queer objects of desire

HOLLY FURNEAUX

By way of an abstract

This essay comes out of Dickens's fascination with stuff: specifically his interrelated interests in strange bodies and strange things. It brings together lines of enquiry inspired by thing theory, queer theory and gender studies to explore Dickens's investment in the imaginative, emotional and erotic appeal of objects. I suggest that in conjunction these approaches reveal the centrality of the material to Dickens's queer imagination, as his thinking on human/object relations participates in his wider scrutiny of the naturalness and inevitability of gender roles, heterosexuality, and, indeed, the human. In this I am particularly inspired by William Cohen's recent treatment of queer, which is not (just) about 'sexual counterortho-doxy' but about a presentation of 'the openness of the body to the world by the senses as a type of permeability, or penetrability, that is not reduc-ible to heterosexuality, nor is it even limited to the realm of the sexual'. Queer theory here meets posthuman and cyborgian approaches, offering a 'critique of the human – with its phantasmatic completeness and integrity' (2008: 134). I take as my focus the bizarre text *Master Humphrey's Clock* as Dickens's most explicit meditation on the joys of object-loving.

Reading Dickensian sex

Dickens's work is 'absolutely saturated', James Eli Adams recently announced, with sexuality (235).[1] Eli Adams reads the sexual as cannily presented by Dickens as blatant public spectacle rather than a hidden truth uncovered

---

[1] Eli Adams uses *The Pickwick Papers* as his central example.

through careful critical excavation. In doing so, he follows a Foucauldian trajectory away from the 'repressive hypothesis' of Victorian prudery. Under this hypothesis, which Michel Foucault firmly refuted, sex was silenced, only speaking its name in the most oblique or covert ways. To recognise the overt presentation of desire in Dickens is to surrender the alluring premise 'that sexuality in the Victorian novel is a largely unwitting or uncanny production, an effect generated by novelists unable to grasp their own dynamics of representation' (Eli Adams 243). Sergeant Buzfuz's over-determined mode of textual scrutiny – Buzfuz produces Pickwick's short note to his landlady requesting 'Chops and Tomata sauce' as evidence of amorous intentions at Pickwick's trail for breach of promise (*Pickwick Papers*, ch. 33: 454) – presents Eli Adams's exemplary case. Via Buzfuz, who urges the court to read for textual absences and silences ('They are not open, fervent, eloquent epistles, breathing nothing but the language of affectionate attachment. They are covert, sly, underhanded communications, but, fortunately, far more conclusive than if couched in the most glowing language and the most poetic imagery – letters that must be viewed with a cautious and suspicious eye' (ch. 33: 454)), Eli Adams points out that a hermeneutics of suspicion is not always the most appropriate mode. Sharon Marcus makes a similar case in her advocacy of a method that she calls 'just reading', which can supplement and provide different interpretations from those offered by 'symptomatic reading'. While 'symptomatic reading' is Buzfuzian in its attention to 'how the marginal and the invisible are central to narratives that apparently occlude them', 'just reading' does not 'claim to plumb hidden depths but to account more fully for what texts present on their surface but critics have failed to notice' (Marcus 76–7).

In seeing Victorian sex as obvious, a given easily discernible rather than a carefully concealed guilty secret, such approaches participate in a turn in Victoriana, in and outside the academy, by which stereotypes of the prudish Victorians have been replaced by their opposite: a widespread fascination with polymorphous Victorian desire. This new wave of speaking sex – a proliferation of discourses comparable to that Foucault identified, contra the repressive hypothesis, as characteristic of the nineteenth century – is especially apparent in reinventions of the Victorians in neo-Victorian fiction, film and television adaptations of nineteenth-century texts and lives, and in academic work.[2] The aura of prudery

---

[2] For detailed work on neo-Victoriana see Kaplan. I discuss the legacy of the

around Dickens has perhaps, given his status in the West as an emblem of wholesome Englishness and icon (if improbably given the details of his work and life) of a particular brand of domestic respectability, been a little slower to dissipate. As we approach the bicentenary of Dickens's birth, the climate of Dickens studies has rather altered from that of 1970, the centenary of his death, when Pamela Hansford Johnson wrote: 'It is due, perhaps in part, to Dickens that so many people believe that the Victorians were totally ignorant about the by-ways of sexual behaviour. The image of the "family" audience became so strong with him that, as he grew older, he failed more and more to use even those liberties that Thackeray and Trollope found available' (173). In this view Dickens is guilty of the form of Podsnappery that he lambastes in *Our Mutual Friend* through the pompous and hypocritical criteria of propriety applied by Mr Podsnap: 'would it bring a blush into the cheek of a young person?' (ch. 11: 132)

Dickens's work has, in recent decades, richly rewarded scholarship on the representation of sexuality, through readings attentive to the speaking silences of his work – the exemplary text of this kind is William Cohen's interpretation of the homoerotic and masturbatory concerns of *Great Expectations* – and interpretations interested in overt, yet long overlooked, aspects of the fiction, such as Marcus's. Cohen advances a nuanced approach to 'sexual unspeakability' which 'does not function simply as a collection of prohibitions for Victorian writers. Rather, it affords them abundant opportunities to develop an elaborate discourse – richly ambiguous, subtly coded, prolix and polyvalent' (1996: 3). Marcus takes a different approach to *Great Expectations* that focuses on what she sees as the blatant, but previously overlooked, spectacle of 'Dickens's unselfconscious exhibition of Miss Havisham's overt relish for Estella' (170). Pip's education in desiring Estella via homoerotic female intimacy is most apparent, Marcus suggests, when the novel is read with an eye to Dickens's acquaintance with the worlds of fashion and dolls, particularly the doll tales owned by his daughters.

Though it is questionable whether Marcus's reading of Dickens is any more about textual surface than the 'symptomatic reading' she critiques, I take seriously the potential of 'just reading' as a move from an implicit assumption that the erotic in Victorian culture is repressed, and that furtive evocations of desire are inevitably transgressive rebellions against

repressive hypothesis in 'Victorian Sexuality' (2011).

cultural prohibitions. Once at least some forms of sensuality and desire are seen as working with, rather than against, the grain of Victorian culture, Dickens's unabashed celebration of a range of eroticisms comes into clearer view. While Marcus's loaded terminology of 'just reading' has come in for some criticism – and it certainly is not helpful to insist on the ascendancy of any one form of textual/sexual scrutiny where others may offer equally vibrant possibilities – attention to 'what texts present on their surface' is particularly appropriate for an author like Dickens, so concerned with the material: the heft and reproduction of manuscript, the book as thing, and the things of the book.[3]

Surface loving in *Master Humphrey's Clock*

Perhaps Dickens's most thorough object lesson in the joys of thing-loving is presented in *Master Humphrey's Clock*, a weekly miscellany which ran from 4 April 1840 to 4 December 1841. This text, Dickens's first effort at a magazine, is perhaps the most overlooked of Dickens's oeuvre. The attempt at a miscellany was a failure, and Dickens, mindful of falling sales figures and muted responses from his readers, quickly abandoned the sketches/letters/short-story format to give his readers what they most wanted from him, serialised novels. By its eleventh week the *Clock* was given over to the serialisation of *The Old Curiosity Shop* (1840–1), followed by *Barnaby Rudge* (1841). Given its short-lived success, the *Clock* material now appears as an odd protuberance, a residue of attempted meta-narrative, with an awkwardly negotiated relationship to the novels it carried. John Bowen, mindful of 'how much Dickens's imagination loved prosthetic things that belong and do not belong to the bodies to which they are attached', suggests in his work on *The Old Curiosity Shop* that we look again at this 'strange supplement, this prosthesis of the novel, Little Nell's wooden leg' (143).[4] The 'just reading' of this material which follows here aims to bring this lesser-known text back into the purview of Dickens studies in order to demonstrate the emphatic ways in which Dickens's work celebrates curious bodies and desires.

---

[3] Kucich, for example, has criticised projects of 'just' and 'surface reading', arguing that they 'inadvertently reveal' 'the categories "visible", "surface" and "literal" to be contingent' (73).
[4] Given the history of publication, however, it seems more appropriate to view Nell herself as a wooden leg, or at least as a prop to the struggling Master Humphrey.

Master Humphrey, the miscellany's elderly, disabled protagonist, explains in the inaugural issue that his attachment to his clock is both aesthetic – he describes the clock's materiality and texture – and nostalgic: 'It is associated with my earliest recollections. It stood upon the staircase at home (I call it home still mechanically), nigh sixty years ago [. . .] it is a quaint old thing in a huge oaken case curiously and richly carved' (10). But the clock's principal attraction springs from the sense of emotional fellowship that it offers its owner. While Master Humphrey shares some clock attributes (describing things 'mechanically', for example) the clock takes on a life of feeling of its own(er): 'I incline to it' Master Humphrey explains 'as if it were alive, and could understand and give me back the love I bear it' (10).

After the usual deliberations Dickens rejected the alternative titles *Master Humphrey's Tale*, *Master Humphrey's Narrative*, *A Passage in Master Humphrey's Life*, in favour of one that presented Master Humphrey's 'prize' possession as eponymous hero.[5] In choosing this title Dickens places the relationship between man and clock at the centre of the miscellany, and the clock is made the mechanism for the generation of narrative throughout. The over-arching framing narrative of the journal is that all its contents, having been written by Master Humphrey and his small, all-male, story-telling society of authors, are placed in the clock case, to be drawn forth as required, supplying the material for nightly manuscript readings:

> In the bottom of the dark old closet, where the steady pendulum throbs and beats with healthy action [. . .] there are piles of dusty papers constantly placed there by our hands, that we may link our enjoyments with my old friend, and draw means to beguile time from the heart of time itself. (12)

The tactile and emotional conduit that the clock provides between members of this circle, and between these putative authors and the readers of the miscellany, is laid out in the introduction to the first manuscript. This is authored by Master Humphrey's best human friend, the deaf gentleman, who is the first member, somewhat surprisingly given his specific disability, to be recruited to the story-telling circle:

> But still clinging to my old friend [the clock], and naturally desirous that all its merits should be known, I am tempted to open (somewhat

---

5   For details of Dickens's deliberation over titles see Forster, I: 176.

irregularly and against our laws, I must admit) the clock-case. The first roll of paper on which I lay my hand is in the writing of the deaf gentleman. I shall have to speak of him in my next paper, and how can I better approach that welcome task than by prefacing it with a production of his own pen, consigned to the safe keeping of my honest Clock by his own hand? (12–13)

This precious 'roll of paper', that furnishes the majority of copy for the miscellany's inaugural instalment, has passed from hand to hand via the 'honest' body of the clock. The felt relationship between people and things, explored through a tactile vocabulary attentive to 'clinging' and the laying on of hands, is established in this first number as integral to the circulation of text.

Authorship and the affective experience of commodity culture

The animation of this clock in Master Humphrey's treatment of it 'as if it were alive' and his imbuing of its wooden form with a 'healthy' heartbeat and with characteristics such as 'honesty' and an aptitude for love, is typical of Dickens's much-remarked fascination with the inanimate made animate and vice versa. Since Dorothy van Ghent drew attention to this feature of his work in 1953, there has been a rich variety of scholarship interested in 'how thoroughly and pervasively Dickens confuses the categories of persons and things. It is', as Michael Hollington puts it, 'a kind of trademark of his imagination' (1). Such work has received new impetus from the development of thing theory, as explored by thinkers such as Bill Brown and Elaine Freedgood, and by the related turn, or turn back, in Victorian studies to material culture.

In her magnificent recent study of *Household Words* (1850–9), Dickens's first successful edited miscellany, Catherine Waters demonstrates the centrality of an interest in commodity culture to Dickens's editorial and journalistic projects. Waters notes the journal's 'fascination with changing relationships between people and things that distinguishes its attempt to come to terms with the mid-nineteenth century development of commodity culture' (16). She points out that 'Dickens filled *Household Words* with articles addressing commodity culture in one way or another: biographies of raw materials; stories spun from advertisements; process articles describing visits to manufactories; tales of the flaneur; and narratives describing those residual or marginal economies in which waste is recycled' (7). Here 'goods seem to take on a life of their own', especially in the journal's many '"biographies" of commodities' (13).

Waters's work is important in recognising a range of responses to commodities in *Household Words*, as diverse contributors offer insights, often ambivalent and conflicting, to the 'increasing presence of the commodity in their daily lives' (7). This variety of relationships with stuff is not so apparent in earlier, more strictly Marxist readings, like van Ghent's, in which Dickens is presumed to share Marx's critical stance on the subordination of use to exchange value, and on the mystification and disappearance of labour in goods as they enter the market. As Waters helpfully glosses Marx, in *Capital* (1867), 'we see an inversion in the "natural" relation between people and things, as objects acquire a life of their own and come to dominate those who produce them' (4). Dickens is certainly critical of forms of mechanistic domination that supplant human relationships. This facet of his work is effectively documented by, for example, Katherine Inglis, who examines the ascendancy of automata and the 'destabilisation of human agency' in Dickens's fiction (1), and Hollington, who observes the malevolence of objects in *The Old Curiosity Shop* as a 'fundamental feature of the novel in its analysis of nineteenth-century capitalism – it depicts a society where people treat other people and even themselves as things to be bought and sold' (1). Hollington notes, however, that the novel is not univocal in its presentation of commodities, 'elsewhere [. . .] objects are represented as faithful companions who share and sympathise with the lives of their owners' (4). Tamara Katabgian has valuably explored the affective capacities of Dickens's machines, arguing in her reading of *Hard Times* 'for a more porous and productive relation between human nature, industrial technology and that most contested of topics – emotion' (650). As Juliet John puts it in the most nuanced reading to date of commodity culture and mechanisation in Dickens's work, 'the problem is not so much the machines, then, but the idea that mechanical or "wholesale" relations between people should replace personal or emotional relations instead of complementing them. For Dickens machines [. . .] can function productively in industrial society if used to further community and intimacy between people' (169). The furthering of community is certainly the emphasised mode of object relations in *Master Humphrey's Clock*. Here Dickens uses extreme, apparently hyperbolic, emotional responses to objects, specifically a range of mechanised objects which are cherished primarily for their sentimental value, to challenge an idea of 'the "natural" relation between people and things'.

Dickens, as a particularly successful artist in the age of mechanical reproduction, astutely working the copyrights and utilising the commercial possibilities of different modes of publication, 'appreciated', as John has shown, 'that mechanical reproduction would bring art closer to the masses spatially and culturally' (166). In *Master Humphrey's Clock*, the Dickens text most transparently concerned with the means of generating narrative (the search for different conceits of manuscript production results in a sometimes dizzying layering of framing devices), Dickens models his relationship to his readers through a tale of intimacy between the human story teller(s) and machine. The relationship between producer and consumer of text is mediated by the benign body of the Clock; here the Clock, a machine capable of fellow feeling, stands in for the printing presses. Furthermore, as a space for the gestation of the production of a number of authors who also act as the audience for each other's works, the line between producers and consumers is blurred as writing and receiving text becomes a shared, communal and collaborative endeavour. The circulation of text through Master Humphrey's Clock, then, reflects Dickens's passionate vision of his intimate and personal relationship with each person within his mass readership, with readers given an active, participatory role.

The *Clock*, somewhat perversely, presents itself as the multi-vocal result of a collective of authors, a model that Dickens had, unwisely, rejected here. Though he initially had hoped to incorporate material from other contributors, he quickly abandoned this idea; Dickens's frequent reference to the logistics of separating profits between contributors suggests that the choice of sole authorship was, at least in part, a financial one at this relatively early stage of his career.[6] He wrote apologetically to his friend Thomas Beard, who he had initially envisaged 'managing the correspondence, correcting proofs and so forth': 'It has been for weeks quite clear to us that I must write it all, if we are to hope for that great success which we expect.'[7] While it cannot, then, offer a range of authorial responses to human/object relations which is distinctive of the later *Household Words*, Dickens anticipates this more successful miscellany in making the lively object the central material of *Master Humphrey's*

[6] See Charles Dickens to John Forster (14 July 1839), Dickens 1965–2002, I: 563–5.
[7] Charles Dickens to Thomas Beard (22 March 1840), Dickens 1965–2002, II: 46.

Clock and by stratifying the *Clock*'s treatment of thing-loving along lines of class and character.

Master Humphrey is an affluent leisured property owner, able to dispense charity and maintain his home without working. He is also physically disabled, walking with a stick and having been perceived as a child as a 'poor crippled boy' (10), and feels himself to be somewhat apart from society. Dickens represents Master Humphrey's affection for domestic objects as directly following from these social circumstances, presenting his past sorrows as the back-story to his particular attachment:

> it may help in some measure to explain why I have all my life been attached to the inanimate objects that people my chamber, and how I have come to look upon them rather in the light of old and constant friends, than as mere chairs and tables which a little money could replace at will. Chief and first among all these is my Clock, – my old, cheerful, companionable Clock. How can I ever convey to others an idea of the comfort and consolation that this old Clock has been for years to me. (10)

Though the Clock uniquely meets Master Humphrey's emotional needs it does not act as a replacement for human fellowship, rather as a conduit to the development of new social bonds. As Master Humphrey invites the deaf gentlemen, two other elderly single men and then Mr Pickwick to join the storytelling circle he calls 'Master Humphrey's Clock', the Clock becomes a communal space as each member places his manuscripts within it. Mr Pickwick proves his credentials of membership through an excess of sensory clock 'admiration', complete with a readiness to anthropomorphise, as he touches and gazes at it:

> I thought he would never have come away from it. After advancing towards it softly, and laying his hand upon it with as much respect and as many smiling looks as if it were alive, he set himself to consider it in every possible direction, now mounting on a chair to look at the top, now going down upon his knees to examine the bottom, now surveying the sides with his spectacles almost touching the case [. . .] (49)

Through the inclusion of Mr Pickwick, Master Humphrey's sociability extends to communities beyond this text and, via Pickwick's entourage of his voluble servant Sam Weller and Sam's coach-driving father Tony, to a more mixed social constituency. The Wellers join with Master Humphrey's housekeeper and her suitor, a local barber, to 'make up', as Sam

describes it, 'a club of our own like the governors does up-stairs' (80). This
down-stairs group take as their 'title and emblem' Mr Weller's Watch, a
piece of portable property only extricated with some difficulty from Tony
Weller's person:

> He laid violent hands upon his watch-chain, and slowly and with
> extreme difficulty drew from his fob an immense double-cased silver
> watch, which brought the lining of the pocket with it, and was not to
> be disentangled but by great exertions and an amazing redness of face.
> (80)

As a coachman by trade, Tony Weller is dependent on the reliability
and durability of this piece of equipment to keep to timetables. He remarks
'with great pride that nothing hurt it, and that falls and concussions of all
kinds materially enhanced the excellence of the works and assisted the
regulator' (80). While Master Humphrey's more cumbersome treasured
possession chimes with his relatively static, homely existence, Weller's
Watch is an appropriately classed emblem of its owner's professional
and personal perambulation. Eventually the upstairs–downstairs hierarchy is dissolved as the 'Watch' group are invited into the 'Clock' circle.
Across social classes, then, Dickens demonstrates a pride and affection
in personal property that, rather than being a cause of alienation, operates to enrich human relationships and affective experiences. Through
the over-determined, though celebrated, emotional response to objects
in this miscellany Dickens resists a thesis of the mechanistic as inevitably
dehumanising. Indeed affective responses to objects in this miscellany are
combined with imaginative acuity; the Clock and Watch are the sites or
totems around which stories are told, generating the manuscript of *Master
Humphrey's Clock*. These powerful reactions to objects also raise interesting questions about the appropriateness of forms of emotional and, as we
will see more clearly anon, erotic attachment.

Curious bodies: mannequin drag and dummy love
For all the attention to Dickens's fascination with the fusion between
human and inorganic matter, criticism has been behindhand in seeing the
queer potential of Dickens's cyborgian imagination. In Donna Haraway's
polemical 'cyborg manifesto', 'a cyborg world might be about lived social
and bodily realities in which people are not afraid of their joint kinship

with machines and animals' (154). These kinships, for Haraway, have the potential to liberate people from life scripts of compulsory heterosexuality and conventionalised gender roles, as reproduction is decoupled from the body: 'The cyborg does not dream of community on the model of the organic family' (151). Dickens's fiction shows that such dreams are not restricted to the 'post-human' climate of late twentieth-century theory. In seeing the enabling (as well as at other times threatening and alienating) possibilities of inter-human/machine or cyborg connections, Dickens presents the kind of non-naturalised opportunities of a cyborg world. He is, perhaps, queerest in his scepticism towards what constitutes the 'natural', and persistently uses an exploration of human/object relations to question whether attributes and responses perceived to be natural or innate, especially in terms of gender and sexuality, are really so.

In both *Master Humphrey's Clock* and its first serial novel, Dickens uses wax dummies to explore the authenticity of gender and sexual relations. *The Old Curiosity Shop*, with its emphasis on commodity value and its population comprising a 'waxwork girl', mechanistic evil dwarf and multiple hybrid bodies from stilt-walkers to the Brass family, is something of an urtext for the analysis of Dickensian object relations.[8] Its many human–object amalgams include, significantly among the more benevolent cast, an animated clock, property of the Jolly Sandboys Public House: 'the very clock had a colour in its fat white face, and looked a clock for Jolly Sandboys to consult' (ch. 18: 143). Through its sustained interest in surface, in this case the waxworks exhibited by Mrs Jarley, this novel also incorporates a startlingly explicit model for the artificiality and theatricality of gender. Under Mrs Jarley's inventiveness the mannequins undergo complete transformations of persona and sex through the slightest adjustment of props:

> Mr Pitt in a nightcap and bedgown, and without his boots, represented the poet Cowper with perfect exactness; and Mary Queen of Scots in a dark wig, white shirt-collar, and male attire, was such a complete image of Lord Byron that the young ladies quite screamed when they saw it. (ch. 29: 221–2)

---

[8] This treatment of the novel began with Theodor Adorno's 1931 'On Dickens's *The Old Curiosity Shop*: A Lecture', a response to the novel's things which was informed by his conversations with close friend Walter Benjamin. Adorno's lecture is printed in *Notes to Literature*, vol. 2, trans. Shierry Weber Nicholsen, ed. Rof Tiedemann (New York: Columbia Univeristy Press, 1992), pp. 171–7. For a discussion of the lecture see Hollington.

The easy transition from queen to lord is effected through nothing more than 'a dark wig, white shirt-collar, and male attire'. The drag act of the queen's model operates with a similar meaning to that assigned by Judith Butler, in the classic theoretical account of gender performativity, to more fleshy drag performances: 'As imitations which effectively displace the meaning of the original, they imitate the myth of originality itself' (1990: 176).[9] As Butler has acknowledged, there are limitations to a theory of drag that assumes radical, transformative potential across a wide variety of acts that may have very different performance motives and constraints; Dickens's waxwork, however, allows a perfect application (because disembodied, and thus divorced from the wide range of specific personal circumstances) of the argument.[10] The fact that the Byron model was formerly known as Mary seems to suggest an original or authentic identity. However, this 'original' is – as is theatrically manifest – a 'fake', merely an approximate representation which places the illusive 'original' at an even greater remove. The dramatic interchangeability of these waxy bodies privileges surface, exposing gender as 'performative', in precisely Butler's terms, in the sense that 'the essence or identity that they otherwise purport to express are *fabrications* manufactured and sustained through corporeal signs and other discursive means' (1990: 173). The culturally encoded materials through which gender is read – the hair and clothes – are here exposed as nothing more than unsophisticated props, whilst the potentially endless re-dressing of the wax figures offers a physical model for the absence of an original, authentic gender.

In the *Clock* material, too, Dickens is preoccupied with the imaginative possibilities of mannequins, specifically with the potential of waxwork to raise questions about the assumed authenticity of gender, sexuality and

[9]   Herbert Sussman and Gerhard Joseph have suggested that Dickens's cyborgs 'foreshadow the post-human dissolution of the unified human subject as self-acting monad with any sort of centralised control and agency' (624). They build on Robert Newsom's earlier reading of *Dombey and Son* which posits a link between Dickens's questioning of bodily coherence and his simultaneous 'undermining [of] conventional expectations about the behaviour of men and women' (209). Newsom concludes that 'when it comes to gender, this novel likes to mix it up with a freedom that is [. . .] remarkable' (211).

[10] As Butler emphasises in the preface to *Bodies that Matter*, gender cannot just be 'donned for the day, and then restored [. . .] to its place at night'. Since, in human acts, embodying gender is more than costume, it is necessary to complicate notions of drag and to 'formulate a project that preserves gender practices as sites of critical agency' (1993: x).

feelings of attachment. He treats dummies, in their approximation of the human form, as a particularly promising medium through which to explore what makes the human and to consider the distinctiveness of human relationships and felt connections. The *Clock* incorporates a bizarre story of dummy loving, told by Sam Weller within the framework of a story-telling meeting of Mr Weller's Watch. Sam's story features a young hairdresser, William Gibbs, with an enthusiasm for the barber-shop window models:

> 'Vun o' these dummies wos a favrite with him beyond the others; and ven any of his acquaintance asked him wy he didn't get married [. . .] he used to say, "Never! I never will enter into the bonds of vedlock," he says, "until I meet vith a young 'ooman as realises my idea o' that 'ere fairest dummy vith the light hair. Then, and not till then," he says, "I vill approach the alter."' (82)

This resolution is similar to the many under-determined prohibitions on marriage characteristic of *The Pickwick Papers*, in which, of course, Sam and his father first appear. In *Pickwick*, a novel which places marital avoidance at its heart in the central incident of Pickwick's breach of promise trial, interpolated tales offer similarly mysterious explanations for the rejection of the marriage plot. In 'The Story of the Bagman's Uncle', for example, the uncle dreams that he has rescued a phantasmal beautiful woman and promised her that he will never marry anyone but her; true to his dream-promise he remains a bachelor until his death.[11]

In Sam's *Clock* (or 'Watch') story, however, the hairdresser does encounter a 'young lady as wos the very picter o' the fairest dummy. "Now" he says, "it's all up. I am a slave."' Things go well until he shows her the source of his passion:

> 'Look up, my love', says the hairdresser, 'behold your imige in my winder, but not corrector than in my art!' 'My imige!' she says. 'Yourn!' replies the hairdresser. 'But whose imige is *that*?' she says, a pinting at vun o' the gen'lmen. 'No vun's my love', he says, 'it is but a idea.' 'A idea!' she cries: 'it is a portrait, I feel it is a portrait, and that 'ere noble face must be in the millingtary!' 'Wot do I hear!' says he, a crumplin' his curls. 'Villiam Gibbs,' she says, quite firm, 'never renoo the subject. I respect you as a friend,' she says, 'but my affections is set upon that manly brow.' (*Master Humphrey's Clock* 82)

11 I discuss this tale within the context of elective bachelorhood in more detail in chapter 2 of *Queer Dickens*.

Having vented his frustration by breaking the dummy's nose and melting it down, Gibbs takes to poetry and gin and water and is later run down by a cab. The young lady, failing to find an original for the wax 'manly brow', pines away, 'by rayther slow degrees', as Sam mischievously narrates it, 'for she ain't dead yet' (83).

Though set in the comic register of the 'downstairs' mode of 'Mr Weller's Watch', which provides a humorous relief from the more tragic melodramas told in the higher-class Clock circle, this narrative provides a clear object lesson in the powerful emotional and erotic appeal of things. The 'gen'lmen' dummy is so appealing to the young lady as a surface onto which she can project the characteristics which she particularly admires, notably military nobility, which her potential life-partner, 'Villiam', conspicuously lacks. In its response to the Pygmalion motif of male love for a statuesque feminine ideal devoid of vitality, this tale neatly revises the classic gendered narrative of mannequin loving. Furthermore in providing a narrative of the apparently under-motivated redirection of desire away from a human object, Sam's story anticipates the case-histories offered in support of early psychological theories of 'fetishism'.

The erotics of things

Alfred Binet first used the term 'fetishism' to describe an erotic response to objects in his 1887 essay, 'Le Fétichisme dans l'amour' (or 'Fetishism in Love') published in *Revue philosophique*. Binet's work was driven by his concern for what he saw as a decadent shift towards a celebration of the artificial over the real, as in, for example, the modern fascination with makeup. As well as individual body parts, he discussed the potential for objects such as bonnets and shoes to stimulate intense desire. In contrast to this, he presented true love as symphonic, an 'emotional "polytheism"', which celebrates all the glories of the beloved not an impoverished "monotheism", which focuses impotently on a single unworthy object'. Reproductive potency, in Binet's thesis, was the aim of 'normal' desire: 'Normal love leads always to the deification of the whole individual, a natural enough consideration given its aim of reproduction' (165–6).[12]

Through comedy, the prevailing tone in Sam's tale and the mode of his 'Wellerisms', Dickens avoids presenting a judgement on these characters'

[12]   Binet's article is cited and discussed by Robert Nye.

mannequin attachments; certainly they are presented as eccentric and anecdote-worthy but the narrative does not call for or generate moral disapprobation. Dickens's emotional sympathies, however, are clearly with the exemplary thing-lover of this miscellany, Master Humphrey, himself. In Master Humphrey's love for his clock, his emotional investments are routed away from genetic formations of family. His clock-loving is as central to his identity as his confirmed bachelorhood and preference for bachelor society. This determinedly non-marital and non-reproductive life story, shared by the other bachelors of the Clock circle (Jack Redburn and Pickwick), is not presented as in any way unnatural. On the contrary, here as across his writing career, Dickens actively celebrates bachelorhood and non-procreative life choices. In *Master Humphrey's Clock*, he combines this with an explicit celebration of affection directed not towards a biological family, but to an object with which Master Humphrey experiences a particular kinship.

Today perhaps the best-known narrative of the love and symbiosis between an old man and his clock is Henry Clay Work's 1876 song, '[My] Grandfather's Clock', from which the term 'grandfather clock' was drawn into everyday use.[13] The subject is a particularly suitable one for Work, who began his career as a printer and composed in his head while working to the rhythm of machinery. The song is said to be based on a real-life tale of the clock at the George Hotel, Yorkshire, which was owned by two bachelor brothers. Having kept unusually good time for a pendulum clock, the clock slowed at the death of the first brother and stopped completely when the second brother died.[14] Work's song imagines a physical parity between an old man and his clock; clock and owner have the same

[13] *The Oxford English Dictionary* lists Work's song as inaugurating this term, followed by various uses in the late nineteenth and early twentieth centuries in histories of watches, in furniture and antiques trading etc. The suggestive cyborgian conjunction 'grandfather clock' shows the particular imaginative possibilities invested in clockwork, and the relationship between this type of mechanism and organic life, from the seventeenth century onwards. In 1675, for example, the poet Richard Leigh described insects as 'like living watches'; 'each of these conceals/ A thousand Springs of Life, and moving wheels'. Clockwork also has a long history of close association with erotica, as the many specimens of 'dirty horology' found at websites such as <http://watchismo.blogspot.com/2009/09/you-dirty-horologist-hardcore-erotic.html> (here examples date from the 1820s) attest.
[14] Details from Zecher. For more on Work's life and music see Bertram Work. He records that the first issue 'Grandfather's Clock' sold over 800,000 copies and that Henry Work received $4,000 in royalties (introduction, unpaginated).

body weight ('It was taller by half/ Than the old man himself/ Though it weighed not a penny weight more') and function by the same life-span:

> It was bought on the morn
> Of the day that he was born
> And was always his treasure and pride
> But it stopped short
> Never to go again
> When the old man died

Dickens's miscellany is also concerned with the clock's fate at its owner's death; rather than plotting an automatic sympathetic response Dickens has Master Humphrey request that the clock be stopped at his death, that 'the voice of his old companion be heard no more' (100). If Dickens's miscellany was another partial source for Work, his song presents a considerably straighter life-story. The key events for Work's clock are marriage and death: 'It struck twenty-four/ When he entered at the door/ With a blooming and beautiful bride.' This union gives rise to further generations, including the grandchild who narrates the song. Master Humphrey, of course, is emphatically not a grandfather.

The elective kinship of Master Humphrey's circle, bonded through the exchange of manuscripts in the clock and mutual experiences of storytelling, rather than by blood or marriage, is typical of Dickens's imagination of domestic happiness. As Karen Chase and Michael Levenson so acutely observe, Dickens has a narrative horror of the isolated marital couple: 'More than a marriage, it is a *household* that Dickens's novels come to seek, and the conditions of the flourishing household require at least three, at least that additional one, to break the close-circuit of romantic love' (94). This Miscellany presents one of Dickens's many thoroughgoing imaginings of a household not shaped by marital or biological bonds. During his lifetime, Master Humphrey's home is the site for a community of men, and after his death, as stipulated in his will, it is tenanted by two of the circle, Jack Redburn and the Deaf Gentleman. While object-loving is at the heart of this narrative, the term 'fetishism' cannot be accurately applied to Dickens's fiction as its etymology, in Marx's usage, and, later, in sexology and psychoanalysis, imbues it with various forms of lack. As Laura Mulvey explains in her theorisation of the connected applications of this term, for Marx, 'it is around the difficulty of establishing the exchange value of actual objects produced under capitalism that commodity fetishism flourishes', while the Freudian fetish 'ascribes excessive value to objects' which are given sexual value as a substitute for something else (2). In *Master Humphrey's Clock*, by contrast, objects can reintegrate their owners into society, offering connection and a coherence of private and public identities, rather than alienation, through an emotional and physical valuation of things that is presented as unproblematic.

Queer Dickens

In this Miscellany Dickens offers a multi-faceted queer vision. It is so in the predominant nineteenth-century sense of 'strange, odd, peculiar, eccentric' (*Oxford English Dictionary*); this is how Dickens uses the term when he has a fictionalised correspondent describe Master Humphrey as 'confounded queer' (28). Dickens's treatment of Master Humphrey's relationships is also compatible with queer as I have defined it in social terms, as 'that which demonstrates that marriage and reproduction are not the only, or indeed the dominant or preferred, modes of being, and, in doing so, undoes an unhelpfully narrow model of identity as determined by a fixed point of sexual orientation' (2009: 9). The *Clock* material is also queer in the wonderfully suggestive sensory lexicon of William Cohen's recent work, cited at the outset.

Cohen is interested in the way that Dickens's fiction 'stages an overlapping series of bodily interactions, which bring the surface and the interior into proximate relation' (2008: 35). His principal figure for this is the keyhole as a constant site of Dickensian interaction. Attending to the keyhole scenes integral to the development of the relationship of Dick Swiveller and the Marchioness in *The Old Curiosity Shop*, he discusses the variety of sensory interchange at this aperture: 'It is a penetration, or more precisely an interpenetration, that involves the breath and the mouth and the eye and the ear; it is a commingling, not a passive receiving, brought into focus through a narrow conduit' (Cohen 2008: 35). Master Humphrey's clock is, perhaps, *the* 'narrow conduit' of Dickens's fiction that, while facilitating bodily interaction, brings 'the surface and interior into proximate relation'. Its porous body, penetrable by the various manuscripts produced by Master Humphrey's storytelling circle and simultaneously inhabited by the productions of these men, offers a device for understanding the interpenetrability through which social connection operates.

The Clock's beloved form, a receptacle for feeling (tactile, aesthetic, nostalgic . . .), also operates as the trusted space in which private writings, sometimes containing autobiographical revelations, go through a gestation, before becoming public texts. As endowed with emotional autonomy the Clock presents, not a passive cavity, but a hospitable, fecund body. Its phallic casing is combined with a womb-like interior, apparently endlessly expandable in relation to the male storytellers' need for their texts to be brought to term. The Clock's mechanical body, a gendered hybrid, infused with human feeling and creativity, offers what Haraway describes as 'cyborg replication', 'uncoupled from organic reproduction' (150). Attention to this neglected *Clock* material shows the way that Dickens's romance with machines and hybridised forms contributes to his queer imagination. These critical lenses can help us to see what Dickens clearly knew: that conventional scripts for relationships organised along biological and marital lines are insufficient to account for the sensory and affective joys of a queer world.

Works cited
Binet, Alfred, 1887. 'Le Fétichisme dans l'amour: Étude de psychologie morbide', *Revue philosophique*, 24: 143–67.
Bowen, John, 2000. *Other Dickens: Pickwick to Chuzzlewit*. Oxford: Oxford University Press.
Brown, Bill, 2003. *A Sense of Things: The Object Matter of American Literature*. Chicago: University of Chicago Press.
Butler, Judith, 1990. *Gender Trouble: Feminism and the Subversion of Identity*. London: Routledge.
Butler, Judith, 1993. *Bodies that Matter*. New York and London: Routledge.
Chase, Karen, and Michael Levenson, 2000. *The Spectacle of Intimacy: A Public Life for the Victorian Family*. Princeton: Princeton University Press.
Cohen, William, 1996. *Sex Scandal: The Private Parts of Victorian Fiction*. Durham, North Carolina: Duke University Press.
Cohen, William, 2008. *Embodied: Victorian Literature and the Senses*. Minnesota: University of Minnesota Press.
Dickens, Charles, 1965–2002. *The Letters of Charles Dickens*, ed. G. Storey, K. Tillotson *et al.* 12 vols. Oxford: Clarendon.
Dickens, Charles, 1997. *Our Mutual Friend*. London: Penguin.
Dickens, Charles, 1999. *The Pickwick Papers*. London: Penguin.

Dickens, Charles, 2005. *The Old Curiosity Shop*. London: Penguin.

Dickens, Charles, 2008. *Master Humphrey's Clock*. Cambridge: Cambridge Scholars Publishing.

Eli Adams, James, 2009. 'Reading with Buzfuz: Dickens, Sexuality, Interrogation', in *Contemporary Dickens*, ed. Eileen Gillooly and Deidre David. Ohio: Ohio State University Press, pp. 231–44.

Forster, John, 1872–1874. *The Life of Charles Dickens*. 3 vols. London: Chapman and Hall.

Foucault, Michel, 1976. *The History of Sexuality: Volume 1*, trans. Robert Hurley. rpt London: Penguin, 1998.

Freedgood, Elaine, 2006. *The Ideas in Things: Fugitive Meaning in the Victorian Novel*. Chicago: University of Chicago Press.

Furneaux, Holly, 2009. *Queer Dickens: Erotics, Families, Masculinities*. Oxford: Oxford University Press.

Furneaux, Holly, 2011. 'Victorian Sexuality', *Literature Compass*, 8: 767–75.

Hansford Johnson, Pamela, 1970. 'The Sexual Life in Dickens's Novels', *Dickens 1970*, ed. Michael Slater. London: Chapman and Hall, pp. 173–94.

Haraway, Donna, 1991. *Simians, Cyborgs and Women*. London: Free Association.

Hollington, Michael, 2009. 'The Voice of Objects In the Old Curiosity Shop', *Australasian Journal of Victorian Studies*, 14: 1–8.

Inglis, Katherine, 2008. 'Becoming Automatous: Automata in *The Old Curiosity Shop* and *Our Mutual Friend*', 19: *Interdisciplinary Studies in the Long Nineteenth Century*, 6: 1–39. <http://www.19.bbk.ac.uk>.

John, Juliet, 2010. *Dickens and Mass Culture*. Oxford: Oxford University Press.

Kaplan, Cora, 2007. *Victoriana: Histories, Criticism*. Edinburgh: Edinburgh University Press.

Ketabgian, Tamara, 2003. '"Melancholy Mad Elephants": Affect and the Animal Machine in *Hard Times*', *Victorian Studies*, 45: 649–76.

Kucich, John, 2011. 'The Unfinished Historical Project: In Praise of Suspicion', *Victoriographies*, 1: 58–78.

Leigh, Richard, 1675. *Poems, upon several occasions, and, to several persons. By the author of The Censure, of the Rota*. London.

Marcus, Sharon, 2007. *Between Women: Friendship, Desire, and Marriage in Victorian England*. Princeton: Princeton University Press.

Marx, Karl, 1995 [1867]. *Capital: An Abridged Edition*, ed. David McLellan. Oxford: Oxford University Press.

Mulvey, Laura, 1996. *Fetishism and Curiosity*. Bloomington and Indianapolis: Indiana University Press.

Newsom, Robert, 1989. 'Embodying Dombey: Whole and in Part', *Dickens Studies Annual*, 18: 197–219.

Nye, Robert, 1993. 'The Medical Origins of Sexuality', in *Fetishism as Cultural Discourse*, ed. Emily Apter and William Pietz. Ithaca and London: Cornell University Press.

Sussman, Herbert, and Gerhard Joseph, 2004, 'Prefiguring the Posthuman: Dickens and Prosthesis', *Victorian Literature and Culture*, 32: 617–28.

van Ghent, Dorothy, 1953. *The English Novel: Form and Function.* New York: Harper and Row.

Waters, Catherine, 2008. *Commodity Culture in Dickens's 'Household Words': The Social Life of Goods.* Aldershot: Ashgate.

Work, Bertram, 1920. *Songs of Henry Clay Work.* New York: Little and Ives.

Work, Henry, 1876. *Grandfather's Clock: Song and Chorus.* New York.

Zecher, Henry, 2005. 'How an Old Floor Clock Became a Grandfather', *The Pride of Olney*, official newsletter of the Lions Club of Olney. Maryland, vol. XXX. Also online at <http://www.henryzecher.com/grandfather_clock.htm>.

Texts, paratexts and 'e-texts': the poetics of communication in Dickens's journalism

JOHN DREW

SINGING my days,
Singing the great achievements of the present,
Singing the strong light works of engineers,
Our modern wonders, (the antique ponderous
    Seven outvied,)
In the Old World the east the Suez canal,
The New by its mighty railroad spann'd,
The seas inlaid with eloquent gentle wires;
Yet first to sound, and ever sound, the cry with
    thee O soul,
The Past! the Past! the Past!
           'Passage to India' (1870)

THE FIRST STANZA of Walt Whitman's extraordinary poem, with its inspired bathos and confident 'poetics of ad-libbing' (Donald Davie's phrase: 59), proclaims its aim to fuse, on both personal and public planes, a sense of the trajectory linking past with present, and today's technology with tomorrow's new possibilities. It also announces the public occasions for this rhapsodic outburst (which actually gets more uncertain the longer it lasts): namely the successful laying of a transatlantic submarine cable allowing telegraphic communication across the Atlantic (July 1865);[1] the junction of the Union and Pacific railroads (May 1869), and the completion of the Suez canal project allowing ships to travel to the East from Europe and the New World without circumnavigating Africa (November 1869). On the one hand, Whitman's celebration looks firmly back to

---

[1] A team from the Anglo-American Telegraph Company aboard the SS *Great Eastern* completed the task, after five unsuccessful or only temporarily successful attempts dating back to 1858 (see Gordon).

Emerson, whose rapturous delivery is emulated, and whose essay 'The Poet' (*Essays*, 1842) was a clarion call for writers to take the marvellous facts of their age and land and transform them into song – or a miscellany:

> Readers of poetry see the factory-village and the railway, and fancy that the poetry of the landscape is broken up by these; for these works of art are not yet consecrated in their reading; but the poet sees them fall within the great Order not less than the beehive or the spider's geometrical web . . .. We do not with sufficient plainness or sufficient profoundness address ourselves to life, nor dare we chant our own times and social circumstance. . . . Our log-rolling, our stumps and their politics, our fisheries, our Negroes and Indians, our boasts and our repudiations, the wrath of rogues and the pusillanimity of honest men, the northern trade, the southern planting, the western clearing, Oregon and Texas, are yet unsung. (229, 241) [2]

On the other hand, as Whitman moves on from concrete examples to what they represent in terms of a revolution in communication and the opportunities for human connection that E. M. Forster questions in his novel of the same name, the poem looks inexorably forward – to the point where a latter day reader can feel excused for reading into it a foreshadowing of the information revolution, and the connectivity of the internet:

> Passage to India!
> Lo, soul! seest thou not God's purpose from the
>   first?
> The earth to be spann'd, connected by
>   net-work,
> The people to become brothers and sisters,
> The races, neighbors, to marry and be given in
>   marriage,
> The oceans to be cross'd, the distant brought
>   near,
> The lands to be welded together.
> (A worship new, I sing;
> You captains, voyagers, explorers, yours!
> You engineers! you architects, machinists,
>   yours!)

---

[2]   Whitman was by no means the first or only poet or journalist to answer Emerson's call. For samples of railway-inspired verse, see Emily Dickinson's lyric 'I like to see it lap the miles' (53–4), Walter Thornbury's 'The Poetry of Railways' (1–6), or the poems of Alexander 'Surfaceman' Anderson.

. . .
Then, not your deeds only, O voyagers, O sci-
    entists and inventors, shall be justified,
All these hearts, as of fretted children, shall be
    sooth'd,
All affection shall be fully responded to – the
    secret shall be told;
All these separations and gaps shall be taken
    up, and hook'd and link'd together;
The whole Earth – this cold, impassive, voice-
    less Earth, shall be completely justified. . ..
                (lines 30–9; 117–21)

Biographical accounts often stress Charles Dickens's quarrel with
America, and perhaps overlook the extent to which he not only found an
instant rapport with American audiences and formed lasting American
friendships, but was transformed in his political thinking and in terms of
self-regard by his experience of the new world.[3] He responded to Emerson
with enthusiasm, as did Whitman to Dickens. Dickens met Emerson on
his first visit to what he had hoped would be 'the Republic of my imagination' in 1842, read the already famous *Essays* and found them 'dreamy
and fanciful . . . true and manly, honest and bold'.[4] As a journalist, Whitman followed Dickens's career closely, and championed his editing of *The
Daily News*; his familiar style of editorial address bears close comparison
with Dickens's.[5] The dates of their Romantic configurations of the contemporary poet's role, quoted above, encompass the years of Dickens's
maturity as a writer.

    In the novel many regard as the greatest achievement of those years,
Bleak House, Dickens is famously scathing about those who hold a place

[3] Sidney P. Moss's account makes the most of the quarrel; for nuanced accounts
in biographical, cultural, and publishing terms, see Slater (1979), John (ch. 2) and
McGill (ch. 3).
[4] 'And therefore', he concluded, 'if I were a Bostonian, I think I would be a
Transcendentalist' (*American Notes* I: 133–4). See also Dickens 1965–2002, III:
156.
[5] See 'Boz and his New Paper' (10 March 1846) in Whitman 256–7; for the
tone, see 'Ourselves and the *Eagle*' ('There is a curious kind of sympathy [haven't
you ever thought of it before?] that arises in the mind of a newspaper conductor
with the public he serves. He gets to *love* them. . . . As for us, we like this. We like
it better than the more "dignified" part of editorial labor' etc. (1 June 1846)), repr.
in Holloway 115.

in society but who fail, as Emerson puts it, to 'address themselves to life', or respond to the challenge of the real:

> ladies and gentlemen of another fashion, not so new but very elegant, who have agreed to put a smooth glaze on the world, and to keep down all its realities. For whom everything must be languid and pretty. Who have found out the perpetual stoppage. Who are to rejoice at nothing, and be sorry for nothing. Who are not to be disturbed by ideas. On whom even the Fine Arts, attending in powder and walking backward like the Lord Chamberlain, must array themselves in the milliners' and tailors' patterns of past generations, and be particularly careful not to be in earnest, or to receive any impress from the moving age. (ch. 12: 224–5)

However, it is not only – and perhaps not so extensively – in his work as a writer of fiction that Dickens himself vigorously took on the role of the Emersonian poet, and the Whitmanesque seer, and circulated impressions of this 'moving age'. Here is a brief excerpt from his 'Preliminary Word' to *Household Words*, the weekly miscellany he founded and edited from 1850 onwards, and which, in its subsequent reincarnation as *All the Year Round*, would reach a vast global audience estimated (in America alone) at 'more than three million readers':

> The mightier inventions of this age are not, to our thinking, all material, but have a kind of souls in their stupendous bodies which may find expression in *Household Words*. *The traveller whom we accompany on his railroad or his steamboat journey, may gain, we hope, some compensation for incidents which these later generations have outlived, in new associations with the Power that bears him onward; with the habitations and the ways of life of crowds of his fellow creatures among whom he passes like the wind*; even with the towering chimneys he may see, spirting out fire and smoke upon the prospect. The swart giants, Slaves of the Lamp of Knowledge, have their thousand and one tales, no less than the Genii of the East; and these, in all their wild, grotesque, and fanciful aspects, in all their many phases of endurance, in all their many moving lessons of compassion and consideration, we design to tell. (*Household Words* [30 March 1850] I, p. 1; my italics)[6]

---

[6] This, and all subsequent items cited from *Household Words* and *All the Year Round* under Dickens's editorship, can be consulted online at <http://www.djo.org.uk>.

Replacing 'tell' here with 'sing' would underscore both the transcendental and the poetic qualities of the passage, which builds towards an exhortatory climax where writer and audience are simultaneously being propelled forwards into what is to come, a futuristic prelude every bit as proleptic as Brian Eno's universally familiar Windows fanfare:[7]

> Thus, we begin our career! The adventurer in the old fairy story, climbing towards the summit of a steep eminence on which the object of his search was stationed, was surrounded by a roar of voices, crying to him, from the stones in the way, to turn back. All the voices we hear, cry Go on! The stones that call to us have sermons in them, as the trees have tongues, as there are books in the running brooks, as there is good in everything! They, and the Time, cry out to us Go on! (2)

In this essay I aim to explore some of the ways in which the texts Dickens handled as a magazine editor – both his own writing and that of others – were imaged, presented, published and distributed by him, and think about the range of different formats and media through which – by design or accident – they were transmitted. It seems to me that his sense of enthusiasm about, and desire to celebrate, the sheer power of the connection between writers and readers that new technological and industrial processes were forging marks out something important about his work as a journalist, that occurs within a definable Anglo-American literary tradition.

There must of course be limits to the extent one can seek to frame Dickens as pre-empting in some historically definable way the communications revolutions of the twentieth century. We are dealing with an artistic sensibility that began to be shaped formally during the Regency of George IV, and a writer whose fiction charts heights and depths that have been traditionally measured (and often superlatively well) by the contours of such period terms as 'the Romantic' and 'the Victorian'. Yet to some of Dickens's contemporaries – Ruskin most famously – he appeared almost unappealingly to have his sights set on the future: 'a pure modernist . . . a leader of the steam-whistle party *par excellence*' (*Works*, XXXVII: 7). In this vein, but without the disparagement, perceptive critics of film – arguably the most powerful new medium developed in the Modernist era

---

[7] Irritating as one may find the fanfare, few sequences of notes represent a greater socio-economic power; see Selvin 43.

– have argued convincingly that Dickens fully anticipates key cinematic techniques such as *mise en scène* and montage in his narrative technique.[8] On the other hand, some of Dickens's most characteristic reportage in both town and country, early and late, shows a remarkable capacity for recording – with a nostalgia that is as often genuine as joking – the effacing of popular pastimes and customs, of traditional ways of life, in the face of industrial and technological progress.[9] Against this apparent conservatism, however, one could then set Dickens's rampant anti-medievalism: his broadsides against the 'Young England' movement in politics, Puseyism in religion and the Pre-Raphaelite Brotherhood in art, all indicative of staunch faith in both Protestantism and progress. His nostalgia for the past perhaps extends no further than the civilised coffee-house eccentrics and the essayists of the reign of Queen Anne.[10] Granted that any brief summary of the positions a writer as abundant as Dickens appears to adopt will tend to fall into a series of oversimplified antitheses like the one just constructed, nevertheless, we may say with some confidence that there are crucial tensions at work here. Nowhere do they appear to me to be more noticeable and interesting than in Dickens's performance as a magazine editor, where the roles of herald as well as chronicler, disseminator as well as creator, service provider as well as content manager, all fall within his purview.

Each format or medium adopted by Dickens and his team for periodical publication of their work has, as part of its strategy of presentation, additional productions – verbal, graphic, typographic, representational, or otherwise – which stand at its material threshold and help determine the work's meaning and guide its reception. These are (to adopt Gérard Genette's useful coinage) its paratexts. Dickens's periodical works are particularly rich in their paratextual apparatus, whether we are thinking in terms of the kind of bibliographical typology that Genette lays out (dedications, prefaces, titles and title-pages, epigraphs, signature or lack thereof, notes, running heads, public and private defences, or 'epitexts')

---

[8] For example, Eisenstein's seminal 'Dickens, Griffith and the Film Today' or Grahame Smith's fuller treatment.
[9] For examples, see 'The Last Cab Driver and the First Omnibus Cad' or 'The First of May' in Slater 1994: 142–50, 168–75; and 'An Old Stage-Coaching House' in Slater and Drew 2000:269–77.
[10] See Gardiner for a lucid account of Dickens's strengths and weaknesses as a historian.

or in terms of related practices he candidly admits he has had to leave out (these would include wrappers, advertisements, fliers, manifestos, mastheads, editorial addresses and illustrations: 404). As I hope to illustrate, the central emphases we may detect in Dickens's paratextual guidance, on immediacy of address, rapidity and extensiveness of circulation, on fluidity of form, on accessibility to the widest range of readers both socially and geographically, justifies (with minimum reliance on poetic licence) the borrowing of the exclusively modern term 'e-text' to indicate certain properties of his periodical writings that lend them a surprising currency and adaptability. In the course of my exploration, I shall draw on the experience of setting up *Dickens Journals Online*, the first open-access online edition of Dickens's weekly journals – now under construction at <http://www.djo.org.uk> – and some of the curious parallels which seem to obtain between the dynamism of modern web publishing and that of the Victorian periodical press. Re-editing Dickens's journals for twenty-first-century readers, albeit in a free format, brings into play key relationships between Romantic idealism and harsh economic realities that obtained just as powerfully at the time of the magazines' first sale and distribution.

The Victorian railway offers a tempting point of departure, given that a convincing case can be made for it as 'nineteenth-century modernity's epitome' (Carter 292). A wide range of commentators put forward *Dombey and Son* (commenced 1846) as the work in which Dickens first engages seriously if ambivalently with the advent of steam locomotion, and its wider implications for society.[11] 1846 was the year he left off his brief editorship of *The Daily News*, citing distrust of what he saw as the paper's dangerously 'one-sided' pro-railway policy and the potentially tainting influence of some of its backers and advertisers as two of the main reasons for his resignation, so the chronology, and the ambivalence, seem reasonable (Dickens 1965–2002, IV: 484; Drew 2000: 82–3). However, in his journalism and letters, Dickens responded to the symbolism of the railway engine and the idea of a railway journey considerably earlier, figuring them as analogues for the editing of a newspaper or periodical. Given Ruskin's comment, this is an interesting connection to make, and Dickens takes it well beyond the vague boast of the editor of the *Eatanswill Gazette* that 'The press is a mighty engine, sir' in the fifth number of *The Pickwick Papers* (August 1836). For

[11]   Carter 72; see also Baumgarten and Schivelbusch.

example, on resigning the editorship of *Bentley's Miscellany* in 1839 and making way for Harrison Ainsworth to take over his position, Dickens abandons the main thrust of his valedictory editorial address (entitled 'A Familiar Epistle from a Parent to a Child, aged 2½ Years') for a much more contemporary and less neo-classical analogy:

> And if I might compare you, my child, to an engine; (not a Tory engine, nor a Whig engine, but a brisk and rapid locomotive;) your friends and patrons to passengers; and he who now stands towards you *in loco parentis* [i.e. Ainsworth] as the skilful engineer and supervisor of the whole, I would humbly crave leave to postpone the departure of the train on its new and auspicious course . . . while, with hat in hand, I approach side by side with the friend who travelled with me on the old road, and presume to solicit favour and kindness in behalf of him and his new charge (Slater 1994: 554)

The little Latin pun is thus not inappropriate, but, more importantly, the passage is the first of a series of semi-heroic comparisons Dickens makes between managing and supervising a train carrying passengers towards their destination and running a magazine that conducts its readers on their journey into the future. A late, ornate expression of it is given in the first passage from the 'Preliminary Word' to *Household Words* quoted above (see my italics), but a simpler version can be found in letters of July 1842, written only a week or so after Dickens's return from America, as he buttonholes the Whig hostess Lady Holland, hoping to secure her influence to help him take over the editorship of a prominent Liberal paper, *The Courier*, which had just folded:

> I need scarcely say, that if I threw my small person into the breach, and wrote for the paper (literary articles as well as political) I could command immediate attention . . . . The notion of this newspaper was bred in me by my old training – I was as well acquainted with the management of one, some years ago, as an Engineer is, with a Steam engine. (Dickens 1965–2002, III: 262, 266)

Dickens, I would suggest, thought habitually in terms of this conceit, investing the role of 'editor' with something of the hazy glamour and sheer, naked power of Turner's 'Steam and Speed', and liked seeing himself in sole control of this kind of transformative energy as it moved along its destined track. He aligns the editor's role with that of a Carlylean

Captain of Industry, master of the technology even while an integral part of it: the reverse hierarchy to that perceived by Gissing's hapless periodical contributor, Marian Yule, in a lower circle of the old British Library Reading Room, who considers herself a 'mere machine for reading and writing' and double-takes at an advertisement for a 'Literary Machine' out of fear that 'an automaton' has been invented 'to supply the place of such poor creatures as herself to turn out books and articles' (*New Grub Street*, ch. 8). While there are darker, more serious and alternative nuances that could be explored, Dickens here focalises a set of relationships that are as remarkable for their positivism and triumphalism as for their boyish enthusiasm. Other interesting examples can be cited of this expressly linear model of press management in his thinking.[12]

It is worth noting, however, that it is a model belonging particularly to the years running up to the successful founding of *Household Words* in 1850: in other words, to the period before Dickens had extended experience of sitting in the driver's cab of a successful periodical. Thereafter, indeed, references in letters together with the establishment of the annual Extra Numbers for Christmas (with titles such as 'A Round of Stories by the Christmas Fire' (1852), 'Another Round of Stories by the Christmas Fire' (1853)), give grounds for suggesting that Dickens's sense of the editor's role assumes a more cyclical and circular model. Writing to Leigh Hunt on 31 January 1855, five years into the management of *Household Words*, Dickens revisits the familiar railway metaphor to offer an image of loss of control, confessing that 'I have been so put about and railroaded, and expressed, and business-pressed, since the day [you wrote me], that my life has been a perfect whirl' (Dickens 1965–2002, VII: 518). Charity reading tours in Berkshire, Yorkshire and Dorset were partly to blame, but also having 'all my children home for the holidays' (nine of them by this date), getting up 'our Annual Fairy Play at home', a bout of influenza, having to go to Paris the following week, and, the litany of busy woes concludes,

---

[12] Cf. 'here's a man for you! – They sent me today the proposed No. 2, in a list of articles. The amazing undersigned feels a little uncomfortable at a want of Household tenderness in it. So he puts away *Copperfield*, at which he has been working like a Steam Engine – writes (he thinks) exactly the kind of thing to supply the deficiency – and sends it off, by this post, to Forster! What an amazing man!' (Dickens 1965–2002, VI: 64)

I don't mention such trifles as that great humming-top *Household Words*, which is always going round with the weeks and murmuring 'Attend to me!' (Dickens 1965–2002, VII: 518)

The periodical is no longer a glamorous vehicle of transportation but something spinning, whirling, demanding regular attention, and – to judge by the way Dickens writes privately about winding himself up to organise the extra Christmas issues – becoming a site of dreary repetition and returns.[13]

In support of these speculations, one could cite the two little-known supplements to *Household Words*, which still await serious academic attention; for, as Marysa Demoor and Kate McDonald have pointed out, 'the study of the evolution of the use of periodical supplements [can] offer an enhanced reflection of the Victorian development of modernity'(108). These are the *Household Narrative of Current Events* (1850–5), a monthly digest of hard news, offering a good example of the expressly linear march through time, and the *Household Words Almanac* (1856–7), emphasising, with its woodcut illustrated calendar, the cyclical nature of life, and the natural

> laws that maintain . . . the Earth, in its appointed place among the stars, and regulate the winds and waters; the principles on which the preservation of our health and cheerfulness mainly depends; the times of the development of the several kinds of trees and flowers, and when the melody of the various sorts of birds is first awakened.[14]

That the one kind of supplement gave way to the other seems a happy coincidence for the hypothesis that Dickens shifted his editorial paradigm, and the point could be reinforced by pointing to the symbolism of the attractive woodcut masthead Dickens commissioned for the inauguration of *All the Year Round*'s New Series in December 1868. Along with its larger type for serial fiction, and improved paper quality, the magazine

[13]   As early as 1859, he had announced himself (to G. H. Lewes; Dickens 1965–2002, IX: 168) 'in a state of temporary insanity (annual) with the Xmas no.' and by 1868 he was (he told Wills; Dickens 1965–2002, XII: 159) 'in a state of positive despair . . . I have invented so many of these Christmas Nos. and they are so profoundly dissatisfactory after all, with the introduced Stories and their want of cohesion or originality that I fear I am sick of the thing.'
[14]   'Our Almanac', *Household Words*, XII: 385 (24 Nov 1855). They are discussed briefly in House 32–3, Drew 128–31, and John 117–18.

now graphically emphasised the cycle of the four seasons, illustrations of which orbit the title text. In announcing the New Series, Dickens also announced the discontinuation – after seventeen years – of the extra Christmas number, 'at the highest tide of its success' (*All the Year Round* XX: 337), as though the mere inscribing of a seasonal message on the masthead could substitute for its detailed textual encoding. The metaphor, we may note, is naturalising and cyclical rather than mechanistic.

We are now firmly in the realm of interpreting the paratexts of Dickens's periodical texts, so it seems appropriate to dwell briefly on their rich variety, which in turn depends on the multiplicity of forms which these texts could take. As Lorna Huett has shown, from its inception, *Household Words* embodied hybridity of form, being transmitted at three distinct frequencies – weekly, monthly, bi-annually – and in as many formats and prices: a 24-page or occasionally 20-page booklet with no wrapper, priced at tuppence, a 9d. 96-page booklet with a duck-egg blue wrapper, and a substantial cloth, or half-leather and board volume, priced at 5s. 6d. With its low-grade paper and two-column typography, reminiscent of the 'penny bloods' and the lowest sector of the market, but with options for high-quality bindings and other markers of social distinction, *Household Words*, as Huett observes, 'combined publishing practices from both ends of the marketplace', a significant and bold editorial step (76, 68). More recent research corroborates this protean quality, both in view of the fact that the weekly incarnation seems actually to have been distributed uncut and unstitched, like the cheapest penny chapbooks – requiring readers to cut tops, bottoms and foredges of pages in order to get at the contents[15] – and that Dickens's editorial methods and agenda withstand serious comparison with those of a lofty quarterly such as the *Edinburgh Review* under Jeffrey and Napier (Crawford).

Such mutability, moreover, extends in other directions. In addition to paying his contributors well for original articles and poems on an encyclopaedic range of subjects, Dickens actively encouraged them to collect and re-edit their own work in volume form, and laid no claim to copyright.

---

[15] Uncut, folded copies of *All the Year Round* and of the *Household Narrative of Current Events* have been viewed in various places: antiquarian booksellers, the St Bride's Printing Library, London, and – most tellingly (because once in private hands) – the Forster Collection at the National Art Library, Victoria and Albert Museum, London.

Innumerable volumes containing or composed of reprinted matter from *All the Year Round* and *Household Words*, by scores of authors, took their place amongst the letterpress of the high Victorian era. A trawl through Anne Lohrli's splendid bibliography to the published index of *Household Words* gives a list of 127 anthologies of this kind, but work on new attributions for the *Dickens Journals Online* website suggests this is merely the tip of an iceberg. Where his own work was concerned, since 1842, Dickens had been contracting with Bernhard Tauchnitz in Leipzig to publish copyright editions of his major works for marketing on the Continent, in the publisher's pioneering 'Collection of British and American Authors': pocketsize editions which often precede the recognised first editions of his work, and which 'are of potential textual significance, having been set from proofs, advance sheets, or corrected editions, or variously adapted to suit the series format'.[16] Copyright editions of volumes of *Household Words*, quite different in presentation and ordering of material from the British edition, were amongst them, although this does not seem to have prevented European newspapers and magazines from freely translating anonymous material from the journals and, in some cases, claiming Dickens as the author.[17]

In America, and particularly after the incorporation of *Household Words* into *All the Year Round* (of which Dickens and his sub-editor were now the proprietors and publishers), an even greater degree of mutation was engineered. The culture of unauthorised reprinting and the 'characteristic decentralisation of American publishing' was – thanks in part to the development of a more unified rail network – giving way to a more integrated market, which promoted exclusive authorisation of various kinds (McGill 270). Dickens was extremely proactive and imaginative in contracting with American publishers to disseminate material from his magazines. One of the most striking was the arrangement whereby

[16]   Strictly, copyright was only enforceable in Prussia, which had enacted reciprocal legislation with Britain, but Tauchnitz undertook to market aggressively in other European countries, to overbear unauthorised reprints.
[17]   Meticulous research undertaken for the forthcoming *Reception of Charles Dickens in Europe* (ed. Hollington) has thrown up examples of translated stories and articles published as far afield as Portugal, Estonia, Sweden, Norway, etc., and wrongly ascribed to Dickens. It presumably did not help that the publisher's frontispiece to one of the 1854 Tauchnitz volumes announced 'Collection /of/ British Authors./Vol. CCCV./*Household Words* by Charles Dickens./Vol. XXVI' – paratextual guidance can be misleading.

installments of the main weekly serial novel from *A Tale of Two Cities*
onwards were published in *Harper's Weekly* before or only shortly after
their appearance in Britain, set from advance sheets of the author's manuscript or early proofs, and 'richly illustrated' by local artists. It is curious
to reflect that the sensation of reading *Great Expectations* was probably
experienced in Rochester (New Jersey) and Richmond (Virginia) before
it was felt by readers in their English namesakes, and that the story of Pip's
lost illusions first unfolded amongst columns of Civil War reporting and
engravings of military manoeuvres. At the same time, Dickens and Wills
made arrangements through Emerson & Co. to have the entire magazine
published in America, simultaneous with its British release, by shipping
to New York the stereotype plates from which it was printed, a fixed
number of days beforehand. At times, this meant bedding down the final
copy a week or more earlier, but Dickens was alive to the potential loss of
topicality, lamenting on one occasion that the 'sliding away of temporary
subjects at which I could dash with great effect, is a *great* loss' (Dickens
1965–2002, X: 202). After the disruption of the civil war, transatlantic
crossing times were substantially reduced, but even before this, Emerson
was able to make the extraordinary announcement to readers cited above
that *All the Year Round* 'now has the largest circulation of any similar publication in the world', with material from its pages finding 'in this country
alone more than three million readers' (IV: 336; 12 January 1861). Had
the transatlantic submarine cable celebrated in Whitman's poem been
capable of achieving transmission speeds of something faster than eight
words per minute, one suspects Dickens would have used it to broadcast
his message internationally.

The mention of words per minute offers a cue for routing back to underscore
the crucial importance of Dickens's experience as a short-hand reporter
to the way he 'addresses himself to life' and receives an 'impress from the
moving age'[18] in his work as a journalist and editor: the very mechanics of
transmission and reproduction of textual material, the variables of speed,
distance and time, were a lifelong preoccupation, to the extent of fascination. For the purposes of this essay, I choose to identify the numerous ways
in which, rhetorically and conceptually, this important aspect of Dickens's
work as a journalist is handled, as constituting a self-conscious poetics of

---

[18]   Emerson's phrase, quoted in paragraph 1 above; his own phrase, ditto.

communication. First, however, I should like to consider the reciprocity between medium and message in Dickens's journals (without necessarily conflating the two). Here is the opening of a leading article that Dickens copy-edited for publication in *Household Words*, breaking up a series of his own leaders that deal with such miscellaneous topics as papal aggression, sanitary reform, social responsibility, Christmas, and education, to make way for it.[19] It is called 'Wings of Wire', and the anonymous author is Charles Knight:

> In an age of express trains, painless operations, crystal palace, revolutions and republics, Mormons and Puseyites, and a hundred curiosities, such as our grandfathers and grandmothers never dreamt about, there is yet little difficulty in saying which of our modern wonders is really the most wonderful. In our last days, we have one thing, above all others, the fastest; in our generation of marvels, we have one thing of all others the most marvelous. We hear of it in conversation; we see it paraded in the newspapers; we are reminded of it in our railway travels, until our very familiarity half blinds us to its merits. Yet among all the useful things which human ingenuity has of late completed, it would not be difficult to show that the Electric Telegraph is one of the most useful. (*Household Words*, II: 241; 7 December 1850)

The opening paragraphs (whether Dickens himself retouched them, as was his wont, need not concern us here) alternate between plain-spoken narrative of the science and the kind of rhapsodic mythologising of the process that I identify as belonging to the Dickensian poetics of communication:

> The old heroes of the race course – the fleet-footed descendants of Arabian deserts . . . have been outdone. Flying Childers is no longer a byword for swiftness; and Eclipse, with his race of a mile a minute is left far, far behind . . .
> This was long work. Watching, deep study, thousands of experiments, suggestions, and reasonings; numberless plans and models – not of one man, or of two, but of thinkers in many countries . . . – until, at last, some shrewd, practical men thought out the final means of turning to

[19] 'A Crisis in the Affairs of Mr. John Bull' (23 November 1850), 'Mr Booley's View of the Last Lord Mayor's Show' (30 November), 'A December Vision' (14 December), 'A Christmas Tree' (21 December), and (with Henry Morley) 'Mr Bendigo Buster on our National Defences against Education' (28 December), all online at <http://www.djo.org.uk>.

a purpose the accumulations of their predecessors; and lo, the hidden vagaries of the element that claims close kindred with the lightning, are reined up and made to do the worldly work of men! (*Household Words*, II: 241; 7 December 1850)

Household Words, to be sure, was a miscellany, and aimed to cover an encyclopaedic range of topics: one article on the electric telegraph does not of itself constitute a strand. But even a rapid glance through the tables of contents for it and for *All the Year Round* indicates how regularly Dickens and his staff foreground practices relating to communication in its widest sense – letter-writing, mail-sorting and delivery, transport networks, official documents and language (whether municipal, legal or parliamentary), advertising, the press itself – not to mention such cognate fields as the spread of banking, paper money, the mechanics of reproduction and distribution in manufacturing, the take-up of industrial innovations and inventions, the spread of banking and new financial systems.[20] The following passage from the opening of Henry Morley's 'The Birth and Parentage of Letters' (another leader) has the air therefore of returning to a theme:

> Letters will hereafter be absolutely sent more rapidly from hand to hand, and, what is more immediately practicable, the powers of the electric telegraph, from being a rare luxury, have to become vulgarised and pressed into service for the important correspondence of the million. Then, too, we may have, some of these days, that is to say, in 'the good time coming', an ocean penny post. (*Household Words*, IV: 1; 27 September 1851)

We do not need to read Dickens's journals as if they were the prophecies of Nostradamus to appreciate their currency (though this is as good a forecast of e-mail as one could reasonably hope to find in a mid-Victorian periodical) but merely to note how their contents echo and reciprocate Dickens's fascination with journalistic communication as evinced by their creation, production and transmission.

---

[20] Online at <http://www.djo.org.uk>: 'A Bundle of Emigrants' Letters' (*Household Words*, I: 30 March 1850); 'Valentine's Day at the Post Office' (ibid.); 'The Doom of English Wills' (II: 28 September 1850 et seq.); 'Our Honorable Friend' (V: 31 July 1852); 'Bill-Sticking' (II: 22 March 1851); 'Review of a Popular Publication' (II: 27 July 1850); 'Discovery of a Treasure near Cheapside' (VI: 13 November 1852); see also articles by Martineau repr. in *Health, Husbandry, and Handicraft*; Dvorak.

In many cases the reciprocity is taken to a further level by a marked tendency to innovate linguistically, and the attempt to develop mimetic and narrative strategies to optimise the reader's engagement and under-standing. As Jonathan V. Farina has recently indicated, *Household Words* consistently 'employs stylistic features of fictional characterisation to describe new abstractions, technologies, and objects as if they too, like fictional characters, were repositories of deep character available for read-ers'(393). To the extent that these varied aspects of Victorian modernity were all potentially commodities of one kind or another, excellent book-length readings by Cathy Waters and Juliet John offer us the wherewithal to perceive how self-consciously Dickens conducted his journals with an intense awareness of their own participation in a commodity culture that they sought both to mystify and explain, and how thoughtfully, if sometimes ambivalently, he engaged on an 'emotional, imaginative, and political [level] with the idea of a mass audience' (John 29). Even return-ing to Walter Benjamin's rather narrower Marxist interpretation of the massification of aesthetic experience[21] in 'The Work of Art in an Age of Mechanical Reproduction' (1935), as John has shown, pays dividends for our understanding of Dickens's response to 'the mightier inventions of the age' and the reproduction of art for the widest of audiences, and in the context of repeated criticisms of the mechanistic repetitions of his fiction (John 163-6). Benjamin's argument outlines a history of modes of perception of works of art which passes linearly from their idolisation for magical or religious purposes (a mode dependent on a sense of the work's authenticity, and physical presence in space and time: its 'aura'), to a secular aestheticising of the work as art *pour l'art*, and thence, in an age of mass reproduction and distribution, to the modern 'emphasis on its exhibition value' (Benjamin 223, 227). It has then becomes 'a crea-tion with entirely new functions, among which . . . the artistic function, later may be recognised as incidental' (227). Benjamin has the plastic and performing arts primarily in mind, particularly what he hails as the revo-lutionary inauthenticity of cinema, but it is worth considering Dickens's publishing and editorial practices in light of what Benjamin has to say about the film industry:

---

[21] 'Massification' (from 'massify', *Oxford English Dictionary*), the act of taking all people together in a group as a whole, without reference to their individual characteristics or needs.

film responds to the shriveling of the aura with an artificial build-up of the 'personality' outside the studio. The cult of the . . . star, fostered by the money of the film industry, preserves not the unique aura of the person but the 'spell of the personality', the phony spell of a commodity. (Section X; 233)

Dickens's repeated attempts to mythologise and make magical some of the agents of mass reproduction and distribution which surround his readers, while simultaneously laying bare their processes – the poetics of communication in his journalism – can be read on one level as an enlightened attempt to restore lost aura, and reanimate a sense of wonder; on another, less benignly, as a cheap trick, 'the phony spell of a commodity'. As I have argued elsewhere, the 'conversion of . . . raw research findings on social, industrial, and cultural matters into stories embroidered by Scheherezade proves to be a key editorial process' in *Household Words* (Drew 115). In Dickens's hands, I read this duality as a redemptive mythology against industrial materialism and 'the iron binding of the mind to grim realities', rather than a fetishising of the commodity, or the result of a leveller's appreciation of how mass production of art would 'destroy . . . the very idea of high culture (in the transcendent sense)' (John 166). While there are a number of ironies involved in maintaining the position, I imagine Dickens to have believed that a high, refined culture and a mass culture were indeed compatible, and that their merging at some unspecified future moment, enabled by unspecified future technologies, would be a transcendental and poetic union worth anticipating and celebrating, in the Anglo-American tradition I have identified.

The shorthand system that Dickens started teaching himself in 1829, perhaps with the assistance of his father and uncle, was set down in a handbook first published in 1750 by Thomas Gurney, called *Brachygraphy; or, Swift Writing Made Easy to the Meanest Capacity*. In the later editions revised by his son Joseph – one of which Dickens almost certainly used – the same combination of myth-making with the setting forth of factual information that is so notable in his weekly magazines, can be detected. The book opens with a series of poems praising the skills which the apprentice is about to learn as something which, in previous eras, would have been condemned as witchcraft; now however, 'Gurney's art contracts the mighty span/And sinks th'immense of science to a span' (Drew 2003: 8). Shorthand, in other words (and in a striking conflation

of Benjamin's distinction between art-as-ritual and art as instrument of
political practice), is simultaneously mechanistic and magical, and its
contractions reduce the entire scope of written language and whatever
it seeks to express, to series of combinations of lines, curves, circles and
points.[22] Only partly tongue-in-cheek, one could recall the metaphorical
importance of all these movements to Dickens's figuring of the editor's
role. More importantly, one can emphasise how the successful manipula-
tion of this system – Dickens was recalled as occupying 'the very highest
rank' among the parliamentary shorthand writers 'not merely for accuracy of reporting but for marvellous quickness in transcript' (Forster I:
69) – involves a series of transformations at high speed through different
character sets and encoding systems. To get a parliamentary speech given
at a late hour set up in type for the next morning's paper, for example,
involved a team of shorthand writers processing chunks of spoken language into brachygraphic code, then shortly afterwards transforming the
code into passages of manuscript text, which would then be passed as rapidly as possible (by coach or railway or both) to a co-ordinating reporter
in the printing-house, who would despatch them to the compositors to set
up in long columns of type. An impression would then be taken to form
galley proofs, which would then be read for accuracy, and the type reset as
required, before locking down each newspaper page for printing; a series of
further journeys at high speed, by coach, post, rail, would intervene before
the finished product met the gaze of the consumer. At key moments in his
career and of nineteenth-century politics, Dickens was involved in setting
up 'special expresses' to convey packages of information along carefully
constructed lines of communication.[23] To liken this set of transformations
to those involved in typing an e-mail and sending it, or downloading an
electronic text, and to call a shorthand writer a word processor, is by no
means a sleight of hand, even if it is all play on words.[24] The processes are

[22] When David Copperfield is apprenticed to 'the savage art' of stenography, he
recalls learning by rote series of 'dots', 'flies' legs', 'circles', 'curve[s]' plus tables
of 'arbitrary characters', personified as 'the most despotic characters ever known'
(David Copperfield, ch. 38, II: 132; Drew 2003: 8 and n.). See Benjamin 1973:
Sections II–IV (222–6).
[23] Drew 2003: 22–3, 26–7, 76–80, 149; Drew 2011 (forthcoming).
[24] To download an e-text from Project Gutenberg, for example, involves
requesting the file containing it from a webserver, which then transmits the file in
data packets containing bytes of information – typically eight 'bits' of binary code
– together with additional binary data consisting of the destination computer's

fundamentally akin, and at the outset of the twenty-first century we are still very much in the days of the 'ocean penny post' so eagerly anticipated in *Household Words*. That continuity is worth emphasising, together with the concept of a 'slow-burn' information revolution, albeit with peaks, dating back through Gurney, to Gutenberg.

Since 1971, Project Gutenberg, the first producer of free e-books, has been giving away easily searchable 'plain vanilla' texts of classic works of literature, premised on what its founder, the late Michael Hart, termed 'Replicator Technology', namely that 'anything that can be entered into a computer can be reproduced indefinitely' (Hart 1992). However familiar we may be with Gutenberg e-texts, and supportive of the Project's philanthropic and educative mission, this is still a striking thought. Project Gutenberg currently offers something over 36,000 scrupulously proof-read e-texts to a target audience defined as no less than '99% of the general public', with works selected which it is hoped 'extremely large portions of the audience will want and use frequently'; 'esoteric materials' are avoided. Leaving aside speculation as to whether Dickens himself, with his qualified support for the abolition of the Newspaper Stamp (Drew 2003: 183–7; John 115–19), would have approved of this anarchic gesture, we can note that the traffic in Dickens material is healthy, and no fewer than 186 separate items (including audio-books and some rather tangential Dickens-related material) were available in June 2011. In the same month, his works formed the third-most popular requests for downloads, after those by Mark Twain and Arthur Conan Doyle.

One might have thought, given the push towards cheapness and the free-flowing reproduction of material that Dickens himself instigated when arranging for *A Tale of Two Cities* to be serialised across multiple formats and outlets in 1859, that free downloads from Project Gutenberg would by now dwarf traditional, commercial forms of delivery, but matters

address, the sender's details, and a packet number. Transmission is routed via network switches comparable to a mail sorting office, or telephone exchange. Depending on the distance to be traversed, the binary switches are converted to series of electrical impulses passing down copper wire and/or to light impulses in fibre optic cable (the latter countering the attenuation of signal in electrical wiring). Where typing is involved (e.g a plain text e-mail) each keystroke in a word is converted into 16 binary bits according to the keycode; formatted e-mail also involves MIME encoding (a redistribution of data packets to circumvent transmission problems).

are complicated by the nature of web statistics. The Project offers detailed 'Top 100' rankings for authors and books, but only over 1-, 7- and 30-day timeframes, rather than offering finite totals. Certainly, the *Tale* was the most popular Dickens title in June 2011, with 9,899 downloads from the main Gutenberg server (mirror site statistics are not included), but compared with claims abroad in 2010 that this particular novel 'has sold more than 200 million copies to date, making it the bestselling novel – in any genre – of all time', this seems small beer (Mitchell 2010). The figure may even reflect the closing stages of a temporary hike in interest due to the selection of the novel, along with *Great Expectations*, as the Christmas 2010 reading choice for the Oprah Winfrey Book Club. Internet statistics such as these, based on self-updating snapshots, are hard to back-project cumulatively, and scarcely look valid as evidence, still less as admissible criteria for forming canonical judgements.

However, much the same could be said of the historical data we have about sales, circulation and readership of Dickens's works, and it is as well to be reminded of the still slender means at the disposal of scholarship when we want either to quantify readers' experiences of a given text, or to extrapolate their qualitative and interpretative conclusions.[25] In some ways, the quantitative/qualitative data currently available online outstrip anything preserved in Victorian ledgers and letters, but it dips from view so quickly that some means of record-keeping surely needs putting into place so that future scholarship will possess both snapshots and aggregates of the kind of information we currently struggle to compile for the nineteenth century. It is ironic that while the splendid 'Reading Experience Database (RED)' (an Open University project online at <http://www.open.ac.uk/Arts/RED/>) is painstakingly documenting a retrospective history of reading in Britain based on individuals readers' comments from 1450 to 1945, the wealth of ongoing reader-response information available through customer reviews on websites is going by the board. One day, the 83 online posts responding to the opening discussion of *A Tale of Two Cities* on Oprah's Book Club ('Rough start with all those big words and long sentences. But after a few days I am actually

---

[25]   Dallas Liddle quotes a telling exchange to this effect between the two scholars who have arguably done most to fill in gaps in our knowledge of such details, Richard Altick and Jonathan Rose (150). In Dickens's case, Ford and Patten are still the cornerstones of our knowledge.

enjoying the book' *et al.*[26]) will have value for researchers, but only if web archiving steps up to the challenge.

The not-for-profit California-based 'Internet Archive' (<http://www.archive.org>) is the only organisation I am aware of that is archiving the web itself, by means of its pioneering 'Wayback Machine'. Although it only trawls and preserves the higher-level pages on individual sites, and will only pick up the limited range of user statistics there displayed, it has at least been doing this periodically since 1998, so that whole series of data – downloads per month for *A Tale of Two Cities* for example – may be constructed. Web users may also be familiar with its rapidly expanding open access Text Archive, which offers public domain titles in complete facsimile form as 'flip-books' – a substantially different basis to Project Gutenberg's plain text supply. It is a good example of what Peter Shillingsburg calls the 'renewed emphasis' in the development of electronic resources, 'on images, not just transcriptions, of original documents, and especially images that . . . highlight the materiality of the originals' (22). It is also significantly larger (over 2.8 million texts in June 2011), and growing more rapidly. Two observations seem relevant. One is that this welcome emphasis on the 'materiality of the originals' restores to the text many of the paratexts which helped mediate its particular encounter with readers at the precise point when it was published. These might include the owner's bookplate, the author's inscription, the binding chosen, as well as what Genette calls the 'publisher's peritext', together with the volume's particular format and typography (16–33; 117–40). I suspect many readers of Project Gutenberg e-texts respond with something like alienation to the standardised way each begins –

> Copyright laws are changing all over the world, be sure to check the copyright laws for your country before posting these files!!
>
> Please take a look at the important information in this header.
>
> We encourage you to keep this file on your own disk, keeping an electronic path open for the next readers. Do not remove this.
>
> **Welcome To The World of Free Plain Vanilla Electronic Texts**

---

[26] <http://www.oprah.com/oprahsbookclub/Oprahs-Book-Club-Producer-Jills-Charles-Dickens-Discussion-1>.

– and which continues, with disclaimers, and appeals for donations, for over 200 lines – because here the e-publisher's peritext obliterates or delays important information about the material book from which the text has been prepared (which edition, which publishing house, what date?) and prevents us from acquiring all that subliminal information that constitutes our sense of a book's history and personality as soon as we encounter it. To denote this the book's 'unique aura' – as opposed to the 'phony spell of the commodity' (in the age of 'Replicator Technology') – would be à propos, if potentially unjust to Project Gutenberg. A great many hours of human work go into the entering, proofreading and checking of any individual Gutenberg e-text, which is also free, and purposefully kept plain and unadorned so as to be portable and lightweight: the very ideal of a 'Cheap Edition' one might think. Its textual accuracy – in terms of words rather than punctuation or pagination – is also paramount for empowering one of the main virtues of electronic editions, rapid searchability. For all their emphasis on materiality and the image, Archive.org e-books do not offer texts proofread by human intermediaries, and searches – as with almost all extant digital archives of newspapers and periodicals – are carried out on less than 100% accurate machine-read transcriptions, produced by Optimal Character Recognition (OCR). Searches thus regularly fail to return complete sets of data, or return false positives.

Dickens Journals Online (DJO), the online edition of *Household Words* and *All the Year Round* under Dickens's editorship that has been under gradual development at the University of Buckingham since 2006, could be described as an attempt to combine in a single interface the advantages of both the Project Gutenberg and Archive.org approaches, together with something crucial but rare to find in a digitised periodical: an anno-tated contributor index.[27] In the early 1990s, when personal computers, the internet itself, and my own periodicals research were all still in their infancy, the way one accessed copies of Dickens's journals was entirely tra-ditional: requesting musty bi-annual volumes from the periodicals 'stack' at the University of London Senate House, or – luxury – reading them from the open shelves in a college library, if they happened to be available.

---

[27] Its immediate inspirations were actually rather different: the *Internet Library of Early Journals* and *The Victorian Literary Studies Archive*, in the early stages of DJO's development, and *The Stormont Papers* and *Australian Newspapers Digitisation Program* in the latter, have all been powerful influences.

Now, however, as with most pre-1870 items in Britain's research libraries, the original bound copies of Dickens's journals are available for reference only, and never for loan. Library readers are probably still frustrated, however, by the lack of any kind of weekly tables of contents or authorship information and may well be unaware that the two indexes and contributor lists compiled in the twentieth-century (one to *Household Words* by Anne Lohrli, the other to *All the Year Round* by Ella Anne Oppenlander) need to be requested separately – if, indeed, the library where one is consulting the journals possesses copies of these rare, out-of-print publications. Although ProQuest's commercial subscription service to digitised runs of hundreds of British periodicals (costing hundreds to thousands of pounds per annum) does offer facsimile images of the contents of Dickens's two journals, neatly packaged by article, it provides no authorship information, and does not facilitate searching on corrected text.

The first premise of *DJO* is that it should be open-access. As one convenor of a vibrant Dickens reading and discussion group wrote, on test-driving a prototype of the site, this is 'the biggest interface issue of all – access to the site should be free . . . . If people can only access the site through university libraries, believe me, it might as well be on the dark side of the moon'.[28] This has multiple implications, and while the aim may only partly square with Dickens's own clearly commercial strategies with his journals, in terms of pursuing a broad 'quality, cheapness and breadth of access' agenda, there is no essential conflict. The second premise is that the browser showing any given page should offer a parallel view (customisable according to readers' preferences) of both the page image, in high resolution, and a plain corrected transcript of it (currently in XHTML), which is therefore searchable to a high degree of accuracy. To achieve this, the project worked in collaboration with Archive.org, which scanned our materials – including the rare *Household Narrative of Current Events*, a supplement to *Household Words* – to create 48 e-books for its own library, and then allowed us access to the resulting image and text-based files to build our own resource. Costs were minimal, but interestingly, the initial impulse to collaborate was based on a misunderstanding Walter Benjamin might have relished. My approach letter specified that I had 'a rare collection of Dickens's journals'[29] that would be well worth making available digitally,

<hr />

[28] E-mail to the author, 14/09/2010.
[29] This was not disingenuous: our set of bi-annual volumes came from the library

and, supposing that these were the personal handwritten diaries of one of the world's most celebrated novelists – rather than mechanically reproduced artefacts – the Director of Collections responded from California with some alacrity. Hence, the Archive.org hosting of our raw materials at <http://www.archive.org/details/djo> has, since October 2007, acted as a kind of basic mirror or back-up site, attracting some interest in its own right: 18,972 individual volume downloads to the end of June 2011.

A major obstacle, however, to *DJO*'s combined 'parallel browser' capability was the intense manual labour that is involved in correcting 'dirty' OCR transcription: proofreading and editing the circa 30,000,000 words of text which *DJO* currently comprises does not happen overnight, and certainly not at standard industry rates of hourly pay, such as suggested by the National Union of Journalists. While Archive.org's mechanical scans return something like a 99.5%+ degree of accuracy, this results in circa 25 errors per page, even before additional editorial policies (such as removing hyphenation) are taken into account. Text correction, in short, looked prohibitively expensive. However, just as the project had encountered an encouraging degree of success with a hybrid community funding model[30] that involved individual members of the public as well as groups of readers, along with providers of research grants, so it took heart from the broad appeal of its key material. Dickens's journals on original publication had created a huge community of readers and followers across the British Empire, and on both sides of the Atlantic: was there not a way of creating a group of volunteer proofreaders and text-correctors working online internationally? The *Australian Newspapers Digitization Program* had done just this in 2008, and published some very encouraging results, including analysis and recommendations for quality control in publishing projects incorporating volunteers, which *Dickens Journals Online* has tried to assimilate (Holley 2009a, b; 2010). According to John B. Thompson's weighty guide to *Books in the Digital Age*, there was even a name for this approach, the 'scholarly community model', in which 'the building of the online community – the e-community – is what matters' (365).

---

of distinguished Victorianist Kenneth J. Fielding (1924–2005); complete runs of this kind seldom become available.

[30]　This puts it favourably; patchwork might be a more accurate description, with no diminution of gratitude to our supporters.

As a result, from January 2011, *DJO* opened up its contents to what – in preference to the somewhat sinister term 'crowdsourcing' – we refer to as public collaborative online text correction, or 'OTC'. In less than eight months, and thanks to a spate of media interest in August 2011, 98% of the total volume of work has been volunteered for, with over 25% already completed to a high standard of accuracy, while various improvements in security and functionality (including a precautionary 'rollback' facility) have been bedded down. Our community of registered 'OTC-ers' has reached the 2,700 mark within a similar period, and although not all are active, it has been fascinating to see how the sharing of what looked originally like hard mechanical labour has spontaneously converted itself into something recreational and educational. I was delighted, for example, to have my attention called to the following passage in a *New York Times* article of 22 March 2011, published with no prior communication between the parties:

> In a Swarthmore [College] lounge where Ms. Buurma's weekly research seminar on Victorian literature and culture meets, Ms. Levine and a handful of other students . . . settled into a cozy circle on stuffed chairs and couches. As part of their class work, they have been helping to correct the transcribed online versions of *Household Words* and *All the Year Round* . . . . On a square coffee table sat a short stack of original issues of the magazine that a librarian had brought from the college's collection to show the class. Students discussed how the experience of reading differs, depending on whether the text is presented in discrete segments, surrounded by advertisements or in a leather binding; whether you are working in an archive, editing online or reading for pleasure.
>
> 'I was more immersed in the fictional world because I was concentrating so much,' Ester Lee, a junior, said, describing her experience of reviewing the online transcriptions for mistakes. 'I was editing word by word by word and noticing more of the details.'
>
> Laura Backup, a senior, had the opposite reaction. 'I couldn't do both at once,' she said of reading and editing. 'I was too focused on finding the errors.'
>
> For Charlie Huntington, a curly-haired junior, neither the pamphlet-sized journal nor the Web made the novel 'feel nearly as important as it does here,' he said, tapping a paperback copy of *Great Expectations*. (Cohen C1)

This is pure paratextual analysis in action, and equally interesting from a theoretical, practical or pedagogical perspective. There are also material, bodily considerations. Another volunteer confides that he finds that 'electronic forms of presentation put much more strain on the eye than well-designed pages on paper do, and often require one to sit upright. Unless an electronic device is light enough to be used in an easy chair and has optical characteristics as benign as black print on white paper, it cannot, I feel, offer a good reading experience'. This has already had us wondering about developing 'Kindle' and 'i-Pad' compatibility, though our volunteer helpfully concludes that 'I enjoy the correcting enough to put up with the eye and back strain'.[31]

Another experienced volunteer has been working sequentially through the volume of *All the Year Round* containing *A Tale of Two Cities* and is intrigued by the sensation of being unable to read the next episode until the text correction for the previous magazine, including other contents, has been completed and approved. She comments that 'the absence of a finite artefact, and no obvious sign as to how far the story has got, makes a significant difference to one's reading experience', and notes the contrast with the easily gratified temptation when reading a paperback novel to 'wolf the text and race to the end . . . lost in a continuous stream of narrative'. Contrary to what we are often told about the relentless forward-impetus involved in the reading of serial novels, this reader/OTCer found that working on discrete installments of the *Tale* 'leads to the counter-intuitive situation of not wanting to finish the novel', of wishing it to continue indefinitely. Its delays and its promotion through advertising within the pages of the journal prompt 'the creation of a fetish for *A Tale* above all the other content' in *All the Year Round*. And finally, as against the 'passivity of reading a novel' in volume form, in a semi-recumbent posture,

> for OTC I'm sat upright, at my desk, work-like . . . I'm interrogating the text in front of me, my mind is fully alert, my hands are a blur of movement[. This] interrogative reading approach, where you correct mistakes, is similar to the treatment you would give a poem or short story. You read it repeatedly, and carefully note punctuation, and graphological detail.[32]

Admittedly, not every volunteer will have the additional energy or acumen to reflect on and articulate the process they are engaged in, but it is already

---

[31]   E-mails to author, 27 and 28 June 2011.
[32]   E-mail to author, 28 June 2011.

becoming clear that the act of involving readers-as-editors (or sub-editors) in their interaction with the e-text of periodicals for which Dickens himself originally performed a similar function is something that can generate an interesting critical penumbra, directly relating to the nature of the material itself.

Gissing's Marian Yule felt disempowered as a periodical contributor, a 'mere machine for reading and writing . . . an automaton', but so far our impression is that – unless a page-saving glitch causes work to be lost (2–3% of cases at present) – OTC contributors feel in control, and enthused. Should volunteer energy and concentration start to dwindle, however, there is a fall-back plan to complete the text correction within a specified time-frame, which is worth mentioning at the end of this brief overview of the currently functioning elements of *DJO*.[33] Amazon Web Services, which already provide additional weekly backups of the content as well as a flexible 'cloud server' web-hosting solution for the main site, offer an additional service, ingeniously named 'The Mechanical Turk'. Contemplation of its methodology affords an example of the manifold parallels that seem to obtain between the dynamism of modern web publishing and that of the Victorian periodical press, and a curious sensation of a wheel somewhere having come full circle. Its commercial interface describes the service as 'a marketplace for work' giving 'businesses and developers access to an on-demand scalable workforce' of casual online labourers who log on and freely select from huge numbers of tiny tasks called HITs (Human Intelligence Tasks), of which 123,517 were available on the last date consulted, payable at rates ranging from $0.01 for a 1–10 minute task, to $12.87 for a 4½ hour task. At one level, it is a clinical operation exploiting and perhaps cementing existing global inequalities between labour markets; on another, it is a recognition that computers are merely human prostheses, and dependent entirely on human willpower and artistry, as the FAQ answer recounting the origin of the idea, explains:

> In 1769, Hungarian nobleman Wolfgang von Kempelen astonished Europe by building a mechanical chess-playing automaton that defeated nearly every opponent it faced. A life-sized wooden mannequin, adorned

---

[33]   I restrict my remarks in this overview to the functions already securely in place on the *DJO* betasite; many others are planned/under development, but it would be tempting fate to discuss them at this stage of the project's history. The 'OTC' project was in fact completed, through volunteer effort alone, on 7 February 2012.

with a fur-trimmed robe and a turban, Kempelen's 'Turk' was seated
behind a cabinet and toured Europe confounding such brilliant chal-
lengers as Benjamin Franklin and Napoleon Bonaparte. To persuade
skeptical audiences, Kempelen would slide open the cabinet's doors
to reveal the intricate set of gears, cogs and springs that powered his
invention. He convinced them that he had built a machine that made
decisions using artificial intelligence. What they did not know was the
secret behind the Mechanical Turk: a chess master cleverly concealed
inside.[34]

Amazon is by no means the only company offering networked services
where human agents perform myriads of outsourced tasks that computers
struggle to do well[35] but its rhetorical and storytelling strategies are perhaps
the most compelling, and reminiscent of the Dickensian poetics of communication, and the way these form a nexus of idealism fully imbricated
with consumerism. Just as Dickens's journals had reached out to a mass
audience, offering to retail them fanciful re-imaginings of the contemporary
scene at an affordable price, to be consumed in moments of leisure, so
'Mechanical Turk' appeals to its potentially vast workforce on the basis of
flexible empowerment, offering them a miscellany of small tasks, nuggets
of paid employment, to be voluntarily selected and carried out to no fixed
routine. The same FAQ answer quoted above goes on to ask questions of its
own: 'What if . . . a computer program could ask a human being to perform
a task and return the results? What if it could coordinate many human
beings to perform a task?' In the case of *DJO*, the answer is already clear,
but if we try to reconfigure the relationships for a moment inserting Dickens
as the programmer, his weekly magazines as the program, and original
readers as the human beings to be coordinated, then one is prompted to
ask a further (and final) question: what tasks was Dickens asking them to
perform through his journals?

The idealistic form of answer was given to Elizabeth Gaskell, when
Dickens wrote to her to solicit contributions for the launch issue of
Household Words: 'the general mind and purpose of the journal . . . is the
raising up of those that are down, and the general improvement of our
social condition' (Dickens 1965–2002, VI: 22). In practice, as Dickens's

---

[34]   <http://aws.amazon.com/mturk/faqs/#What_is_Amazon_Mechanical_
Turk>.
[35]   <http://www.microtask.com> offers 'human powered document processing'
and claims to solve 'one billion tasks per day'.

journals go on to address themselves to life with plainness and profound-
ness, this takes on transcendent overtones: the Whitmanesque sense that
'God's purpose' is for 'the earth to be spann'd, connected by net-work,/ . . .
/ All these separations and gaps [to] be taken up, and hook'd and link'd
together'. The consumerist form of answer is that Dickens's readers are
asked to participate in, and celebrate, acts of communication that are
themselves being performed, and to an extent fetishised. There was, arguably – and perhaps still is, if the early experience of *DJO* is anything to go
by – as much aura about the poetics of communication in Dickens's journals as there is phony consumerism, so perhaps it is our own linear models
of media-communications development that need to be questioned, after
all. Is it always a straight line of progress, or are there not curves, points
and circles? Orthodox histories opt for the straight line: first the computer, then the e-text; after the e-text, then the e-book; which, thanks to the
revolutionary e-book reader, comes out of the office or deskspace where
it had been chained to a monitor, and into the pocket. *Plus ça change plus
c'est la même chose*, however . . . . The Tauchnitz copyright editions of
Household Words were smaller and lighter than a Kindle, contained two
to three months' worth of fiction, poetry and journalism, and have presented a stable browsing interface for over 150 years. Of one collection of
popular essays republished from *All the Year Round* in 1860, an anonymous
reviewer in *The Morning Post* wrote, simply, 'a pleasant book . . . for railway
travellers' (3).[36] Consumers of Dickens's weekly magazines, whether in
their original Victorian forms or in modern digital online format, are constantly invited to participate in texts that in and of themselves celebrate
the Romantic connectivity of the publishing practices that have brought
author and reader into anonymous communion in the first place.

Works cited

Altick, Richard D., 1957. *The English Common Reader; A Social History
of the Mass Reading Public 1800–1900*. Chicago: University of Chicago
Press.
Anderson, Alexander ('Surfaceman'), 1878. *Songs of the Rail*. London:
Simpkin Marshall.
[Anon.], 1859. 'Literature', *The Morning Post*, 26842 (29 December
1859), p. 3, col. d.

[36]   The book was Charles A. Collins's *A New Sentimental Journey* (1859).

Baumgarten, Murray, 1990. 'Railway/reading/time: *Dombey and Son* and the Industrial World', *Dickens Studies Annual*, 19: 65–89.

Benjamin, Walter, 1973 [1935]. 'The Work of Art in the Age of Mechanical Reproduction', repr. in *Illuminations*, ed. H. Arendt; trans H. Zohn. London: Fontana.

Carter, Ian, 2001. *Railways and Culture in Britain.* 'Studies in Popular Culture'. Manchester: Manchester University Press.

Cohen, Patricia, 2011. 'Giving Literature Virtual Life', *New York Times* (21 March) 'Books', p. C1, <http://www.nytimes.com/2011/03/22/books/digital-humanities-boots-up-on-some-campuses.html>.

Clayton, Jay, 2003. *Charles Dickens in Cyberspace: The Afterlife of the Nineteenth Century in Postmodern Culture.* Oxford: Oxford University Press.

Crawford, Iain, 2011. '"Faithful Sympathy": Dickens, the *Edinburgh Review*, and Editing *Household Words*', *Victorian Periodicals Review*, 44: 42–68.

Davie, Donald, 2000. *Two Ways out of Whitman; American Essays.* Manchester: Carcanet Press.

Demoor, Marysa, and Kate MacDonald, 2010. 'Finding and Defining the Victorian Supplement', *Victorian Periodicals Review* 43: 97–110.

Dickens, Charles, 1842. *American Notes.* 2 vols. London: Chapman and Hall.

Dickens, Charles, 1852–3. *Bleak House.* 4 vols. Copyright Edition. Leipzig: Bernh. Tauchnitz Jr.

Dickens, Charles, ed., 1850–9. *Household Words* I–XIX. London: Bradbury & Evans. Online at <http://www.djo.org.uk>.

Dickens, Charles, ed., 1859–70. *All the Year Round* I–XX, ns I–IV. London. Online at <http://www.djo.org.uk>.

Dickens, Charles, 1910–12 (1850). *David Copperfield* 2 vols. 'Centenary Edition'. 36 vols. London: Chapman and Hall.

Dickens, Charles, 1965–2002. *The Letters of Charles Dickens*, ed. G. Storey, K. Tillotson *et al.* 12 vols. Oxford: Clarendon.

Dickinson, Emily, 1959. *Selected Poems of Emily Dickinson*, ed. James Reeves. Oxford: Heinemann.

Drew, John M. L., 2003. *Dickens the Journalist.* Basingstoke: Palgrave.

Drew, John M. L., Hazel Mackenzie and Ben Winyard, eds. and intr., 2012 (forthcoming). 'Introduction' to *All the Year Round*, vol. I. Buckingham: University of Buckingham Press.

Dvorak, Wilfred P., 1984. 'Dickens' Ambivalence as a Social Critic in the 1860s: Attitudes to Money in *All the Year Round* and *The Uncommercial Traveller*', *Dickensian*, 80: 89–104.

Eisenstein, Sergei, 1949 [1942]. 'Dickens, Griffith, and the Film Today', in Jan Leyda, ed. and trans., *Film Form*. New York: Harcourt, Brace, pp. 195–255.

Emerson, Ralph Waldo, 1906? [1842]. 'The Poet' in *Essays*, vol. 1 of *The Works of Ralph Waldo Emerson*. London: George Routledge.

Farina, Jonathan V., 2009. '"A Certain Shadow": Personified Abstractions and the Form of *Household Words*', *Victorian Periodicals Review*, 42: 392–414.

Ford, George H., 1955. *Dickens and His Readers. Aspects of Novel Criticism since 1836*. Princeton, New Jersey: Princeton University Press.

Forster, John, ed., 1928 [1872–4]. *The Life of Charles Dickens*, ed. J. W. T. Ley, 2 vols. London: Cecil Palmer.

Gardiner, John, 2008. 'Dickens and the Uses of History', in *A Companion to Charles Dickens*, ed. David Paroissien. Oxford: Blackwell, pp. 240–54.

Genette, Gérard, 1997 [1987]. *Paratexts: Thresholds of Interpretation* trans. Jane E. Lewin. Cambridge: Cambridge University Press.

Gissing, George, 1891. *New Grub Street*. 3 vols. London: Smith, Elder & Co.

Gordon, John Steele, 2002. *A Thread across the Ocean; the Heroic Story of the Transatlantic Cable*. London: Simon & Schuster.

Gurney, Thomas, 1817 [1750]. *Brachygraphy; or an Easy and Compendious System of Short-hand . . . brought still nearer to perfection . . . by Joseph Gurney*. London.

Hart, Michael, 1992. 'The History and Philosophy of Project Gutenberg', <http://www.gutenberg.org/wiki/Gutenberg:The_History_and_Philosophy_of_Project_Gutenberg_by_Michael_Hart>.

Holley, Rose, 2009a. 'Many Hands Make Light Work: Public Collaborative OCR Text Correction in Australian Historic Newspapers', National Library of Australia (March), <http://www.nla.gov.au/ndp/project_details/documents/ANDP_ManyHands.pdf>.

Holley, Rose, 2009b. 'A Success Story – Australian Newspapers Digitisation Program', *Online Currents*, 23.6: 283–95. <http://www.nla.gov.au/ndp/news_and_events/documents/ANDPSuccessstory_OnlineCurrentsDec2009.pdf>.

Holley, Rose, 2010. 'Crowdsourcing: How and Why Should Libraries Do It?', *D-Lib Magazine*, (March/April), 17 <http://www.dlib.org/dlib/march10/holley/03holley.html>.

Hollington, Michael, ed., 2012 (forthcoming). *Reception of Charles Dickens in Europe*. London: Continuum.

Holloway, Emory, ed., 1921. *The Uncollected Poetry and Prose of Walt Whitman*. 2 vols. New York: Doubleday, Page & Co.

House, Humphrey, 1942 [1941]. *The Dickens World.* 2nd edn. London: Oxford University Press.

Huett, Lorna, 2005. 'Among the Unknown Public: *Household Words, All the Year Round* and the Mass-Market Weekly Periodical in the Mid-Nineteenth Century', *Victorian Periodicals Review*, 38: 61–82.

John, Juliet, 2010. *Dickens and Mass Culture.* Oxford: Oxford University Press.

Liddle, Dallas, 2009. *The Dynamics of Genre: Journalism and the Practice of Literature in Mid-Victorian Britain.* Charlottesville, Virginia: University of Virginia Press.

Lohrli, Anne, 1973. *Household Words, . . . Table of Contents, List of Contributors and Their Contributions &c.* Toronto: University of Toronto Press.

Martineau, Harriet, 1861. *Health, Husbandry, and Handicraft.* London: Bradbury and Evans.

McGill, Meredith L., 2002. *American Literature and the Culture of Reprinting, 1834–1853.* Philadelphia: University of Pennsylvania Press, 2002.

Mitchell, David, 2010. 'David Mitchell on Historical Fiction', *The Daily Telegraph*, Reviews (8 May 2010), <http://www.telegraph.co.uk/culture/books/bookreviews/7685510/David-Mitchell-on-Historical-Fiction.html>.

Moss, Sidney P., 1984. *Charles Dickens' Quarrel with America.* Troy, New York: Whitston Publishing Co.

Oppenlander, Ella Ann, 1984. *Dickens' All the Year Round: Descriptive Index and Contributor List.* Troy, New York: Whitston Publishing Co.

Patten, Robert L. 1978. *Dickens and his Publishers.* Oxford: Oxford University Press.

Rose, Jonathan, 2010 [2001]. *The Intellectual Life of the British Working Classes.* 2nd edn New Haven, Connecticut: Yale University Press.

Ruskin, John, 1903-12. Letter to C. E. Norton (19 June 1870), in *The Works of John Ruskin*, ed. E. T. Cook and Alexander Wedderburn, 39 vols. London: George Allen.

Schivelbusch, Wolfgang, 1986 [1977]. *The Railway Journey.* Berkeley, California: University of California Press.

Selvin, Joel, 1996. 'Q and A with Brian Eno', *San Francisco Chronicle* S (2 June) , p. 43 <http://www.sfgate.com/cgi-bin/article.cgi?file=/chronicle/archive/1996/06/02/PK70006.DTL>.

Shillingsburg, Peter, 2010. 'The Impact of Computers on the Art of Scholarly Editing', in Gabriel Egan, ed., *Electronic Publishing: Politics and Pragmatics.* Tempe, Arizona: Iter Inc. & ACMRS, pp. 17–29.

Slater, Michael, ed. and intr., 1979. *Dickens on America and the Americans.* Hassocks, Sussex: Harvester Press, pp. 1–67.

Slater, Michael, ed., 1994. *Sketches by Boz and Other Early Papers, 1833–39.* 'Dent Uniform Edition of Dickens' Journalism', 4 vols; vol. 1. London: J. M. Dent.

Slater, Michael, and John Drew, ed. and intr., 2000. *The Uncommercial Traveller and Other Papers, 1859–70.* 'Dent Uniform Edition of Dickens' Journalism'. 4 vols; vol. IV. London: J. M. Dent.

Smith, Grahame, 2006. *Dickens and the Dream of Cinema.* Manchester: Manchester University Press.

Thompson, John B., 2005. *Books in the Digital Age: the Transformation of Academic and Higher Education Publishing in Britain and the United States.* Cambridge: Polity.

Thornbury, Walter, 1861. *Cross Country.* London: Sampson Low.

Todd, William B., and Ann Bowden, 1988. *Tauchnitz International Editions in English, 1841–1955: A Bibliographical History.* New York: Bibliographical Society of America.

'Todd-Bowden Collection of Tauchnitz Editions', British Library <http://www.bl.uk/reshelp/findhelprestype/prbooks/tauchnitz/index.html>.

Waters, Catherine, 2008. *Commodity Culture in Dickens's 'Household Words'.* Aldershot: Ashgate.

Whitman, Walt, 1920. *The Gathering of the Forces. Editorials, Essays . . . written by Walt Whitman as Editor of the Brooklyn Daily Eagle* &c., ed. Cleveland Rodgers and John Black, The Knickerbocker Press. New York: G. P. Putnam's Sons.

Corpus stylistics – Dickens, text-drivenness and the fictional world

MICHAELA MAHLBERG

Introduction

Accounts of Dickens's language highlight the variety of stylistic devices that can be found in his writings (cf. e.g. Stewart, Plummer). Ingham observes that Dickens 'deploys every available linguistic resource' (126). However, relatively little attention seems to have been given to specific patterns and the functions they fulfil in the creation of fictional worlds. This article sets out to illustrate how computer-assisted methods can support the analysis of linguistic devices and the effects they create in the text. The focus will be on two resources in particular: repeated sequences of words and suspended quotations. The strength of computer-assisted approaches is typically seen in the potential that quantification offers, for instance, for the comparison of stylistic features in writings of different authors. The present approach, however, is less interested in the detailed quantification of features than in the functions of the patterns that become visible when a number of examples form the evidential basis for textual analysis. When cues in the text guide an analysis it becomes text-driven. This article will show how links can be made between a text-driven approach and wider concerns in literary criticism – in particular the creation of characters in fictional worlds. I will look at how descriptions of body language contribute to the externalised techniques of characterisation which John has argued are rooted in Dickens's narrative prose. Patterns that are found with the help of corpus methods also relate to linguistic resources that Rosenberg describes as the 'language of doubt'. The article argues that corpus methods can help to view patterns as part of a bigger picture that includes both striking linguistic devices but also patterns that receive less conscious attention from the reader – or the critic.

The first section begins with a brief background on the corpus stylistic approach adopted in this article before the second section introduces 'clusters' as building blocks of fictional worlds. The third section discusses the implications of a text-driven approach for a conception of characterisation as externalisation, which leads to an outline of the text-driven cline of highlighting and contextualising functions in the fourth section. The final section shows how the investigation of specific places in the text – as opposed to repeated patterns – contributes to the functional continuum outlined in the fourth section. While the text-driven approach presented in this chapter is based on the study of a corpus of twenty-three texts by Dickens, an extended example that focuses on Rigaud in *Little Dorrit* serves to illustrate how linguistic devices function in their textual context in the construction of a particular character.

Corpus linguistic methods and the analysis of literary texts

The use of computers and quantitative methods for the analysis of literary texts is not a new development (for overviews see, for instance, Hockey, Biber (2011)). However, the term 'corpus stylistics' has only recently become popular. It refers to approaches that seek to employ corpus methods to address questions in literary stylistics and criticism, or as Carter puts it: 'Corpus stylistic analysis is a relatively objective methodological procedure that at its best is guided by a relatively subjective process of interpretation' (67). A 'corpus' is usually regarded as a relatively large collection of computer-readable texts used for linguistic analysis. General corpora contain a range of texts from newspaper articles to transcriptions of conversations. Corpus software can count and display linguistic units in a number of ways. Below is a concordance for the word *nose*. A concordance displays the search word with a specified amount of co-text on either side. In Concordance 1, the co-text is sorted according to the first word on the right of *nose*. The concordance illustrates repeated patterns such as *nose blowing, nose for, pay through the nose for, nose job, nose operation.* The patterns do not always appear in the exact same forms, as the examples of 'breaking someone's nose' (lines 15, 24, 30) or 'nose blowing' (lines 1, 3, 4, 6) show. Most of the instances of *nose* are nouns, but there is also a verb in line 2. A key observation in corpus linguistics is that the meanings of words are associated with the patterns in which the words occur. For instance, the meaning 'to pay too much money for something' is associated with the

```
 1                   News Motorist fined for blowing nose A motorist was fined by
 2        Rugby Harinordoquy masters Munster to nose Biarritz into the final
 3                  vigorous exercise at 7.9% and nose blowing at 5.4%. These were
 4                   News Video Baby scared of nose blowing becomes internet hit A
 5              champagne gets right up my nose By Harry Mount Food and
 6            sex and even blowing one's nose can burst blood vessels in
 7                Andrew tries to keep his nose clean in Indonesia By Andy
 8  Pushing envelopes Pushing envelopes: red nose day Pride and embarrassment
 9                 has to pay through the nose for using tissue at the
10          Welsh are paying through the nose for insurance' Do you live
11              Oil and Gas A bloody nose for Sir William Castell at
12          home Peter Simon shows his nose for a good bargain on
13            free Andy Coulson had a nose for the view of the
14        Things Are: The shoebill - a nose for the unusual By Mike
15  Japan Elderly woman breaks student's nose for failing to give up
16      Doctor, doctor: Why does my nose get blocked? 'I worry this
17      Snooker: No skin off snooker's nose if Rocket quits, says Davis
18          Surgery: Ed votes for a nose job Miliband hopes for better
19        Dianna Agron admits to having nose job Glee star Dianna Agron
20  continued with plastic surgery' after nose job patient dies from heart
21          Does Mike Tindall need a nose job? He's set to wed
22      volume reveals brutality of early nose jobs 19th century book for
23              that he has a red nose: like all of us, he's
24 Advertisement sport Meagan Duhamel breaks nose of Eric Radford at World
25      Ed Miliband Ed Miliband undergoes nose operation for sleep apnoea
26      Politics Ed Miliband Ed Miliband nose operation satisfies surgeons
27      Miliband Ed Miliband to undergo nose operation on NHS Ed Miliband
28    UK Politics Ed Miliband undergoes nose operation Wednesday, 27 July
29          Ed Nose Day' Ed Miliband's nose operation could prove
30  vigilante Phoenix Jones suffers broken nose Phoenix Jones, the masked
31          Science News Having a big nose prevents sniffles Having a
32        Sunday | Home More on: runny nose Refine: immune hay fever
33      Blog home Should schools ban nose studs? They're against
34      Great Dane bites off courier's nose The owner of two barking
35          1837: Woman bites off man's nose The Guardian reports on a
```

Concordance 1. Thirty-five examples of *nose* retrieved with WebCorp[*]

pattern *pay through the nose* where the meaning of *nose* is very different from the meaning of the word in *blowing one's nose*. Concordance 1 also shows that the patterns of a word reflect the register they come from. The sample of the word *nose* has been retrieved with the tool WebCorp that accesses the Web as corpus. The search was limited to webpages of United Kingdom broadsheet newspapers. The nature of newspaper articles is apparent in references to accidents where noses get broken or bitten off, or to issues that

[*] (*WebCorp*, Research and Development Unit for English Studies, Birmingham City University (1999–2011) <http://www.webcorp.org.uk/>)

```
1    chair, with a white face and a frosty nose (but still clawing), she stretches
2      r hearts!" As Mr. Snagsby blows his nose and coughs his cough of sympathy, a
3   ins him to secrecy; he rubs it over his nose, and it sharpens his scent; he sh
4    ays Mr. Snagsby with his finger on his nose, "don't allude to it!" For some
5      regularly and keeps putting it to his nose and taking it away again all the e
6    tasting it, first with one side of his nose and then with the other, Mr. Bucke
7   ns Mr. Tulkinghorn, quietly blowing his nose. "But I don't ask what you think o
8    y, eh?" returns the lawyer, rubbing his nose with the key. "Yes. What is it
9    orner of his eye, and having given his nose one triumphant rub with his forefin
10  ollar, with a moist eye and an inflamed nose, who modestly takes a position nea
11    ed by the solar rays from the judicial nose, who calls in at the shell- fish s
12     scratch my chair and table merchant's nose, which has no pimple on it. His r
13    el with HIM? If I have a pimple on my nose which is disagreeable to my landlor
14    e of lady with spectacles, a prominent nose, and a loud voice, who had the effe
15    lady in a large cap, with rather a red nose and rather an unsteady eye, but sm
16  essed about the waist, and with a sharp nose like a sharp autumn evening, incli
17   h acids, they held, had mounted to the nose and temper of the patient. With wh
```

Concordance 2. Examples of *nose* in *Bleak House*

seem to be of interest to society such as celebrities' nose jobs. The examples also show the topicality of the newspaper articles. The repeated reference to the Labour leader Ed Miliband's nose operation reflects the fact that I ran the concordance a few days after he had his operation.

Large corpora that contain a variety of texts are used, for instance, in lexicography to describe the meanings of words that occur frequently in a language. When corpus methods are applied to the study of literary texts, one factor that can play a role is the amount of data that is available. Concordance 2 contains all the occurrences of *nose* in *Bleak House*. We might expect differences between patterns of *nose* in a novel as compared to a corpus of newspaper articles, but the patterns that we can observe are also limited in frequency when the focus is on one particular text. While Concordance 1 only contains a sample of the instances that can be retrieved from the Web, Concordance 2 provides all occurrences of *nose* in *Bleak House* (sorting at the first word to the left). Patterns that are visible include *rubbing* or *blowing one's nose* (lines 2, 3, 7, 8), as well as a preceding third person possessive determiner (*his*) and the modification of *nose* by adjectives (*frosty, inflamed, judicial, prominent, red, sharp*), pointing to the function of *nose* in the description of characters. A concordance analysis is only one example of frequently used methods in corpus linguistics. Examples of studies that use computer-assisted methods specifically for the study of texts by Dickens are Hori and Tabata.

Clusters as building blocks for fictional worlds

A concordance analysis begins with a specific search word. Another start-ing-point to find patterns that are associated with meanings is to generate clusters. 'Clusters' are repeated sequences of words, such as *at the same time* or *I don't know*. While concordances illustrate more flexible patterns around search words, clusters are defined as verbatim repetitions of words in a sequence without specifying which words are to be included in the sequence. Studies in corpus linguistics have shown that very frequent clusters are associated with register-specific discourse functions (cf. e.g. Biber 2006). In Mahlberg (forthcoming), I present an approach to fictional worlds that focuses on five-word clusters, i.e. repetitions of sequences of five words, in a 4.5 million word corpus of twenty-three texts by Charles Dickens.[1] Such clusters can be interpreted in terms of areas of meanings in or building blocks for the fictional world. Without going into detail as to the retrieval of clusters, Table 1 contains an overview of the areas of meanings that are reflected by clusters. Clusters are initially classified on the basis of features on the textual surface: Labels contain names or are part of expressions that are used to refer to characters or themes; clusters that are only found in one single text in the Dickens corpus are also clas-sified as Labels. Speech clusters contain first- or second-person pronouns or possessives. Body Part clusters contain a Body Part noun. *As if* clusters contain *as if*. Time and Place clusters are or contain time and place refer-ence expressions. The functional interpretation of the clusters is shown in Table 1 by the information following the category names: Labels refer to or identify characters and themes, Speech clusters are typically found in character speech, Body Part clusters describe body language, *as if* clus-ters provide comments and interpretations by the narrator and Time and Place clusters function as time and place references.

Unsurprisingly, some of the clusters draw attention to linguistic features that are included in accounts of Dickens's language under various other headings, for instance, character 'tags' or 'speech tics', and I will discuss some examples below. A crucial point that the text-driven corpus approach emphasises is that such striking patterns are part of a bigger picture. Clus-

---

[1]   The frequency thresholds for the clusters in the Dickens corpus are less selective than in studies that investigate more general discourse functions. For details see Mahlberg (forthcoming). Very frequent clusters are also called 'lexical bundles', cf. Biber (2006).

ters can be interpreted on a functional continuum with highlighting and contextualising patterns as the two extreme points, as I will explain in the fourth section. Especially the first four areas of meanings outlined in Table 1 are of particular relevance to the creation of characters. By concentrating on the functions of textual cues it is possible to see links between seemingly different views on characterisation in Dickens. In the next section I will focus in particular on John's approach to the externalisation of character and Rosenberg's discussion of Dickens's language of doubt. Because of the range of possible patterns of textual cues, the headings in Table 1 indicated in italics relate to broad areas of meanings in the fictional world that can be realised by a number of patterns. Five-word clusters only present a small section of the range of textual patterns that affect the creation of fictional worlds. In the last section, I will address the issue of the variety of patterns by looking at 'suspensions'.

Table 1. Areas of meanings in fictional worlds characterised by clusters (cf. Mahlberg forthcoming)

Labels   *References to and identification of characters and themes*

. . . and the *young lady with the black* eyes and the fur round the boots, whispered something in Emily's ear, and then . . .

Speech clusters   *Character speech*

. . . Thank you, Mr. Bumble, sir, *I am very much obliged* to you, I'm sure.'

Body Part clusters   *Body language*

. . . said Riderhood, when his visitor sat down, resting his chin on his hand, *with his eyes on the* ground.

As if clusters   *Narrator comments and interpretations*

Exceedingly red-eyed and grim, *as if he had been* up all night at a party which had taken anything but a convivial turn, Jerry Cruncher worried his breakfast rather than ate it, . . .

Time and Place clusters   *Time and place references*

Kit stood *in the middle of the* road . . .

Interpreting external features of characters

Characters in Dickens have been discussed from various angles – ranging from their popularity and cultural impact to techniques of characterisation that are interpreted as resulting in 'flat characters' or 'types'. In this section, I want to look at two approaches that deal with the interpretation of external features of characters. As will be shown in the following section, clusters play a specific role in the textual presentation of such external features. The first approach I want to look at is John's account of characterisation that sets Dickens's narrative prose in the context of his views on popular entertainment. John argues that Dickens's techniques of characterisation are based on the externalised methods of popular melodrama. Emotions shown in an exaggerated way, gesture, speech and outward appearance are all external features that are clues to a character's nature. An example is provided by Rigaud, whose dark cloak is 'a familiar uniform for stage villains' (John 103), the description of his face, in particular his eyes, nose and moustache, as well as his language and gestures reflect his wickedness. Emphasising Dickens's vision of the novel as theatre, John explains Dickens's melodramatic writing through his anti-intellectual project: 'the passion [. . .] and the distinctive presentational techniques of melodrama are formative in Dickens's anti-intellectual ideologies' (109). A point in John's argument that is crucial to the text-driven approach to fictional worlds is that she highlights the need for close analysis of Dickens's prose: 'Dickens studies has failed to analyse adequately the melodramatic poetics informing Dickens's prose' (John 108). However, merely equating Dickens's techniques of characterisation with the techniques of popular melodrama would be a simplification. John addresses this issue when she discusses how melodramatic models of character work in the context of the novel. She argues that Dickens succeeds in rendering extreme, violent emotion credibly, and not only comically, because of the context provided by his descriptive prose, or more specifically 'the melodramatic substructure of Dickens's descriptive prose' (John 105). In this substructure, it is the interaction between animate and inanimate world that is described and 'rendered passionally and melodramatically' (John 105). Thus the melodramatic model of character works because the characters' behaviour is part of the bigger picture of the fictional world. To stay with an example from *Little Dorrit*, focusing on the opening passage, John shows how Dickens's description of Marseille is melodramatic – exaggerated, externalised, highly emotive and attributing life to the inanimate world (112).

John's approach provides an explanation for some of the linguistic features we can find in Dickens's novels through his anti-intellectual ideologies. Her approach also raises questions that warrant more detailed investigation from a linguistic point of view. These questions relate specifically to the transfer of the model of characterisation from melodrama to the novel. John tackles the 'descriptive prose' or the 'narrative environment' by drawing on textual examples to illustrate her points. What I want to ask from a text-driven point of view is what linguistic patterns, i.e. linguistic similarities between examples, we can find that contribute to the creation of characters in the fictional world. Gestures or other habitual behaviour that externalise a character have to be packaged in linguistic forms, and this is where a crucial difference between novel and theatre needs closer attention. Similarly, while heightened emotion might be conceived in the theatre through loudness of the actor's voice or the tone in which he or she speaks, how is this tone conveyed in a novel? In the nineteenth century, actors could consult acting manuals to see specific facial expressions that would be associated with particular emotions, but can it simply be deduced that theatrical conventions are also reflected through conventional linguistic expressions in the novels? When studies point out what 'favourite' stylistic devices Dickens liked to use, we might almost believe so. However, with the text-driven approach I want to argue that the picture is more complex, with a variety of forms that includes very recognisable patterns that have not gone unnoticed in the literature but also with more subtle structures that might not easily receive attention.

Rosenberg is also concerned with patterns that are repeatedly found in Dickens and that relate to characterisation. He subsumes these patterns under the notion of the language of 'doubt' and argues that Dickens is less a straightforward and confident novelist than a novelist of conflict and contradiction (Rosenberg 22). While detailed descriptions in Dickens have often been interpreted as clear presentations of the fictional world that would lend themselves easily to film adaptations, Rosenberg claims that too much detail creates the opposite of clarity: 'The greater the number of details presented, the greater the need for the processing of information; the more complex the relations among the details, the more difficult it becomes to assemble them into a coherent whole' (Rosenberg 53-4). With regard to the readers' perception, this means that character is not transparent, but an attempt to approximate the way in which people are perceived in the real world, where external clues for interiority are partial and unreliable. We can see a link between Rosenberg's approach and the cognitive stylistic approach to characterisation put forward by Culpeper (2001) in that Rosenberg focuses on readers' reactions to textual cues. His concern is with 'textual details in order to understand the reactions they typically elicit' (Rosenberg 29).

The role of the reader also seems to be hinted at by John. The melodramatic model of character depends on the audience accepting (and knowing) the conventions for the presentation of specific character features (cf. also John 111). In the novel, this 'acceptance' can to some extent relate to trusting the narrator, who selects which external features are presented and who determines the degree of directness with which surfaces are described. In contrast to the theatre, where the actor on the stage presents the outward appearance of a character in full, the novel only contains partial information on characters, and what is not spelled out explicitly can be provided by the reader, who constructs impressions of characters in the mind. Comments by the narrator then affect the construction of these impressions. This is where the patterns described by Rosenberg come in, even if one may not want to automatically see them as expressions of doubt on the part of the author. The presence of a narrator who not only describes but also comments on and interprets the fictional world for the reader also makes it possible to complicate melodramatic techniques of externalisation.[2] Fully and straightforwardly transparent character would not need comment by the narrator. John argues that in particular in his later novels, 'Dickens foregrounds the self-consciousness of his own melodramatic art' (198).

Both John and Rosenberg can be read as providing support for the need to pay closer attention to the linguistic detail of Dickens's fictional worlds. Such linguistic detail is also important in cognitive stylistics. Culpeper describes characterisation as a cognitive process in the reader's mind that combines both top-down and bottom-up processes, i.e. it combines knowledge about people in the real world with cues that the reader finds in the text. What the cluster approach illustrates is that readers may be aware of these cues to various extents. There will be character information in the text that is striking, for example, because emotional outbursts are depicted in an exaggerated way or characters are explicitly described

---

[2]   John points out that '[w]hile Dickens's non-fictional statements suggest his championing of a transparent model of individuality', his novels 'complicate this ideal' (173).

in terms of their outward appearance. But there will also be character information that is present in a less straightforward way, and the reader may not even explicitly notice the cues while reading. It is for the discovery of such patterns that corpus methods are particularly useful.

Textual cues for the creation of characters

The definition of a 'cluster' is based merely on formal criteria, i.e. the repetition of a specified number of words in a sequence. Clusters are useful devices for linguistic analysis, as work in corpus linguistics emphasises that patterns of words are associated with repeated meanings. While five-word clusters only present a very limited set of linguistic patterns, viewing their functions along a continuum of highlighting and contextualising effects also contributes to a bigger picture. Clusters that most straightforwardly are associated with highlighting functions are found in the group of Labels. For instance, the five-word cluster *put too fine a point* is part of Mr Snagsby's phrase *not to put too fine a point (up)on it*. One could argue that in order to establish the existence of such clusters we do not even need a computer. Habitual phrases in the speech of a particular character or repeated phrases used by the narrator to refer to a character are sometimes called character 'tags' (cf. Newsom 555) and are among the devices that figure in accounts of Dickens's style or the devices he used to create characters. Brook speaks about the '"signature tune" by which a character may be recognized' (144). He views the habitual phrase as 'one of the simplest linguistic devices that can be used as an aid to characterization' (143). He points out that such repetitions may be crucial to Dickens's success as an author, as repeated phrases are easy to remember and give 'pleasure to unsophisticated readers and audiences because it reminds them of other amusing contexts in which the phrase has been used' (143–4). The accessibility of repeated phrases addresses the same point that John makes when interpreting Dickens's narrative prose in terms of melodramatic models. The repeated phrase is a device in the novel that is similar to stylised gestures or stock phrases in melodrama in that it appeals to the masses and can contribute to the creation of what Forster has called 'flat' characters.[3] Because they are striking,

---

[3]   Forster points out that 'The really flat character can be expressed in one sentence' (47). He also emphasises that flat characters are easily remembered (47–8) and as much required in novels as round characters are (49).

features referred to as character tags, speech tics, leitmotifs or by any other terminology, are picked up by critics to characterise Dickens's style, praise his skill or equally criticise the inflexibility of his characters.

In the categorisation of clusters, character 'tags' fall into the group of Labels. The boundaries to the categories of Speech clusters and Body Part clusters are to some extent fuzzy (for a more detailed discussion see Mahlberg forthcoming), but a main point is that both Speech and Body Parts clusters also contain patterns that are not as striking as Labels and less specific in functioning as unique identifiers for characters. Examples of Speech clusters are (1) and (2). These clusters are classified as speech because they contain first- or second-person pronouns which are interpreted as signals of interaction between characters. The examples illustrate polite-ness formulae (as in 1) or expressions of stance (as in 2) that occur in the speech of a number of different characters and also appear across different texts by Dickens. So although both examples illustrate the speech of Mr Snagsby, the clusters are quite different from his favourite phrase.

(1) 'It was very good-natured of you, sir,' says Mr. Snagsby, 'and *I am obliged to you*.'[4] (*Bleak House*, ch. 19)

(2) 'Rents ARE high about here. *I don't know how it* is exactly, but the law seems to put things up in price. Not,' adds Mr. Snagsby [. . .] (*Bleak House*, ch. 32)

Detailed investigations of such Speech clusters might link in with argu-ments about the use of language that varies with the social class a char-acter belongs to, but this aspect cannot be followed up in the context of the present paper. I want to concentrate on examples of body lan-guage. There is a difference between patterns of speech and patterns of body language. Character speech, when presented as direct speech, will always be less mediated by the narrator than a description of body language (cf. also Page 3). In any given situation, the description of body language by the narrator is a choice of what to present. By what is known as the principle of minimal departure, readers assume that the fictional world is like the real world unless they are told otherwise. With

---

[4]   I do not provide page numbers for a specific edition, because I have taken all examples from the electronic editions in the Dickens Corpus that were originally downloaded from Project Gutenberg <http://www.gutenberg.org/>.

regard to body language that means when a conversation is presented readers automatically assume that the characters accompany their words with looks and movements. When any of this body language is made explicit it takes on extra significance.[5]

With the highlighting and contextualising continuum we can address the question to what extent a single instance of body language is part of a larger pattern. If we return to the example of Rigaud, we find that a five-word cluster associated with Rigaud is *and his nose came down*. Concordance 3 contains all seven instances of this cluster in *Little Dorrit*. In each line Rigaud's nose is described together with his moustache, although the five words *and his nose came down* form the longest sequences that is repeated verbatim seven times. In the first chapter of the novel, before Rigaud's name is revealed the reader learns that he has a 'hook nose' and a 'thick moustache' – features which are part of his external appearance that reflects his wickedness. Later in the chapter the reader encounters the cluster *and his nose came down* for the first time in example (3). The cluster is then repeated another two times in the same chapter. In example (3) the narrator describes what Rigaud looks like when he laughs and the typical movement of his moustache and his nose is commented on as 'sinister and cruel'.

(3) When Monsieur Rigaud laughed, a change took place in his face, that was more remarkable than prepossessing. His moustache went up under his nose, *and his nose came down* over his moustache, in a very sinister and cruel manner. (*Little Dorrit*, book 1, ch. 1)

The cluster *and his nose came down* has a highlighting function in the novel. When it first occurs it is in a context that gives emphasis to the description of the external features of Rigaud. It is made explicit that the cluster relates to permanent features and this permanence is underlined through the repetition of the cluster in the same chapter. The narrator's comment on the sinister and cruel manner of Rigaud's laugh is complemented by the point of view from which Rigaud is described. Chapter 1 opens with a description of Marseilles that then narrows in on the 'villainous prison' and the chamber of the two prisoners – one of whom is Rigaud. The

[5] Cf. also Korte, who points out that 'non-verbal behaviour in literature is always "significant": it is integral to the text's artistic design even when it cannot be read as a sign with a clearly defined meaning' (5).

description of the environment in which Rigaud is found moves to the description of his external features and his name is only revealed when the prison-keeper uses it. The point of view thus supports John's observation on the melodramatic rendering of the inanimate world which surrounds the characters.

```
1  of his triumph, his moustache went up and his nose came down, as he ogled a g
2  saluted him with another parting snap, and his nose came down over his moustac
3  his moustache went up under his nose, and his nose came down over his moustac
4  his moustache went up under his nose, and his nose came down over his moustac
5    goes.' Again his moustache went up, and his nose came down. 'What's the h
6  ellow-prisoner, his moustache went up, and his nose came down. 'How do you f
7  His moustache went up under his nose, and his nose came down over his moustach
```

Concordance 3. All seven occurrences of *and his nose came down*
in *Little Dorrit*

In chapter 11 of the first book, the point of view from which Rigaud is described mirrors that of the first chapter. He is first presented as a lonely figure in the landscape of a 'fitful autumn night' that seems to react to his presence. Although he is described as a stranger it is clear that the figure is Rigaud. When he enters an inn to take a break from his journey, the characteristic movement of his moustache and nose shows when he looks at the landlady (line 4, in Concordance 3) and when he talks to her she also observes 'the nose coming down and the moustache going up', i.e. a variation of the *and his nose came down* pattern. Although Rigaud does not want to reveal his identity to the people in the inn, the reader knows who he is because he has encountered Rigaud before. Because of his external features it is also clear to the reader that Rigaud and Blandois are the same person. When Rigaud comes to Mrs Clennam's house he introduces himself as Blandois. However, from the way in which he approaches the house in chapter 29 of book 1, there is no doubt that Blandois is Rigaud. Affery has locked herself out of the house and finds herself outside in a thunderstorm. Her first impression of Rigaud is the feeling of a hand on her shoulder before she actually sees a man that looks like a foreigner. She notices his moustache and his nose and her shock is met by his character-istic laugh (example 4 corresponds to concordance line 3).

(4) He laughed at Mistress Affery's start and cry; and as he laughed, his moustache went up under his nose, *and his nose came down* over his moustache. (*Little Dorrit*, book 1, ch. 29)

Both chapters 11 and 29 are similar in that the characters who encounter Rigaud do not know who he is but they perceive him in similar ways. Although he might be able to change his name, he has other features that identify him. The characteristics that contribute to the externalisation of his character are not only his looks but also the language he uses, and it is those external features that eventually help Arthur identify Rigaud (for a more detailed discussion see Mahlberg (forthcoming)).

The brief discussion of the textual context of *and his nose came down* shows the highlighting function of the cluster. The cluster is not only repeated but it is part of a more complex description of the external features of a character. There is also support for the significance of the cluster from outside the text of the novel. In his working notes for *Little Dorrit*, Dickens includes for chapter 1: 'Rigaud, with his nose going up & his moustache coming down' (cf. Stone 271).

Another aspect to viewing functions of clusters along a continuum of highlighting and contextualising is the distribution of a cluster across a corpus of Dickens's texts. The cluster *and his nose came down* only appears in *Little Dorrit* which underlines its specific function in the novel. A cluster that is also found in contexts where it functions more towards the contextualising end of the cline is *his hands in his pockets*. The five-word cluster *his hands in his pockets* occurs ninety times and in twenty texts in the Dickens Corpus. It appears eight times in *Little Dorrit*, where it does not identify a character uniquely. Below are four of the eight examples. In (5) *his hands in his pockets* is part of Rigaud's body language when Clennam confronts him. Rigaud meets Clennam with defiance, which is reflected by his relaxed posture, leaning against the bedstead and lounging with his hands in his pockets. In (6) Flintwinch's putting his hands in his pockets is a sign of his having given up in his fight with Rigaud. In (7), by contrast, the narrator interprets the speaker (who turns out to be Mr Meagles) putting his hands in his pockets as part of a determined position. Thus examples (5) to (7) illustrate a variety of meanings that are associated with the same pattern. Although example (8) is another example of a cluster that refers to Meagles, here the body language less clearly expresses a particular meaning. It accompanies Meagles's speech and the more meaningful external information refers to the expression of his face. While the function of the cluster in (8) is less specific, it still contributes to the authentication of the character's speech by providing body language. Such contextualising examples shade into what Korte might see as semantically 'empty' body language (190–1). Overall, to assess the functions of the clusters along the highlighting and contextualising continuum it is important not to view them in isolation but in combination with other patterns.

(5) Glancing round contemptuously at the bedstead, which was turned up by day, he leaned his back against it as a resting-place, without removing his hat from his head, and stood defiantly lounging with *his hands in his pockets*. (*Little Dorrit*, book 2, ch. 28)

(6) Mr Flintwinch had made a run at her, but Rigaud had caught him in his arms midway. After a moment's wrestle with him, Flintwinch gave up, and put *his hands in his pockets*. (*Little Dorrit*, book 2, ch. 30)

(7) The speaker, with a whimsical good humour upon him all the time, looked over the parapet-wall with the greatest disparagement of Marseilles; and taking up a determined position by putting *his hands in his pockets* and rattling his money at it, apostrophised it with a short laugh. (*Little Dorrit*, book 1, ch. 2)

(8) 'Just so,' said Mr Meagles, with *his hands in his pockets*, and with the old business expression of face that had belonged to the scales and scoop. (*Little Dorrit*, book 1, ch. 16)

It is tempting to read the occurrences of body language mainly as evidence for the externalisation of characters. However, the various ways in which body language is described are also relevant. Examples (5) to (8) show that the same cluster can take on different functions depending on the context in which it occurs. This context can also contain comments by the narrator, who not merely shows the body language but also interprets its significance for the reader. Narrator comments contribute to the patterns that Rosenberg views as the language of doubt. Rosenberg claims that Dickens (or more precisely the narrator) sometimes draws straightforward inferences that are based on appearance (56–7), but can also create the opposite effect when the descriptions are unvisualisable: 'his [Dickens's] language suggests serious doubts about the potential for any observer to extract reliable meaning from the external world and for any writer to present the truth in words' (62). Among the linguistic features that Rosenberg observes are *as if* and *as though* constructions that relate to the *as if* clusters presented in Table 1. Rosenberg suggests that analogies to *as if* or *as though* might be 'Dickens's favorite device' because they allow 'comparisons simultaneously to be introduced and rendered doubtful' (60).

Rosenberg's observation that similar forms of what he regards as tentative or doubtful language can be used in different ways – i.e. to express clear inferences or create a blurred picture – is to some extent similar to viewing repeated patterns on a continuum of contextualising and highlighting functions. Equally, the emphasis that he gives to the reader and the reader's reaction to the information in the text chimes in with the notion of text-drivenness. However, the conclusions that he draws from his analysis of narrative prose are more difficult to accept from a text-driven point of view. Rosenberg reads Dickens's narrative prose as evidence of the author's 'doubt about the efficacy of language' (145) and concludes that 'Characters that seem initially to be thoroughly knowable prove in the end to be as present and absent, definite and indefinite, as shadows' (149). However, a crucial point is that the detail that is provided on physical appearance, speech, gesture and habits is not seen directly by the reader, but is mediated by the narrator. Even if body language is not commented on by the narrator the fact that it is made explicit already gives it significance. In this sense the efficacy of language that Rosenberg views as doubtful is effectiveness in another sense, i.e. effectiveness as cues for the reader's imagination. This kind of effectiveness seems to be addressed by Brook when he interprets the 'as if' construction as the 'fanciful' as if (33). This interpretation is more in line with viewing Dickens's narrative prose within the context of popular entertainment. Patterns that have the potential to highlight the narrator's presence would thus have similar effects to the repeated patterns described above. Even if they do not problematise character, they add to creating effects that contribute to engaging the reader in the experience of reading.

For *as if* patterns the highlighting and contextualising continuum is more complex than for patterns of body language, because the links between the two elements that are connected with *as if* can take many shapes and the five-word *as if* clusters only capture parts of the patterns. Here are two examples.

(9) When he came back, he was very pale indeed, and greatly agitated, and even looked *as if he had been* shedding tears. (*Dombey and Son*, ch. 48)

(10) . . . he looked *as if* the clouds were hurrying from him, *as if* the wail of the wind and the shuddering of the grass were directed against him, *as if* the low mysterious plashing of the water murmured

at him, *as if* the fitful autumn night were disturbed by him. (*Little Dorrit*, book 1, ch. 11)

In example (9) the *as if* pattern describes the effects of body language without explicitly providing the details of the body language: the reader does not know whether it is the captain's red eyes, traces of tears, or anything else that would indeed be visible evidence of the narrator's interpretation. Still, example (9) illustrates a contextualising function, as the schema that is evoked is closely linked to the concrete detail of external appearance. In example (10),[6] by contrast, the repeated *as if* constructions highlight how the narrator conveys a particular view of Rigaud. In John's framework, Rigaud is part of an inanimate world that is presented passionally and thus reflects his character.

Suspensions – extending the range of text-driven patterns

It is clear that five-word clusters only present a very limited collection of patterns that contribute to the creation of fictional worlds. There are different options to find further patterns; we could, for instance, investigate clusters of different lengths and look at patterns that are non-continuous. In this section, I want to illustrate another option. Instead of starting with words and their patterns, it is also possible to focus on specific places in the text. The places that this section looks at are 'suspensions'. A 'suspension' is as a span of (narrator) text which interrupts a span of quoted speech. It must be in the same orthographic sentence as the speech it interrupts and contain at least five or more words (Mahlberg and Smith 2010). This definition is based on Lambert's concept of the suspended quotation. Suspensions are defined in purely formal terms so that they can be automatically marked up in the text and searched with the help of corpus software. Thus 'quoted speech' is initially anything between quotation marks – which can also be thought or writing.

Suspensions are places that potentially provide character information and thus relate to the patterns illustrated by clusters. Suspensions seem to be particularly useful places to look for body language, because they provide context for a character's speech. Similar to clusters, suspensions can provide character information that is presented as part of a wider

---

[6]   Rosenberg also quotes this example when he argues that too many possibilities create a blurred picture (60).

context so that it supports the information presented in the character's speech or adds to the authentication of the fictional world. In example (11),[7] Jarndyce's looking at his watch supports his comment on the time he has spent with Esther. An example where the significance of the body language receives more emphasis is (12). David's aunt does not simply lay her hand on the table, but does so 'with melancholy firmness', i.e. the narrator does not describe the precise movement, but interprets its meaning.

(11) 'Now, little housewife,' said my guardian, looking at his watch, 'I was strictly timed before I came upstairs, for you must not be tired too soon; and my time has waned away to the last minute. (*Bleak House*, ch. 35)

(12) 'I am convinced,' said my aunt, laying her hand with melancholy firmness on the table, 'that Dick's character is not a character to [. . .].' (*David Copperfield*, ch. 23)

The information in suspensions can also enforce characters' typical behaviour or highlight when a character's behaviour differs from what readers would normally expect. In example (13), Mrs Clennam speaks in 'her usual strong low voice', while in example (14) Twemlow's tone is 'rather less mild than usual'.

(13) 'Flintwinch,' returned Mrs Clennam, in her usual strong low voice, 'there is a demon of anger in you. Guard against it.' (*Little Dorrit*, book 1, ch. 15)

(14) 'Pardon me, sir,' says Twemlow, rather less mildly than usual, 'I don't agree with you. [. . .]' (*Our Mutual Friend*, book 4, ch. 17)

In addition to providing a place for information on body language, in suspensions the narrator can also provide direct characterisation of a fictional character, as in example (15), where the suspension contains a long relative clause that describes how Mrs Micawber likes to see herself.

(15) 'Then,' said Mrs. Micawber, who prided herself on taking a clear view of things, and keeping Mr. Micawber straight by her woman's

[7] I thank Catherine Smith for providing the technology to retrieve the examples used in this article. For a fuller account of the concept of suspensions and the computer-assisted analysis of them see Mahlberg and Smith (2012).

wisdom, when he might otherwise go a little crooked, 'then I ask myself
this question. If corn is not to be relied upon, what is? [. . .]' (*David
Copperfield*, ch. 28)

The above examples all relate to different characters. Suspensions also
offer the opportunity to see patterns for specific characters. While this
goes beyond the scope of the present article, an example is provided in
Mahlberg (2012) with a comparison of Bucket and Tulkinghorn in *Bleak
House*.

Conclusions

This article provided examples of how computer-assisted methods can
contribute to the study of characters in Dickens. In the text-driven
approach that is presented in this article clusters and suspensions are only
some of the examples that play a role in the creation of the fictional world
and further patterns still need to be studied. However, it already becomes
clear that patterns that are described in the literature as Dickens's favourite linguistic devices are part of a much larger picture, where they only
present the more striking and recognisable examples. By focusing on linguistic patterns as the basis for areas of meanings in the text, the approach
provides textual cues that potentially contribute to the processing of the
text in a bottom-up fashion. The bottom-up processes work together with
top-down processes which are guided by the readers' literary competence
as well as their real-world knowledge shaped by the cultural context. A
text-driven approach can thus help to provide the linguistic detail for
accounts of Dickens's strategies of characterisation and their reception by
readers. The questions that the description of a cline of patterns raises will
require more detailed studies that also involve experiments to test readers'
reactions to and awareness of a range of linguistic features. The ground-
work that is done by a detailed account of linguistic patterns can further
serve as a basis for comparisons between Dickens and other authors. It
can also contribute to the investigation of the development of Dickens's
techniques of characterisation from his earlier to his later novels. Most
importantly, however, I hope to have shown that detailed language analysis is not a technical exercise even if it is aided by technology.

Works cited

Biber, Douglas, 2006. *University Language. A Corpus-based Study of Spoken and Written Registers.* Amsterdam: John Benjamins.

Biber, Douglas, 2011. 'Corpus Linguistics and the Scientific Study of Literature: Back to the Future?', *Scientific Study of Literature* 1: 15–23.

Brook, G. L. 1970. *The Language of Dickens.* London: Andre Deutsch.

Carter, Ronald, 2010. 'Methodologies for Stylistic Analysis: Practices and Pedagogies', in *Language and Style*, ed. Dan McIntyre and Beatrix Busse. Basingstoke: Palgrave Macmillan, pp. 55–68.

Culpeper, Jonathan, 2001. *Language and Characterisation. People in Plays and Other Texts.* Harlow: Pearson Education.

Forster, E. M., 1974. *Aspects of the Novel and Related Writings*, ed. Oliver Stallybrass. London: Edward Arnold.

Hockey, Susan, 2002. *Electronic Texts in the Humanities.* Oxford: Oxford University Press.

Hori, Masahiro, 2004. *Investigating Dickens' Style. A Collocational Analysis.* Basingstoke: Palgrave Macmillan.

Ingham, Patricia, 2011. 'The Language of Dickens', in *A Companion to Charles Dickens*, ed. David Paroissien. Oxford: Wiley-Blackwell, pp. 126–41.

John, Juliet, 2001. *Dickens's Villains. Melodrama, Character, Popular Culture.* Oxford: Oxford University Press.

Korte, Barbara, 1997. *Body Language in Literature.* Toronto: University of Toronto Press.

Lambert, Mark, 1981. *Dickens and the Suspended Quotation.* New Haven and London: Yale University Press.

Mahlberg, Michaela, forthcoming. *Corpus Stylistics and Dickens's Fiction.* London: Routledge.

Mahlberg, Michaela, 2012. 'The Corpus Stylistic Analysis of Fiction or the Fiction of Corpus Stylistics?', in *Corpus Linguistics and Variation in English: Theory and Description*, ed. Joybrato Mukherjee and Magnus Huber. Amsterdam: Rodopi, pp. 77–95.

Mahlberg, Michaela, and Catherine Smith, 2010. 'Corpus Approaches to Prose Fiction: Civility and Body Language in *Pride and Prejudice*', in *Language and Style*, ed. Dan McIntyre and Beatrix Busse. Basingstoke: Palgrave Macmillan, pp. 449–67.

Mahlberg, Michaela, and Catherine Smith, 2012. 'Dickens, the Suspended Quotation and the Corpus', *Language and Literature* 21 (1): 51–65.

Newsom, Robert, 2000. 'Style of Dickens', in *The Oxford Reader's Companion to Charles Dickens*, ed. Paul Schlicke. Oxford: Oxford University Press, pp.553–7.

Page, Norman, 1988. *Speech in the English Novel*. Atlantic Highlands, New Jersey: Humanities Press International.

Plummer, Patricia, 2003. *Stil in Charles Dickens' 'Oliver Twist': Formen – Funktionen – Kontexte*. Trier: Wissenschaftlicher Verlag Trier.

Rosenberg, Brian, 1996. *Little Dorrit's Shadows. Character and Contradiction in Dickens*. Columbia and London: University of Missouri Press.

Stewart, Garrett, 2001. 'Dickens and Language', in *The Cambridge Companion to Charles Dickens*, ed. John O. Jordan. Cambridge: Cambridge University Press, pp. 136–51.

Stone, Harry, 1987. *Dickens' Working Notes for his Novels*. Chicago and London: University of Chicago Press.

Tabata, Tomoji, 2002. 'Investigating Stylistic Variation in Dickens through Correspondence Analysis of Word-Class Distribution', in *English Corpus Linguistics in Japan*, ed. Toshio Saito, Junsaku Nakamura and Shunji Yamazaki. Amsterdam: Rodopi, pp.165–82.

Things, words and the meanings of art

JULIET JOHN

We next went to the School of Language, where three Professors sate in Consultation upon improving that of their country.

The first Project was to shorten discourse by cutting Polysyllables into one, and leaving out Verbs and Participles, because in reality all things imaginable are but Nouns.

The other Project was a Scheme for entirely abolishing all Words whatsoever; and this was urged as a great Advantage in point of Health as well as Brevity. [. . .] An Expedient was therefore offered, that since Words are only Names for Things, it would be more convenient for all Men to carry about them, such Things as were necessary to express the particular Business they are to discourse on. [. . .M]any of the most Learned and Wise adhere to this New Scheme of expressing themselves by Things, which hath only this Inconvenience attending it, that if a Man's Business be very great, and of various kinds, he must be obliged in Proportion to carry a greater Bundle of Things upon his Back, unless he can afford one or two strong servants to attend him. I have often beheld two of these Sages almost sinking under the Weight of their Packs, like Pedlers among us; who when they met in the Streets would lay down their Loads, open their Sacks and hold Conversation for an hour together; then put up their Implements, help each other to resume their Burthens, and take their Leave.

[. . .]

Another great Advantage proposed by this Invention, was that it would serve us as an Universal Language to be understood in all civilized Nations, whose Goods and Utensils are generally of the same kind, or nearly resembling, so that their Uses might easily be comprehended.

Swift, Gulliver's Travels, part III, ch. 5: 167–9

THERE WAS A TIME not too long ago when the idea of making things central to literary analysis was novel if not controversial. The influence of 'thing theory' has been such, however, that for the past five to ten years, Victorianists, and perhaps particularly Dickensians, have been, like Swift's sages, 'almost sinking under the weight' of things and the critical conversations they have generated. Thing theory developed partly as an attempt to counter the widespread critical assumption if not orthodoxy in the 1980s and 1990s that things in Victorian literature, as products of an industrial marketplace, were most meaningfully understood as commodities. In an effort to move away from the Marxian ideology that had surrounded analysis of literary things as commodities, Bill Brown argued for 'a new idiom' in critical thinking about things, involving 'the effort to think with or through the physical object world, the effort to establish a genuine sense of the things that comprise the stage on which human action, including the action of thought, unfolds' (Brown 3). Key questions for Brown as a leading exponent of thing theory concern 'why and how we use objects to make meaning, to make and re-make ourselves' (Brown 4) in ways that eschew the logic of capitalism. Another influential voice in thing theory, Elaine Freedgood (2006), maintains that a 'thing culture' may have preceded commodity culture, tracing the histories and 'fugitive meanings' behind literary things. David Trotter has distinguished different strands within thing theory, the 'phenomenological or psychoanalytic approach' and the historicist approach (Trotter 5). It is the latter that has been most influential in Victorian studies; in particular, Freedgood's determination to 'literalise' the reading of objects, to read as a 'collector' rather than an allegorist, has provoked both imitation and dissent (2006: 106).

The fact that these arguments will be familiar if not tired to many in the critical community is evidence of the widespread influence of thing theory. So many fine critics have now dedicated themselves to this 'New Scheme of expressing themselves by Things' (Swift 169) that it is fair to say that two of the main purposes of thing theory have been accomplished: things are no longer peripheral to academic debate and the assumption that things function simply as commodities in literary texts is no longer a widespread or even respectable critical position. It is also true, however, that much of the best recent work on literary things disputes or perhaps refines tendencies in thing theory that Swift would no doubt have satirised, in particular the habit of reading as a collector, reinscribing the histories of objects that seem unimportant within literary texts. Freedgood herself, for example, maintains in a recent essay that 'The Dickens novel is more ambivalent about things than we are in our criticism of it' (Freedgood 2009: 164).

The moment of thing theory has thus now perhaps passed or at least a second wave of interest in literary things is exploring the implications of Freedgood's own suggestive notion that a 'rhetorical hierarchy' (Freedgood 2006: 2) exists within texts which works to ascribe more meaning to some things than to others. Trotter's brilliantly nuanced corrective to first-wave thing theory, for example, reminds us that objects in novels function differently from things in the world and that objects can carry variable meanings and emphases in literary texts. To Trotter, genre works to create proportion and 'Where there is proportion [. . .] there can be meaning' (7). In a similar vein, Pettitt examines the workings of memory and time in Dickens's fiction to ensure that 'some kinds of description carry more value than others' (Pettitt 9).

This essay joins the call for more sensitivity to aesthetic texture in our consideration of how literature represents things, though it maintains that in Dickens's case, meaning, value and proportion depend on lateral as well as hierarchical modes of differentiation. He is conscious, in other words, of the constructedness as well as real power of hierarchies of value. Aware of its place in a mass-cultural marketplace, Dickens's thing art represents and critiques the new ways in which value was being configured and contested. A main premise of what follows is so simple that it should not need stating: things in Dickens's writings are not things but words representing things. It is in one way remarkable that the relationship between material things and words in Dickens has been, as far as I know, largely ignored by thing theory. But in another way, the critical silence is unsurprising: the relationship between things and the signifiers used to represent them seems to take us back to a 'spent' critical moment: to structuralism and post-structuralism, which in Victorian studies have given way to the material turn. But the relationship between things and words, and indeed signifying systems more broadly, is important in Dickens, and subject to conspicuous and self-conscious scrutiny; Dickens is fascinated by how things mean. My concern is thus not just with language systems but with the relational way in which Dickens views things, never existing in isolation, as Trotter points out, always existing within a representational frame or frames. A second premise of this essay is that we can learn more about Dickens's things, and indeed about his sense of the relationship between art and things, if we are generically inclusive in our critical investigations. Thing theory, specifically as applied to Dickens, has fixated on fiction whereas for Dickens, aesthetic boundaries were more permeable than has been understood.[1] Thus while I share Trotter's urge to reinstate proportion and a sense of representational and generic environment in order to better understand the specific workings of literary and artistic things, in Dickens's case, the nature and function of art and 'literature' in creating that proportion in the modern world can, counter-intuitively, most fully be understood by examining his non-fiction alongside his fiction.

Perhaps the most fascinating example of Dickens's treatment of the relationship between material things and the words or language systems used to represent them appears in his travel book, *American Notes* (1842). In it Dickens recounts the history of Laura Bridgman, a deaf, dumb and blind girl who was also 'destitute of smell' (Dickens 2000, I, ch. 3: 40). Laura relies on the sense of touch and as a child explores her home environment by becoming 'familiar with the form, density, weight, and heat, of every article she could lay her hands upon' (Dickens 2000, I, ch. 3: 42). Laura joined the Perkins Institution in Boston at the age of eight and stayed there for the rest of her life. She was the first known deaf and blind person to be successfully educated, later becoming a needlework teacher. Dickens takes much of his account of Laura verbatim from a pamphlet by the director of the institution, Dr Samuel Gridley Howe (1801–76), including the following description of the means by which she was taught to communicate with others:

'[. . .] the attempt was made to give her knowledge of arbitrary signs, by which she could interchange thoughts with others.

'There was one of two ways to be adopted: either to go on to build up a language of signs on the basis of the natural language which she had already commenced herself, or to teach her the purely arbitrary language in common use: that is, to give her a sign for every individual thing, or to give her a knowledge of letters by combination of which she might express her idea of the existence, and the mode and condition of existence, of any thing. [. . .] I determined [. . .] to try the latter.

'The first experiments were made by taking articles in common use, such as knives, forks, spoons, keys, &c. and pasting upon them labels with their names printed in raised letters. These she felt very carefully, and soon, of course, distinguished that the crooked lines *s p o o n*, differed as much from the crooked lines *k e y*, as the spoon differed from the key in form.

---

[1] Catherine Waters's excellent book on *Commodity Culture in Dickens's Household Words* is an exception in concentrating on Dickens's journalism but Waters does not identify herself as a thing theorist.

'[. . .] she repeated the process first from imitation, next from memory, with only the motive of love of approbation, but apparently without the intellectual perception of any relation between the things.

'After a while, instead of labels, the individual letters were given to her on detached bits of paper: they were arranged side by side so as to spell *b o o k*, *k e y*, &c.; then they were mixed up in a heap and a sign was made for her to arrange herself, so as to express the words *b o o k*, *k e y*, &c.; and she did so.

'Hitherto, the process had been mechanical, [. . .] but now the truth began to flash upon her: her intellect began to work: she perceived that here was a way by which she could make a sign of any thing that was in her own mind, and show it to another mind; and at once her countenance lighted up with human expression: it was no longer a dog, or a parrot: it was an immortal spirit'. (Dickens 2000, I, ch. 3: 43)

Once Laura has learned to express herself using words made up of letters made from metal type, she is taught to 'represent the different letters by the position of her fingers, instead of the cumbrous apparatus of the board and types' (Dickens 2000, I, ch. 3: 44).

What is immediately striking about Howe's account is that 'knowledge of the physical relation of things' is inextricable from knowledge of a language system by which those things and the 'relation between the things' can be understood (Dickens 2000, I, ch. 3: 44). If Laura had remained in the condition of Swift's absurd Sages, reliant on things alone to communicate with others, she would, to Dr Howe, have lacked a human and a spiritual life: she would have been an animal. Howe does not explain with any precision how Laura manages to move beyond a thing- and noun-centred understanding of the world to a comprehension of immaterial concepts like the 'immortal spirit' which he attributes to her. The inhabitants of Swift's Laputa, for example, are 'wholly strangers' to 'Imagination, Fancy, and Invention', because they do not have 'any Words in their Language by which those Ideas can be expressed' (Swift, part III, ch. 2: 146). The suggestion in the Laura Bridgman section of *American Notes* is that the ability to relate things to an idea of things as expressed by a separate, abstract and arbitrary language system or systems is the precondition – in Howe's view exclusive to humans – of understanding and experiencing the immaterial aspects of life.

This is Dr Howe's account, of course, and not Dickens's own, but apart from the fact that the lengthy account is not contradicted or questioned, the entire Dickens oeuvre suggests his own fascination with a relationship he presents as symbiotic between things, language and ideas. Dickens's preoccupation with money is an especially complex example. While it is well known that Dickens was obsessed with money, it is not so well known that the physical material of money, particularly paper money, absorbed his imagination to an excessive degree. On his late American reading tours, for instance, the most memorable images from the correspondence are Dickens's descriptions of himself literally (or perhaps materially) staring at his money: there is 'such an immense untidy heap of paper money on the table that it looks like a family wash' (Letter to Miss Mary Dickens (11 December 1867); Dickens 1965–2002, XI: 508). The images almost remind us of Fagin except for the fact that Dickens seems to experience an uncanny alienation from his money rather than a joyous absorption: 'The manager is always going about with an immense bundle that looks like a sofa-cushion, but is in reality paper-money, and it had risen to the proportions of a sofa on the morning he left for Philadelphia' (Letter to Forster ([5 January 1868]); Dickens 1965–2002, XII: 5). It is tempting to write off this preoccupation with the paper material of money by connecting it with Dickens's well-known distrust of the American dollar. But on the British reading tours also, Dickens plays with the materiality of monetary forms of exchange – this time cheques – in his correspondence. He tells Georgina, for instance: 'They turned away hundreds, sold all the books, rolled on the ground of my room knee deep in checks, and made a perfect pantomime of the whole thing' ((20 August 1858); Dickens 1965–2002, VIII: 629). He reports similarly to Edmund Yates: 'There were 2,300 people, and 200 guineas. The very books were all sold out, early in the evening, and Arthur bathed in checks – took headers into tickets – floated on billows of passes – dived under weirs of shillings – staggered home, faint with gold and silver' ((21 August 1858); Dickens 1965–2002, VIII: 631). Dickens uses metaphor – rather than simile – to comically emphasise the 'thingness' of money.

He has no interest here in the relationship between money and the terms used to describe it – whether dollars, cheques, pounds or whatever: his interest is in money as a physical 'thing' which also functions as a signifying system or language. The sight of paper money seems to have raised, for Dickens, the kind of questions asked by Kevin McLaughlin in *Paperwork* about the substantiality or otherwise of a material whose primary function, when used to make money, is figural. It may also have raised in the most extreme and paradoxical way the sorts of problems pondered by thing theory about how far the meaning of things in capitalist societies eludes the logic of commodity fetishism. Certainly, for Dickens, paper money seems to have had a life of its own, though he sometimes struggles to believe in its primary meaning as a material sign of wealth. It is as if he can imaginatively transform the appearance of money into most things other than the actuality of a 'richer' life. How can paper 'things', in other words, *mean* so much?

The power of things to mean, and the arbitrariness of the meanings they generate, are everywhere in Dickens. One of the best fictional examples occurs at the beginning of his historical novel, *Barnaby Rudge*, in which Dickens fictionalises objects with a 'real' physical and historical existence:

In the year 1775, there stood upon the borders of Epping Forest, at a distance of about twelve miles from London – measuring from the Standard in Cornhill or rather from the spot on or near to which the Standard used to be in days of yore – a house of public entertainment called the Maypole; which fact was demonstrated to all such travellers as could neither read nor write (and at that time a vast number both of travellers and stay-at-homes were in this condition) by the emblem reared on the roadside over against the house, which, if not of those goodly proportions that Maypoles were wont to present in olden times, was a fair young ash, thirty feet in height, and straight as any arrow that ever English yeoman drew.

The Maypole – by which term from henceforth is meant the house, and not its sign – the Maypole was an old building, with more gable ends than a lazy man would care to count on a sunny day; huge zig-zag chimneys, out of which it seemed as though even smoke could not choose but come in more than naturally fantastic shapes, imparted to it in its tortuous progress; and vast stables, gloomy, ruinous and empty. The place was said to have been built in the days of King Henry the Eighth; and there was a legend, not only that Queen Elizabeth had slept there one night while upon a hunting excursion, to wit in a certain oak-paneled room with a deep bay window, but that next morning, while standing on a mounting block before the door with one foot in the stirrup, the virgin monarch had then and there boxed and cuffed an unlucky page for some neglect of duty. The matter-of-fact and doubtful folks, of whom there were a few among the Maypole customers, as unluckily there always are in every little community, were inclined to look upon this tradition as rather apocryphal; but whenever the landlord of that ancient hostelry appealed to the mounting block itself as evidence, and triumphantly pointed out that there it stood in the same place to that very day, the doubters never failed to be put down by a large majority, and all true believers exulted as in a victory. (Dickens 2003, ch. 1: 7)

Immediately interesting, for my purposes, is the fact that 'the emblem' of the historical maypole is used to signify both the maypole of old and the pub named the Maypole for the many travellers who 'could neither read nor write'. Furthermore, Dickens carefully differentiates in his own designation of 'the term' 'The Maypole' between 'the house', which is his concern, 'and not its sign'. His self-consciousness here about the fact that things need languages (whether verbal or visual) to mean is as striking as his awareness that there is nonetheless a distinction between things and the signs attributed to them. We do not need Saussure, or even Dr Howe, to be clear from this description that the relationship between things and the signs used to give them intelligible meaning is constructed rather than inherent.

Dickens's sense of the ways in which the meaning of things is constructed by the framework of interpretation that is imposed upon them extends beyond a sophisticated sense of language or signs, moreover, to an awareness of the mutually constitutive relationship between stories and/ or histories and things. Thus in this opening passage from *Barnaby Rudge*, for example, those who doubt that Queen Elizabeth slept in the Maypole and boxed a page while there are shown 'the mounting block itself as evidence', with the result that 'the doubters never failed to be put down by a large majority, and all true believers exulted as in a victory'. Though Dickens is sceptical at best about this piece of local history, the passage demonstrates not only the way in which histories bind communities, but the importance of physical objects to the construction of history – and indeed to a sense of 'heritage', defined by David Lowenthal as 'not an inquiry into the past but a celebration of it, not an effort to know what actually happened but a profession of faith in a past tailored to present-day purposes' (x). The converse of this, evidently, is that the inert mounting block itself is elevated by the history with which it is framed to the status of religious relic, like so many of the 'things' that are the mainstay of the heritage industry (and indeed of today's Dickens industry).[2]

Things can function similarly, of course, in the realm of personal history. In *American Notes*, when Laura Bridgman is reunited with her mother after spending six months apart from her in the Perkins Institution, she does not initially recognise her mother by touch but shows 'much joy'

---

[2]   See John 240–72 on 'Heritage Dickens' and the role of things in the heritage industry.

(Dickens 2000, I, ch. 3: 47) when she is given a string of beads, instantly
understanding that the string was from home. It is only when another
object from her home is presented to her that she makes the connection between the things resonant of home and the past and the weeping
woman before her who she finally recognises as her mother. Pettitt has
sensitively demonstrated the way in which Peggotty's workbox in *David
Copperfield* functions as a marker of memory in the novel; itself a souvenir,
it demonstrates that 'it is the active accrual of meaning over time that
makes things cherished and luminous with meaning' (5). Personal and
cultural memories then are reliant on things just as things rely on the
stories and patterns of time embedded in histories for their immaterial
resonance.

Trotter focuses on household clearances in Victorian fiction to differentiate – using Heidegger and Jameson – between objects that carry
'meaning and value' and 'matter, or stuff' (Trotter 6, 9). Household
clearance scenes in fiction, to Trotter, are 'profoundly disturbing' because
they show us 'a household turned inside out for inspection, laid bare in
its material being; indeed, understood as matter' (Trotter 1, 3). Whereas
so much of thing theory, according to his account, has been preoccupied
with the ways in which objects illuminate subjectivity, auction or 'selling
up' scenes 'imagine the object's double reduction: from household god to
commodity; from commodity to matter, or stuff'; they deprive 'the objects
awaiting disposal not only of their past, but of their future as well' (15).
Trotter's larger argument is that

> the task (of philosophy, of art, of politics) is not to heal this fundamental
> rift, but to exacerbate it and hold it open. Earth/Matter is not passive,
> but comes about precisely as that which cannot be generalized from,
> as anti-system to World/History's system. At the very moment when
> we have become convinced that the World is all World, art discloses
> the Earth within it, alien and inseparable [. . .] we need to believe that
> some at least of the stones arranged in works of art, philosophy, and
> politics have not been put there for a purpose, and that they do not
> explain us to ourselves. (Trotter 10)

His analysis works superbly to enforce the importance of 'rhetorical hierarchy' (Freedgood 2006: 2) in fiction, to account for the emergence and
function of naturalist description in the nineteenth century, and to reinstate the importance of proportion and the aesthetic to the ways in which
we read literature. It is perhaps significant, however, that Dickens makes

only a fleeting appearance in his essay because Dickens's representation of objects is in many ways atypical in nineteenth-century writing and certainly differs from that of the realist and naturalist ficton which comprises Trotter's main subject. Freedgood's recent, nuanced work on Dickens (2009) attempts to explore the ways in which Dickens's 'thingfulness' (153) is more complex than 'commodity criticism' has allowed it to be, but cannot perhaps free itself enough from the critical dialogue with discourses of commodification to fully tease out the complexity of Dickens's thing art. In Dickens's fiction, as so many have commented, subjects and objects are often inextricable; the animate and inanimate worlds are difficult to differentiate, and things flagrantly announce their intention to mean.[3] The narrator of the original version of *The Old Curiosity Shop*, for example, muses that 'We are so much in the habit of allowing impressions to be made upon us by external objects, which should be produced by reflection alone', that 'without such visible aids', the plight of others can escape us.[4] Of Dickens's letter-writing, Forster claimed, 'Not eternal [*sic*] objects only, but feelings, reflections and thoughts, are photographed into visible forms' (Forster 246).

An account of the posthumous auction of Dickens's own belongings provides an interesting appendix to Trotter's account of the relationship between objects and value in the nineteenth century. After Dickens's death, his 'representatives' organised a public sale of Dickens's (mainly domestic) belongings, that met with opposition among many. In a report in *Chambers Journal*, though the journalist attempts to show support for the sale (claiming that 'Charles Dickens was far too free-handed and generous a man to die rich'), his distaste for proceedings is apparent in the ambivalent conclusion that 'No living Englishman for certain, and perhaps no Englishman of the future, will ever see such a sale again' ([Anon.] 1870: 503, 505). The public sale for money of the domestic belongings of England's foremost author seemed in dubious taste in any case, but especially so because the objects sold seemed to fall 'far short of first class' ([Anon.] 503) – no *Pickwick* manuscripts, but unimpressive pictures, drawings and art objects, as well as Dickens's stuffed pet raven, which he

---

[3] See for example, Van Ghent, Meier and Hollington (2009).
[4] This quotation occurred in part 4 of the original serialisation of the novel in *Master Humphrey's Clock*, but was omitted from the first chapter of the novel when it was published in book form. It is cited on p. 19 of the Clarendon edition of the novel.

had kept on his desk and which had inspired Grip the raven in *Barnaby Rudge*. In other words, to the *Chambers* journalist, Dickens's things are nothing but 'matter, or stuff', to use Trotter's terms.

What is interesting, however, is that this was not how the public in attendance at the auction saw his things. The nature of Dickens's fame meant that the crowd at the sale was 'more motley' than those usually in attendance at the sales of 'desirable properties' of 'gentlemen of taste recently deceased' ([Anon.] 1870: 503). Furthermore, the 'positive fanaticism' of 'the assemblage' resulted in behaviour more typical of a large-scale sporting or entertainment event – for example, the mass chanting of 'slogans' from Dickens's novels like Grip the Raven's catchphrases, '"I'm a devil"'and '"Never say die"' ([Anon.] 1870: 504). In almost parodic verification of Dickens's ideal of an imagined community or friendship existing between himself and his readership, one man confides to the journalist on the sale of a gong that Dickens was '"always fond of gongs" (as if we were brothers, though we had never spoken before)' ([Anon.] 1870: 504). For the majority of the public, comprised in large measure of Dickens 'fans', the things on sale were neither simply stuff nor were they meaningful because of their economic worth or cultural capital in the sense that the journalist would have understood such capital. They were valuable because of their connection with Dickens, who is viewed by the crowd as both a friend and a celebrity. His celebrity, a new form of cultural capital, gives his things their value, as indeed does his death.

Trotter does not distinguish between the household clearances of dead people and of living ones, nor between those of public figures and less-fêted citizens, but these are important distinctions. In this highly unusual example of a public auction of belongings, things are not 'reduced', as in Trotter's account, but animated. Though the majority of the public in attendance did not manage to purchase anything and seemed interested in the spectacle above all, one striking aspect of the posthumous sale is the economic effects thereby manifested of the emotional 'aura' bestowed on things by death, particularly the death of a celebrity.[5] The sums raised were 'so enormous' that they were 'out of all proportion to their intrinsic worth' ([Anon.] 1870: 503). Dickens was fascinated by corpses partly because they reduced people to a state of inanimation or matter. The emotional effect of death on the living can be to transfer the life of the

---

[5]   See p. 129 n. 11 for Benjamin on the 'aura' in art.

person onto his/her things: loss can bring things to life. It is not the things that change, in other words, but the context, the frame.

In Dickens's case, the auction makes visible a new cultural frame, one which is implicit rather than explicit in Trotter's account of the relationship between art and objects in the nineteenth century: that is, the emergence of a mass-cultural marketplace. In this marketplace, the newly evident phenomenon of celebrity is most obviously embodied by Dickens: as the subsequent history of celebrity has shown, a form of objectification and commodification in itself, celebrity confers value both economic and emotional to objects. Arguably, objects transformed into commodities make up the language of celebrity. The concept of celebrity has been subject to a great deal of criticism.[6] As I have argued at length elsewhere (2010), Dickens was both complicit in his own celebrity and commodification and sought an older model of community in his relationship with the public. Indeed, according to the *Chambers* journalist reporting on the sale of his belongings, 'it was Dickens's express desire that this sale took place' ([Anon.] 1870: 503). The sale suggests his living consciousness that fame and posthumousness could transform even the most vulgar of objects into 'artefacts', as the *Chambers* article calls them, and into money ([Anon.] 1870: 504). In the evidence it suggests of both communal and market relations, the posthumous auction of Dickens's things would have pleased him. But the key point is that Dickens's things became objects of value during the sale because he was dead and because he was Dickens.

It is curious that though Dickens condoned the sale of his belongings, he left specific instructions in his will that he should *not* be made 'the subject of any monument, memorial or testimonial whatever' and that he was to be buried in 'an inexpensive, unostentatious, and strictly private manner' ('Charles Dickens's Last Will and Codicil' (12 May 1869 and 2 June 1870); Dickens 1965–2002, XII: 730–3 (p. 732)). Though the desire for privacy in death was surprising coming from the most publicly visible author in Britain, it is his desire not to be memorialised as a physical object which interests me here. Why would Dickens object to this? It is tempting to argue that the reduction of his life to an inanimate, stone object would have disturbed him. His novels after all regularly feature inanimate people who have no emotional, moral or spiritual selves, '"stuffed people"', as they are described in *Bleak House*, 'a large collection, glassy eyed, set up

[6] On Dickens and celebrity, see Marsh.

in the most approved manner on their various twigs and perches, very correct, perfectly free from animation, and always in glass cases' (ch. 37: 532). But Dickens worked with a stuffed raven on his desk, presumably an object of inspiration and the same raven that he knew would be auctioned to the public.[7]

My suggestion is that Dickens's objection to being memorialised as a statue – and his dislike of statues generally – stems from the objectification of cultural hierarchy which statues can be seen to signify: statues of historical personages affect to give them transcendence, to separate them from the quotidian, to elevate them out of the community. Dickens's will and the sale together highlight a certain doubleness in his attitude to his own cultural legacy that also pervades his attitude to heritage more generally. Neither a private funeral nor a sale of second-rate effects would have threatened Dickens's idea of the friendship that existed between himself and an intimate public by elevating him above others.[8] Dickens is acutely conscious of the power of veneration or emotional hierarchy in the way in which we remember the past. This veneration is not always represented negatively – as we have seen in the *Barnaby Rudge* example, Dickens demonstrates the way in which it can work to bond communities – but he is highly conscious of both its constructedness and its reliance on physical objects as potential signifiers of difference or hierarchy. Interestingly, though Dickens is ambivalent, as I have stated, about the commodification of culture and indeed his own celebrity, he is more overtly hostile to the idea of transcendence or disconnection suggested by statues than he is to the idea that cultural objects can operate within a mass-cultural marketplace.

As part of an increasingly though not exclusively commercialised world of objects, art for Dickens thus worked to differentiate but also to connect, to reveal the constructedness and even arbitrariness of hierarchies of differentiation, including its own. While Dickens was a loud and uncharacteristically vocal proponent of 'the spirit of fiction', for example,

---

[7] See pp. 124–5 on *Barnaby Rudge*'s Grip and his stuffed prototype. Animals are perhaps a special case and the relationship between objects and animals would include rich materials for a study outside the scope of the present essay; talking animals are particularly complex, of course, in respect of relations between language, the animate and the inanimate worlds.

[8] Dickens described his 'particular relation' with the public as 'personally affectionate and like no other man's' (Forster 646).

in his view of cultural formations its work spread beyond the realms 'of art, philosophy, and politics'.[9] The Maypole regulars, for Dickens, are as capable as an artist or philosopher of animating an object. This does not mean, however, that the Dickens world is a world without differentiation. In *American Notes*, Laura Bridgman's 'disposition to imitate' is her first means of communicating with others (42); she learns to sew and knit a little through imitation, even before she is subject to Dr Howe's system of education. In *Mimesis*, Aristotle identifies imitation as the mainspring of art, that instinct to represent ourselves as the same as others even though we are different. When Laura begins to learn the language system her 'intellectual perception of any relation between the things' (43) involves the perception of connectedness as well as of differentiation. In Dickens's worldview, it is not simply 'art' formally defined or indeed intellectual culture more generally that imitates, that connects, that differentiates. It is the imagination or 'Fancy' informing art and indeed life at its best which is the intellectual and emotion agent for the 'perception of any relation' between things, and indeed between people and things. In the 'Preliminary Word' to *Household Words*, for example, he argues:

> In the bosoms of the young and old, of the well-to-do and of the poor, we would tenderly cherish that light of Fancy, which is inherent in the human breast [. . .] to teach the hardest workers at this whirling wheel of toil, that their lot is not necessarily a moody, brutal fact, excluded from the sympathies and graces of imagination. (Dickens 1850: 1)

Fancy stops people being turned into things by acting as an agent of connection between people. It differentiates between people and things but the activity of imagination or Fancy is dependent on things for its sustenance as well as its symbolic code. As Dickens famously wrote in the Preface to *Bleak House*, his aim was to represent 'the romantic side of familiar things'.

It is a cliché of Dickens criticism that people and things, subjects and objects, are difficult to distinguish. What is newer is that it is not always easy to differentiate in Dickens's world between artefacts and 'stuff', commodities and things, art and commerce. The publication of his fiction in his own journals is one obvious physical manifestation of the way in

---

[9]   See, for example, the anonymous essay 'The Spirit of Fiction' (1867) in his journal *All the Year Round*.

which Dickens refused to objectify art as a separate realm. He is highly conscious, nonetheless, of the ways in which the imagination – and art as a vehicle of imagination – creates proportion. Indeed, Dickens's art makes such play of proportion that it is not infrequently figured as 'grotesque'.[10] The most obvious and extreme example of his grotesque art is *The Old Curiosity Shop*, a novel whose setting is a commercial outlet for old things whose value derives as much from the fact that they are old and 'curious' or different as from their values as markers of aspiration or commodities in a system of exchange. The things all have their histories and their strange appearances invite interpretation – appearing to suggest something intrinsically 'curious' about the things – but those histories are inert without a human frame, without 'curiosity'. Dickens is careful to attribute curiosity to the as yet unnamed girl (Nell) who 'stole a curious look' at the narrator's face and to the narrator ('my curiosity and interest were at least equal to the child's', ch. 4: 8). The noun 'curiosity' refers both to the curious things themselves and to the feeling and/or process that can turn things into curiosities, as well as informing the adjective 'curious'. Curiosities as peculiar things embody the metamorphic threshold between things, emotions and the processes of interpretation by which meaning is generated; like Dickens's art more generally, they blur boundaries between subject and object. The flagrantly fantastical nature of curiosities draws attention to the 'ideas in things', to use Bill Brown's term, but the fact that they are also reliant on curiosity as well as the original imagination of the craftsman to generate meaning suggests the Hegelian saw that 'there are no Things but in ideas' (Brown 2).

As a novel, *The Old Curiosity Shop*, initially narrated by Master Humphrey, is highly conscious of frames or representational systems as producers of signification or aesthetic agents. Like Dickens's novels, the shop does not simply sell things: it frames and exhibits them. In holding objects up for view, in announcing their status as anthropomorphic spectacle, Dickens simultaneously announces their constructedness and intensifies their presence or 'aura', to use Walter Benjamin's term.[11] Dickens's characteristic anthropomorphism, for example, is a means not only to suggest

---

[10] See, for example, Hollington (1984).
[11] Benjamin defines the 'aura' as the idea of a 'unique existence' or 'authenticity' which, in traditional theories of art, seems to attach itself to the great work of art or artists (2002: 104, 103).

the power of objects in Victorian society, but to distance readers at the
same time as drawing them in imaginatively. The environment inhabited
by Dickens's fictional things is some way between a shop and a museum.
Because *American Notes* is a travelogue, the generic frame is obviously
different, but as in *The Old Curiosity Shop*, Dickens makes sophisticated
and conspicuous use of framing mechanisms: Laura's story, for example,
is relayed to us by Dickens, who quotes the educational report of Dr
Howe. In *American Notes*, the things used to educate Laura are neither
commodities nor curiosities; they are everyday objects which gain their
value from the connections she is able to make between them and the
letters of the alphabet. In Dickens's letters, the fascination with money
is motivated not simply by avarice but by Dickens's curiosity about the
processes by which people have framed pieces of paper, wilfully invested
them with such meaning, that they have the power to change lives and
reorder societies.

Dickens's writing is thus a form of thing art, self-conscious about
the creative, representational, emotional and economic ways by which
things mean or confer value – both in writing and in the new mass society
where oppositions between people and things, art and commerce, were
being eroded and refigured. His self-consciousness about the relationship
between words and things, and their mutual dependence in forging meaning, mirrors his larger awareness of the mutually constitutive relationship
between literary and material culture. Notable critics have taken the
implications of this further: for example, Nancy Armstrong and J. Hillis
Miller have argued that nineteenth-century fiction represents not things
but ideas or images of things. But the philosophical debate about how far
we can ever know or understand things in themselves is not my principal
concern. I wish to join the critical appeal for more attention to representational texture in our analysis of objects in nineteenth-century writing
but to urge that this attention understands 'literature' and fiction as part
of a nuanced and differentiated cultural landscape. Ideas of rhetorical
hierarchy, generic difference, aesthetic proportion, and temporal change:
these are all important and necessary to a nuanced understanding of the
representation of things in nineteenth-century culture. But for Dickens, it
is not art as traditionally defined that carries out the work of creating proportion, which in turn creates meaning. It is rather 'Fancy', imagination,
the agent of art but evident for Dickens in all areas of life including the
commercial, which creates proportion but also, importantly, connection.

Aesthetic categories function as framing mechanisms, but they are unstable products of history, time and indeed fancy. Art works to differentiate but also to connect and include; art in the industrial age, for Dickens, should fuse an impulse to inclusivity with an acknowledgement of hierarchies of value. The idea of thing art encapsulates this fusion and the modernity of Dickens's aesthetic practice. To Dickens, modern artists in a world where objects have new power should respond not by objectifying the idea of art, but by animating, extending and rejuvenating the realm of the aesthetic.

Works cited

[Anon.], 1870. 'At Dickens's Sale', *Chambers Journal of Popular Literature, Science, and Art*, 345 (6 August): 502–5.

[Anon.], 1867. 'The Spirit of Fiction', *All the Year Round*, 18 (27 July): 118–20.

Armstrong, Nancy, 1999. *Fiction in the Age of Photography: The Legacy of British Realism*. Cambridge: Harvard University Press.

Benjamin, Walter, 2002 [1936]. 'The Work of Art in the Age of its Technological Reproducibility' (second version), in *Walter Benjamin: Selected Writings*, ed. Howard Eiland and Michael Jennings. 4 vols. Cambridge, Massachusetts: Belknap Press, III (1935–8): 101–33.

Brown, Bill, 2003. *A Sense of Things: The Object Matter of American Literature*. Chicago: Chicago University Press.

Dickens, Charles, 1850. 'Preliminary Word', *Household Words*, 1 (30 March): 1.

Dickens, Charles, 1948 [1852–3]. *Bleak House*, New Oxford Illustrated Dickens. Oxford: Oxford University Press.

Dickens, Charles, 1965–2002. *The Letters of Charles Dickens*, ed. G. Storey, K. Tillotson *et al.* Pilgrim edition. 12 vols. Oxford: Clarendon.

Dickens, Charles, 1997 [1840–1]. *The Old Curiosity Shop*, ed. Elizabeth M. Brennen. Oxford: Clarendon Press.

Dickens, Charles, 2000 [1842]. *American Notes for General Circulation*, ed. Patricia Ingham. London: Penguin.

Dickens, Charles, 2003 [1841], *Barnaby Rudge: A Tale of the Riots of 'Eighty*, ed. John Bowen. London: Penguin.

Forster, John, 1928 [1872–4]. *The Life of Charles Dickens*, ed. J. W. T. Ley. London: Cecil Palmer.

Freedgood, Elaine, 2006. *The Ideas in Things: Fugitive Meaning in the Victorian Novel*. Chicago: Chicago University Press.

Freedgood, Elaine, 2009. 'Commodity Criticism and Victorian Thing Culture: The Case of Dickens', in *Contemporary Dickens*, ed. Eileen Gillooly and Deirdre David. Columbus: Ohio University Press, pp. 152–68.

Hollington, Michael, 1984. *Dickens and the Grotesque*. London: Croom Helm.

Hollington, Michael, 2009. 'The Voice of Objects *In the Old Curiosity Shop*', *Australasian Journal of Victorian Studies*, 14: 1–8.

John, Juliet, 2010. *Dickens and Mass Culture*. Oxford: Oxford University Press.

Lowenthal, David, 1998 [1996]. *The Heritage Crusade and the Spoils of History*. Cambridge: Cambridge University Press, 1998.

McLaughlin, Kevin, 2005. *Paperwork: Fiction and Mass Mediacy in the Paper Age*. Philadelphia: University of Pennsylvania Press.

Marsh, Joss, 2011. 'The Rise of Celebrity Culture', in *Dickens in Context*, ed. Sally Ledger and Holly Furneaux. Cambridge: Cambridge University Press, pp. 98–108.

Meier, Stefanie, 1982. *Animation and Mechanization in the Novels of Charles Dickens*, Swiss Studies in English, CXI. Zurich: Francke Verlag Berne.

Miller, J. Hillis, 1992 [1971], 'The Fiction of Realism: *Sketches by Boz, Oliver Twist* and Cruikshank's Illustrations', in *Realism*, ed. Lilian R. Furst. Modern Literatures in Perspective. London: Longman, 1992, pp. 287–318.

Pettitt, Clare, 2009. 'Peggotty's Work-Box: Victorian Souvenirs and Material Memory', *Romanticism and Victorianism on the Net*, 53: 1–9 <http://www.erudit.org/revue/ravon/2009/v/n53/029896ar.html>.

Swift, Jonathan, 1972 [1726]. *Gulliver's Travels*, ed. Angus Ross. London: Longman.

Trotter, David, 2008. 'Household Clearances in Victorian Fiction', *19:Interdisciplinary Studies in the Long Nineteenth Century*, 6: 1–19 <http://19.bbk.ac.uk/index.php/19/article/viewFile/472/332>.

van Ghent, Dorothy, 1953. *The English Novel: Form and Function*. New York: Rinehart.

Waters, Catherine, 2008. *Commodity Culture in Dickens's 'Household Words': The Social Life of Goods*. Aldershot: Ashgate.

Dickens and the circus of modernity

MICHAEL HOLLINGTON

IT IS WIDELY ACKNOWLEDGED that, on the basis above all of A *Christmas Carol*, Dickens had a hand in the invention of modern Christmas. I want here to put forward a lesser but not unconnected claim, the exploration of which brings into focus an equally rich and international cultural context. During my childhood in London in the years immediately following the Second World War, Christmas meant a great deal to me, as a time of then uncharacteristic cornucopia, of plentiful food and drink, present-giving and entertainment. Two Dickensian forms of the latter were *de rigueur* in my family: a visit to the pantomime at Golders Green Hippodrome, and above all my highlight of highlights, a visit to Bertram Mills's circus at Olympia.

Bertram Mills's circus originates from 1920, that is to say from the aftermath of another cataclysmic war, when likewise 'normality' gradually returned, and with it, a renewed and heightened craving for diversion and entertainment. Mills himself was a well-connected member of British society's upper crust, and he hoped to make money by filling expensive seats as well as cheap ones. So he garnered support from people like Winston Churchill and Ramsay MacDonald to try to overcome a traditional distaste for the circus amongst the middle and upper classes which we shall encounter here more than once. That the tide was already turning, at least in some sections thereof, might be shown by the fact that many of the 'Bloomsberries' were circus devotees. Desmond McCarthy's *Memories*, for instance, describes travels in France with Roger Fry to select paintings for the First Post-Impressionist Exhibition of 1910–11, in the course of which they took time out to go to 'a very good circus' in Meaux (Shone 64), and Duncan Grant's *Juggler and Tightrope Walker* of 1918 is a significant British contribution to the mainly European circus art of the period (Shone 203, Spalding 225). Above all, perhaps, there is that hugely sympathetic representative of her class, Mrs Ramsay, in Virginia Woolf's *To the Lighthouse* of 1927, obviously an avid circus fan. 'Let us all go!' she exclaims 'with child-like exultation' as she sees a man with one arm on top of a ladder pasting a bill that unfolds the delights it announces in fragmentary, piecemeal fashion, as 'each shove of the brush revealed fresh legs, hoops, horses, glistening reds and blues, beautifully smooth, until half the wall was covered with the advertisement of a circus: a hundred horsemen, twenty performing seals, lions, tigers. . .' (Woolf 14).

Now it is my contention that Dickens had a considerable amount to do with this cult of the circus in modern times. I use here, in quite distinct but interconnected ways, the two terms 'Modernism' and 'Modernity'. The first means the great revolutionary flowering in all the arts in the late nineteenth and early twentieth centuries, during which, it can easily be shown, the circus is an almost obsessive reference point in music, in painting, in drama and film, and in literature. 'Modernity' means here the experience of social life, and perhaps particularly of social change, common to people in advanced industrial societies since Dickens's death in 1870, which may be largely negative, made up of alienation and fragmentation, or positive, made up of enthusiasm and awe, or a mixture of both.

I shall be interested here in both 'Modernism' and 'Modernity', and in their interaction. I shall give particular attention to the idea of the society of the circus as a utopian alternative to modernity, suggesting that Dickens is one of the first, if not *the* first, to put forward this conception, in *Hard Times*, in a strong and coherent way. I shall be much interested in the role of humour, suggesting perhaps that it is only through humour that the circus utopia can have any convincing purchase. This would mean that the circus clown is a key figure in establishing its credentials, and I shall borrow from Willson Disher the term 'joke of joy' to conceptualise this aspect of his role. Disher defines it thus: 'This is the joke a clown exploits when he stands before the footlights smiling inexplicably' (Disher 1925: 23), and we can find a fair visual representation of it in Kees van Dongen's *The Clown who believed himself to be the President of the Republic*, which also gives us a handy entrée into the idea of circus as utopia. A clown dressed in an ill-fitting tuxedo, with a grotesquely tilted stovepipe hat on his head, faces us in the full-frontal pose reserved in medieval paintings for Christ alone. But his eyes are shut as he appears to meditate contentedly on the circus utopia of his imaginary republic, represented by a secular trinity of riding-master, horse and ballerina in the background.

It's a humorous painting, of course, and as we explore imaginary circus republics here we shall find they are in fact subject to many 'dystopian' intrusions from the world of modernity, perhaps increasing with its progress towards overwhelming dominance. We might even say that something of a blur sets in with the passing of time, as the prestige of the circus declines and the word itself gets borrowed for metaphorical application in negative contexts, of which perhaps the idea of a 'media circus' is perhaps the most familiar to us nowadays. But even these parody 'anti-circuses' are anticipated in *Hard Times*, where, as Paul Schlicke remarks, 'Dickens's presentation of the world of fact treats it as a grotesque perversion of the circus' (Schlicke 175).

I start inevitably with the first appearance of the circus in *Hard Times*, which takes place, appropriately, at the margins, in the 'neutral ground upon the outskirts of the town, which was neither town nor country, and yet was either spoiled . . . a space of stunted grass and dry rubbish' (Dickens 1998, I, iii: 13, 15) – in short, thinking of a central Modernist text by an admirer of Dickens, one which in fact initially bore a title taken from his writings, a veritable 'waste land'. In this symbolic wilderness Mr Gradgrind is horrified to find his son and daughter abasing themselves to catch glimpses of Sleary's circus through nooks and crannies of fence and tent. How can this be? he asks of the pair, and receives a memorable reply from Louisa: 'I was tired, father. I have been tired a long time . . . I don't know of what – of everything, I think' (17).

The fifteen-year-old Louisa shows herself here to be a child of modernity imagined as a negative. In her commentary on this passage in *The Companion to 'Hard Times'*, Margaret Simpson provides some memorable contextual writing from Victorian contemporaries of Dickens which connects her expression of *anomie* and alienation with a gathering mood of anxiety about the direction of modern 'civilisation'. She quotes John Ruskin, averring that 'these are much *sadder* ages than the early ones; not sadder in a noble and deep way, but in a dim wearied way, – the way of ennui, and jaded intellect, and uncomfortableness of soul and body', and Matthew Arnold, reflecting on how the 'predominance of thought, of reflection, in modern epochs is not without its penalties; in the unsound, in the over-tasked, in the over-sensitive, it has produced . . . the feeling of depression, the feeling of *ennui* . . . these are the characteristics stamped on how many of the representative works of modern times!' (Simpson 70)

But if the circus, which rose to its apogee at much the same time, might in any way be counted as amongst the 'representative works of modern times', it is clear that it cannot simply be arraigned alongside other, quite dissimilar cultural manifestations of the new era. It could be constructed, and was, by Dickens himself and later artists, as an alternative world for which Louisa seems to yearn, as a means of counteracting her *ennui*. It is Jean Starobinski, writing in 1970, who perhaps gives the best general description of this opposition between what the circus stood for for Dickens and later artists and the forces of industrialised modernity: 'Le monde du cirque et de la fête foraine représentait dans l'atmosphère charbonneuse d'une société en voie d'industrialisation, un îlot chatoyant et merveilleux, un morceau demeuré intact du pays d'enfance, un domaine où la spontanéité vitale, l'illusion, les prodiges simples de l'adresse ou de la maladresse mêlait leurs seductions pour le spectateur lassé de la vie sérieuse' ('The world of circus and fairground represented in the grimy atmosphere of a society in the process of industrialisation an islet of shimmering miracles, an intact fragment of the world of the child, a domain in which spontaneous vitality, illusion, and the simple prodigies of grace or clumsiness mingled their charms for the spectator tired of the monotony of the tasks of serious life', Starobinski 7, my translation).

I need first, then, even at the risk of running over ground made familiar by Schlicke's splendid account of the novel, to provide some outline contours of the circus utopia presented in *Hard Times*. It is a utopia with three rings, so to speak: first, the level of social relationships between humans; second, the level of relationship between humans and animals (and indeed things, if we had time to explore this issue); and third, that of interpersonal relationships.

Concerning the ideals of circus society in *Hard Times*, we may stress how the novel emphasises the circle of the circus as a symbolic space, a 'round table' where democracy, equality and mutual support prevail under the auspices of a benign ringmaster, Sleary, who occupies its centre and makes it cohere. In the dramatic scene, for instance, where it becomes apparent that Sissy's father has disappeared, the room she and her father have occupied gets metamorphosed into a circus space: 'Mr. Sleary stood in the middle of the room, with the male members of the company about him, exactly as he would have stood in the centre of the ring' (Dickens 1998, I, vi: 51). As it progresses we gain a firm impression of the company as a unit, acting and reacting as one, in ways not unlike those of the chorus in Greek tragedy, as when Sissy turns to face Gradgrind: 'The whole company perceived the force of the change, and drew a long breath together, that plainly said, "she will go!"' (50) They are portrayed as representing a kind of ideal community – 'there was a remarkable gentleness and childishness about these people, a special inaptitude for any kind of sharp practice, and an untiring readiness to help and pity one another' (46) – manifestly unlike the society that surrounds them. Indeed the idea of the circus as a kind of Noah's Ark saved from the waters of destruction about hovers at one point, in the significant context of the relation between humans and animals, when it is joked that the absent dog Merrilegs, 'that respectable ancestor of the highly trained animal who went aboard the ark, might have been shut out of it, for any sign of a dog that was manifest to eye or ear in the Pegasus's Arms' (37).

Turning to humans and animals, the fact that Pegasus the flying horse gives his name to the inn where these people are lodged during their stay in Coketown suggests that it is an animal rather than a human being who presides over the circus world of the novel. As Margaret Simpson notes, Pegasus had been a *leitmotif* of the circus since its modern reconstitution by Astley in 1768 – Hughes's rival Royal Circus had adorned its roof with a statue of the mythical creature, and the great equestrian performer Ducrow had a favourite horse named Pegasus who was one of the team that pulled his wife's funeral casket (Simpson 91). Here humans and animals appear as if interchangeable – Sleary offers the remarkably low-keyed assurance to Sissy that if she decides to stay with him rather than to go to school with Gradgrind she will be treated in the same way as he treats horses: 'I never did a horthe a injury yet, no more than thwearing at him went, and that I don't expect I shall begin otherwise at my time of life, with a rider' (Dickens 1998, I, vi: 50). Indeed, one at least of the circus folk is represented as a kind of hybrid, half-horse, half-human – Childers, who 'looked the most remarkable sort of Centaur' (38).

As with the communal level in the circus world of *Hard Times*, so with the personal – indeed the two can be said to interlock. Sissy and her father form an eccentric version of that rarity in Dickens – a happy, strongly bonded family: 'those two were one . . . they were never asunder,' says Childers (43), and Sissy herself confirms this to Louisa 'he carried me about with him when I was quite a baby. We have never been asunder since that time' (I, ix: 77). But these bonds are not exclusive and nuclear, and Sleary can assure Sissy that, despite the grievous loss she suffers when

Jupe disappears, 'Emma Gordon, in whothe lap you're a lying at prethent, would be a mother to you, and Joth'phine would be a thithter to you.' (I, vi: 50)

The lap in question is that of a pregnant woman who will be well into her second marriage by the novel's end, and *Hard Times* makes it plain in mid-Victorian terms that this is a society where, in a climate of sexual attraction between men and women, procreation thrives. The novel presents 'two or three handsome women' amongst the circus people, 'with their two or three husbands, and their two or three mothers, and their eight or nine little children' (45), the casual numbering perhaps suggesting some laxity in the domestic arrangements whence this fertility springs. Childers's name anticipates the title of Joyce's fragment of work in progress published in 1931 – *Haveth Childers Everywhere* – and 'Kidderminster' (presumably born haphazardly on tour at that place) appears to double it.

At this point I take a leap to Picasso and Spanish Modernism. Even if, as we shall see, Dickens and *Hard Times* certainly figured significantly in Modernist circles in Spain in the early twentieth century, I do not think it necessary to speculate whether Picasso knew either the book or the author to put forward the claim that his wonderful stage curtain for the Diaghilev ballet *Parade* of 1917 can be approached as a visual expression of a similar circus utopia. The sleeping dog in the foreground captures the atmosphere of peace and harmony, presided over again by Pegasus the winged horse, who dominates the left side of the painting. Fertility figures prominently – the Pegasus is significantly female, and suckles a foal – and so, obviously, does sexual love, particularly at the table laden with fruit on the right. The pyramid of figures on the left (which also parallels Dickens's circus family pyramids in *Hard Times*) culminates in a monkey, not a man.

But for Spanish Modernist circus art that is clearly directly related to Dickens and *Hard Times* we must turn to Rafael Barradas, the subject of an excellent *Dickens Quarterly* article by Beatriz Vegh published in March 1998. Barradas was a Uruguayan of Spanish parentage who spent most of his short adult life and career in Spain in the era of High Modernism, frequenting *avant-garde* cafés in Madrid and Barcelona, and in particular the *tertulia* or literary discussion group founded by Ramon Gomez de la Serna, author of the single most important Modernist book on the circus. Here he met Gregorio Martinez Sierra, the publisher of *Ediciones Estrella*, largely dedicated to writing that attacked social injustice. Perhaps because of his admiration for the Dickens admirer George Bernard Shaw, Sierra chose to include *Hard Times* in this series in 1921 and asked Barradas, as on numerous previous occasions, to provide the illustrations. These are uncompromisingly Modernist, and of high quality and interest. As Vegh notes, they represent free imaginative responses to the novel rather than specific literal illustrations to accompany individual scenes, employing a pattern of imagery in which flowers figure prominently. These are particularly associated with Sissy, who figures yet more prominently in Barradas's illustrations than in Dickens's novel (thus for instance the illustration to *Hard Times*, I, iii, 'A Loophole', portrays neither Louisa nor Tom Gradgrind but Sissy standing by the fence at the circus). The illustrations are often structured in binary fashion, with stylised representation of the circus in the foreground pitted against stylised factories and chimneys in the background. And in one of the most striking of them we have another version of the Dickensian circus idyll – a waste land dotted with flowers in which Sissy is centrally seated against a tree that ascends towards two stylised clumps of foliage, with a dog peacefully stationed nearby and a horse calmly grazing in a kind of fenced *hortus conclusus* – set against the chaotic Expressionist angular backdrop of the industrial world.

With Ramon Gomez de la Serna we encounter an important Modernist whose book *El Circo* of 1917 – the subject of a brilliant 1927 review by Walter Benjamin – marks a kind of crossroads where the idea of a circus utopia not dissimilar to that in Dickens meets a version of surrealism *avant la lettre*. After Ramon, surrealist elements are to be frequently encountered in representations of the circus: Sylvia Plath's early poem 'Circus in Three Rings', for instance, written before 1956, displays its surrealist credentials in lines such as 'my demon of doom tilts on a trapeze,/winged rabbits revolving about his knees' (Plath 322). This is true even of certain circus films that might seem to belong to popular culture rather than to High Modernism, such as those by Chaplin and the Marx Brothers. And of course – though I can do no more than mention it here – there is, much later, the 'inimitable' *Monty Python's Flying Circus*.

El Circo is full of extravagant, tongue-in-cheek hyperbole about what the circus means for humankind. '¿No se curará el cáncer con el espectáculo del circo?' he asks hyperbolically: 'Can't watching the circus cure cancer?' (de la Serna 51), continuing mischievously with the idea that it can restore sexual happiness: 'Señoras casadas, de vida triste, que sonrien otra vez como solteras, curadas y consoladas' ('Married women, leading sad lives, who are cured and consoled and smile again as they once did as young girls', de la Serna 51). Circus people themselves in de la Serna's book, as in *Hard Times*, enjoy happy marriages: 'Las artistas de circo se suelen casar y hacen muy feliz a su marido' ('as a rule, women circus artists get married, and make their husbands very happy', 92).

For de la Serna as for Starobinski and Dickens himself, the circus is a means of travelling back in time to childhood and beyond. Jumping on to a safety net from a height is like a child jumping on its pillow, whilst, again jokily, de la Serna asserts that contortionists and rubber men take us right back to the womb, and that gynaecologists in the audience gasp in recognition of what they see: 'El contorsionista recuerda, en el momento más difícil de su trabajo, cuando se hace un ovillo, la sobrecogida postura que tuvo antes de nacer en el viente de su madre. Retorcido sobre sí mismo hace exclamar a los ginecólogos: "¡Lo mismo! ¡Lo mismo!"' ('At the most difficult part of his performance, when he makes himself into a ball, the contortionist reminds us of the terrified position of the infant in the mother's womb prior to birth. Folded back over himself, he makes gynaecologists cry out: "it's the same! It's the same!"', 88). Exploring here the idea of the birth trauma, de la Serna is in territory adjacent to that of his contemporary Freud, as he enlists the circus for an archaeological dig back into the foundations of the psyche, in order to make it whole again.

But it is Benjamin who perhaps best brings out the political rather than psychological meaning of de la Serna's circus book, praising it for its refusal to write any 'Traktat über den Zirkus als »Symbol« neueren Lebensgefühles' ('tract about the circus as "symbol" of a new sense of life', Benjamin 70). He reminds us in Brechtian fashion of de la Serna's emphasis on the essential absence of theatrical illusion in the circus: that is to say, what takes place under the big top are actual physical exploits of men and animals often involving considerable danger. Circus acts are essentially *presentations* rather than *representations.*

For Benjamin, de la Serna's book offers us a vision of an exemplary world in which social harmony between the classes remains intact in an era largely characterised by its absence. He picks up on a kind of prayer for peace at the very end of de la Serna's book, which had of course particular resonance in 1917 – 'La soñada paz universal se firmará en un gran circo una de esas noches en que sobre la alta cucaña humana se displiegan todas las banderas en verdadera confraternidad' ('that universal peace of which we dream will be signed in a great circus tent on one of these nights, when, on top of the high human pyramid all flags will fly in a display of real confraternity', de la Serna 223) – and wittily sharpens it. Yes, indeed, writes Benjamin, a true peace could only be drawn up in a circus and guaranteed by two professions – mathematicians and clowns, 'die Meister des abstrakten Denkens und der abstrakten Physis' ('the masters of abstract thinking and of abstract physicality', Benjamin 71).

Even more arrestingly, it would be supervised not by humans but by animals. In one of the most beautiful pieces of writing about the circus that I know of, inspired by de la Serna, Benjamin sketches a portrait of an ecological paradise, in which circus people and those who temporarily enter the precincts in which they live and work learn from animals, and not vice versa:

Denn das ist ja das Geheimnis des besonderen Gefühles, mit dem ein jeder den Zirkus betritt: Im Zirkus ist der Mensch ein Gast des Tierreiches. Die Tiere stehen doch nur scheinbar unter der Botmäßigkeit des Dompteurs, die Kunststücke, die sie machen, sind ihre Art den jüngeren Bruder zu unterhalten und zu zerstreuen, da sie ja Besseres mit ihm nicht anfangen können. Die Zirkusleute haben von ihnen gelernt, wie Vögel von Ast zu Ast, so fliegen von Trapez zu Trapez Akrobaten, die Hände des Zauberers schießen durch den Raum wie zwei Wiesel, als Schmetterling läßt auf den Pferderücken die Schulreiterin sich nieder, der dumme August schnuppert wie ein Tapir sich durch den Sand der Manege und nur der Stallmeister mit der Peitsche fällt als der Herr der Schöpfung aus dem anarchischen Tierparadiese heraus. Wie sie so ist im Zirkus auch alles andere bis in die Umgänge, Passagen, Tore hinein von animalischem Leben erfüllt. In den Pausen drängt sich das Publikum zum Buffet, den nichts macht Appetit wie ein Abend im Zirkus.

Because that is the secret of the special feeling that everyone gets entering a circus: that in the circus the human being is a guest of the animal kingdom. For the animals only give the appearance of being under the command of their trainers, and the works of art they perform are their way of conversing with and amusing their younger brother, because there is no way of venturing anything better than that. Circus people have learnt from them. Acrobats fly from trapeze to trapeze like birds from branch to branch, conjurors hands shoot through the air like a couple of weasels, the riding girl lands like a butterfly on the backs of the horses, the silly clown snuffles in the sawdust of the ring like a tapir, and only the ringmaster with his whip behaving like the king of creation is left out of this anarchic animal paradise. In the circus everything else is full of animal life as well, right out into the surrounds and passageways and entrances. In the intervals the audience rush to the cafeteria, because nothing brings on an appetite as much as an evening at the circus. (Benjamin 72; my translation)

Shortly after writing this passage, Benjamin would turn his attention, under the twin influence of Philippe Soupault and Theodor Adorno, to Dickens himself. The former – a genuine 'official' Surrealist – wrote an essay on Chaplin in 1928 pointing out the link between Chaplin and Dickens, the latter an essay on *The Old Curiosity Shop* in 1931. Before going on later to read Dickens under their influence, and commenting on his novels in the *Arcades Project*, Benjamin had already remarked of Soupault's insight, in his 1929 review of it and of Chaplin's *The Circus*, that it might lead to 'further reading and investigation' ('die man nachlesen und weiterverfolgen kann', Benjamin 159).

It will come as no surprise, in the context of Benjamin's enthusiasm for de la Serna, that he regards Chaplin's *The Circus* as a masterpiece, in fact as 'das erste Alterswerk der Filmkunst' ('the first work in which the art of the cinema comes of age', 157). For him as for Soupault it is to be approached as a form of poetry with the musical structure of a theme and variations that Benjamin also finds in Russian film-makers of the period, and with a disdain for linear plot suspense to be applauded. Chaplin is for Benjamin a poet of the city, specifically, like Dickens, of London, whose art achieves universality because of its firm rooting in a habit of local and specific observation practised during long walks in the streets. The laughter he generates, Benjamin concludes, following Soupault again, is the rarest and most potentially revolutionary of achievements, all the more precious because of its capacity for universal dissemination.

The connection between Chaplin and Dickens has become a commonplace since Benjamin and Soupault. But what is of special interest to me here is how *The Circus*, in the post-First World War era, tracks away from the utopianism of Dickens and the early Modernists, opening in a thoroughly dystopian manner which presents the polar opposite of the harmonious father–daughter relationships in *Hard Times* (Jupe–Sissy, Sleary–Josephine). Here the tyrannical father/ringleader of a failing circus berates his daughter for 'missing her tip' (i.e. failing to go through the hoops as she circles the ring on horseback), and punishes her in a profoundly Dickensian way by denying her food, and vents un-Sleary-like fury on his inadequate clowns.

Enter Chaplin as tramp to share his sandwich with Merna and save the circus, initially in a completely unwitting and unrehearsed way, his spontaneous appearances in the ring causing uproarious laughter and applause. But no sooner is he established as the 'star' of the circus than more chicanery sets in – the boss seeks to conceal from Chaplin the extent of his success, and so gives him all kinds of menial jobs as cleaner and master of props. Here the great tradition of zany relation between humans and things, stemming from Dickens and Grimaldi and beyond, is reinvigorated in magical moments such as Chaplin in his zeal taking the fish out of their bowl and cleaning them. *Don Quixote* is another great comic reference point in the scene where Chaplin finds himself in a lion's cage but manages, with Merna's help, to escape as the fearsome creature sleeps peacefully on.

Such scenes belong amongst the highest achievements of Chaplin, and hence of all comic art. Yet there remain many dissonances, especially in the domain of sexual love and fulfilment. Chaplin is led to believe that he and Merna might get together as a couple, but the moment he prepares to act on this assumption Merna in fact falls for Rex, a handsome and suavely presented tightrope walker. The result is that Chaplin – in the Gogol/ Woody Allen tradition – turns his back on comedy: he too now wants to be a tightrope walker rather than a funny man. His clown performances deteriorate, and he gets no laughs. Instead he devotes himself to mounting higher and performing more daring deeds than Rex. Class discords set in ('Rex', the king, is a socially superior, more suitable match for Merna, acceptable to the tyrannical father) and murderous psychological impulses invade the tramp's unconscious mind (in one Expressionist scene he actually does kill Rex in fantasy).

So, despite the sublime hilarity of Chaplin's eventual 'triumph' over Rex (when he at last does mount higher than his rival, a pack of monkeys debag him, and he floats up and down with them attached to his underwear) there remains a bitter-sweet quality about the film's happy ending. Circus unity is restored, but this is achieved only because Chaplin, like Jupe in *Hard Times*, sacrifices himself for the sake of Merna's happiness, accepting the fact that she loves someone else. If, as in Northrop Frye's terms, comedies attempt to end with as many marriages as possible and maximal inclusion of all the protagonists in the concluding dance, then here Chaplin remains excluded, wandering off into the distance to continue the itinerant life of the outsider.

The Marx Brothers at the Circus of 1939 is a more superficial and less problematic work, though again it provides not a few good laughs which can be described as utopian 'jokes of joy', even if they too are under threat. We again encounter a circus in difficulties, though this time these have nothing to do with failure to attract audiences, or the personality of the owner: the problem lies instead with a creditor's implacable hostility towards him. Grotesque accomplices – contrasting 'bad apples' in the company, a midget and a strong man – are hired to steal the ten thousand dollars he has earned to pay back his debts, so as to make him default.

As in *Hard Times*, the eventual saviour is to be an animal. The Marx Brothers, hired to track down the perpetrators of the theft, prove absurdly incompetent, especially in one hilarious scene where they attempt to get back the money in the sleeping strong man's bedroom, and succeed only in creating a snowstorm of feathers issuing from the pillows and mattresses they rip apart. But then Groucho has the idea of entertaining Geoff's rich aunt Mrs Dukesbury (the class theme resurfacing in the Dickensian ono-mastic name) not with the symphony orchestra she has ordered for her dinner guests but with a circus performance on her lawn that will win her and her class over as circus devotees (just as Sleary does Gradgrind, and Bertram Mills sought to do after the First World War). He succeeds in this, despite the villain's attempts to stop the show, and despite the fact that Mrs Dukesbury, in obvious homage to Chaplin, is also reduced to her underwear on the high trapeze. But it is only the supreme trapeze artist, the gorilla, who can scamper up the rope to the summit of the big tent and overpower Geoff's enemy. The film ends with the gorilla on his perch – above them all, as in Picasso – counting out the recovered ten thousand, in ironic corroboration of Benjamin's assertion that we in the circus are beholden to the animals we supposedly master, and not they to us.

Cecil B. DeMille's 1952 *The Greatest Show on Earth* is easily the worst film I shall consider here – indeed it is regularly voted amongst the worst Oscar-winning films of all time. A bloated, pedestrian pseudo-documentary on the Ringling brothers' circus, it would not deserve mention here were it not for two considerations. First, it shows that even bad films about the circus owe something to Dickens's *Hard Times*, even when they share none of its values and concerns, and second (moreover) it may serve as an illustration of what the parodic 'anti-circus' of modernity might mean.

What links it to *Hard Times* is a straight pilfer, concerning the clown Buttons, played by James Stewart. DeMille stitches together two plot-motifs in Dickens's novel – Bounderby's mother Mrs Pegler, who travels incognito to Coketown once a year to admire her son's status and wealth, and the idea of Sleary's circus hiding a fugitive from the law by concealing Tom Gradgrind under grotesque make-up. Fitfully and superficially, eschewing psychological depth or formal complexity, DeMille fills one of the three rings of his plot with the outline of a tale of a young doctor compelled to carry out the mercy-killing of his sick wife and hence on the run from the law. He seeks refuge as the clown Buttons in the circus and never takes off his make-up, even when his mother comes to the circus – once a year, like Mrs Pegler – to keep him abreast of attempts to track him down. Brad the circus manager, played by Charlton Heston, also vaguely resembles Sleary in his attempt to protect Buttons from the attentions of the FBI.

The array of stars – besides Charlton Heston and James Stewart, we have Betty Hutton, Dorothy Lamour and Gloria Grahame – in itself indicates that this is not a film where the idea of circus democracy and solidarity prevails. The plot and its ideological values revolve instead around a fascination with the jealousies and rivalries of 'star' egos competing for money, professional pre-eminence and sexual gratification. Family solidarity in the face of danger and possible death, as in *Hard Times*, is replaced by aggressive competition between isolated individuals, as the two top trapeze artists, male and female, duel from the start for pre-eminence in a series of dares which ends with 'The Great Sebastian' seriously injuring himself in a fall. In this film, the circus appears as a world where everyone seems out to spike someone else.

But 1952 saw the appearance of another film with recognisable links to *Hard Times*. In its focus on the Calvary of the central protagonist Calvero, Chaplin's *Limelight* develops further the 'tragic clown' theme of Signor Jupe, the ageing comedian more and more frequently 'missing his tip', and performing in front of audiences who deride him, or simply leave, or fail to show up. And – consciously or unconsciously echoing Dickens's own wish to 'die in harness' (Dickens 1965–2002, VIII: 89) – Chaplin has his hero die backstage of a heart attack at his Farewell Benefit Performance whilst his protégée dances on.

It is not difficult to show that the supposed communist Chaplin's film far surpasses that of the McCarthyite DeMille. It returns to the issues of Louisa Gradgrind's modern *anomie* – the state of having been 'tired a long time . . . I don't know of what – of everything, I think', as it explores

Thereza's psychosomatic illness, the loss of the use of her lower limbs as a result of a conviction of 'the utter futility of everything'. Once more, it offers the circus and pantomime as part of a cure, once when Thereza appears in a ballet version of the death of Columbine, with Chaplin appearing as Clown, and twice in the unforgettable flea-circus routine where the fleas Henry and Phyllis are addressed in impeccably polite upper-class tones and chased through the recesses of the clown's pants. It is instructive that where DeMille goes for gigantism, Chaplin should seek to distil the meaning of his life's work in such miniaturised circuitry.

And so to my last circus utopia, Angela Carter's *Nights at the Circus*. What distinguishes it from any previous example is the sharp, particular focus on the idea of a *feminist* utopia, but it would once more be a mistake, I think, to see it as a simple partisan tract. Like some other texts stretching back to Dickens examined here, it too takes up the idea of the circus as a place where values that transcend the merely human sphere are presented by a menagerie of wise pigs, mocking apes and learned horses. We mere human beings are privileged to enter into their sanctum, for in the circus cloakroom 'one left behind the skin of one's own beastliness so as not to embarrass the beasts with it' (Carter 105).

And so the book resonates with humanist jokes like the mocking quotation from *Hamlet* ('what a piece of work is man!'– 238). In absurd allegory, the circus chimpanzees revolt against their keeper Lamarck and take over the running of their own show, and then decide to duck out of the circus altogether rather than follow it to Siberia. Their act puts 'their studious observations of ourselves to use in routines of parody, of irony, of satire' (141–2), and they look on in amusement as Mignon dances with a tiger in another *Quixote*-inspired *rapprochement* between humans and ferocious big cats. The Orpheus theme to be found in *The Marx Brothers at the Circus*, where Harpo charms lions and tigers with his harp, resurfaces here, as the Princess accompanies the dance on the piano with a Tchaiko-vsky waltz, and the chimpanzees politely applaud: 'few of the non-simian habitués of the circus could have behaved with more decorum as they clapped' (163).

Music, indeed, especially through the Mignon theme, is a major vehicle of the novel's utopian values. Carter picks up on two of the Mignon songs from Goethe's *Wilhelm Meister* in their Schubert settings. 'Kennst du das Land?', the first of them, asks – 'Do you know the land where the lemon trees grow?' (155) – and Mignon sings it to the tigers, eliciting impassioned narrative commentary: 'might not this land be the Eden of our first beginnings, where innocent beasts and children play together under the lovely lemon trees, the tiger abnegates its ferocity, the child her cunning? Is it, is it?' (155) The intensity of the writing recurs in a later passage asserting that 'Mignon's song is *not* a sad song, not poignant, not a plea. There is a grandeur about the questioning' (249).

To me it is this 'grandeur of the questioning' that characterises the meaning and purpose of *Nights at The Circus* – couched as these are in essentially comic, often surreal terms – and not any formulaic set of answers. Mignon's other song expresses, however, what, in terms of gender politics, that questioning is about – how to achieve a translation to the state imagined by Mignon where 'Sie fragen nicht nach Mann und Weib' ('they don't ask about man and woman'). But firstly that seems to be only one aspect of the utopia imagined in and through the circus, and second, its realisation seems to be resistant to human calculation and engineering. In the joke allegories of the plot, the clock is lost (but in any case it always stood only at noon or midnight) – as we move towards 1900, the supposed point in time when the new era is supposed to dawn. This notion is mocked from the perspective of a global democracy, a plebiscite as a result of which 'the twentieth century would have forthwith ceased to exist, the entire system of dividing up years by one hundred would have been abandoned, and time, by popular consent, would have stood still' (265).

So Fevvers – in a novel that moves towards a punning encounter with shamans – has to be seen, I think, essentially as a sham, a winged circus descendant of Dickens's original Pegasus 'with real gauze let in for his wings, golden stars stuck all over him, and his ethereal harness made of red silk' (Dickens 1998, I, vi: 36). One of her wings gets broken, and the myth of her virginity gets exploded, as she falls in love with Jack Walser and has sex with him. If she takes up a position on top in their love-making, this is for the mundane practical reason that she has a broken wing, not because some huge advance in the status of women is being signified. Like Chaplin and the Marx Brothers, and unlike Cecil B. DeMille, *Nights at the Circus* mocks height contests, and realises that the ideals it urges can only be realised, in the present time of the novel at least, in the realm of the comic imagination.

Carter's novel dates from 1984, and it may be that the line of thinking about the circus as an alternative utopia that begins with *Hard Times* more or less comes to an end with it. This probably has to do with the fact that since the closure of Bertram Mills's Olympia circus in 1967 the circus itself has fallen on 'hard times', especially in Anglophone countries, where protest against the perceived cruelty of the conditions under which circus animals are kept and trained has been at its strongest. Mills's son Cyril Bertram Mills writes of his father that 'if he resented anything it was the wholesale and indiscriminate attacks made by some animal-protection societies against everyone. He knew that animals could be and were being trained without cruelty in circuses and elsewhere and he did everything he could to demonstrate the truth of this, but at the same time he was the first to agree that if there were black sheep in the circus fold they should be rooted out and prosecuted' (Mills 12).

To me, it seems something of a tragedy that so rich a cultural pheno-menon as the traditional circus, inspiring such great works of art in such a variety of media – from Dickens through Seurat and Picasso to Stravinsky and Chaplin and beyond – should now amongst many have something of pariah status, whilst in the same era 'shlock horror' circus movies with the power permanently to desensitise and degrade their consumers should flourish. And I suspect that Dickens, and certainly Mr Sleary, might have agreed with Bertram Mills in thinking that tighter regulation of the treatment of animals in circuses rather than the outright erasure of their presence might be the better way to go. At any rate the latter has very clean hands, for the worst he can think of by way of punishment for circus animals that 'miss their tip', when it comes to pinning down Bitzer, and thus rescuing Tom Gradgrind, is as follows: 'If my dog leth thith young man thtir a peg on foot, I give him leave to go. And if my horthe ever thtirth from that thpot where he beginth a danthing, till the morning – I don't know him!' (Dickens 1998, III, viii: 386)

Works cited

Benjamin, Walter, 1980 [1972]. *Gesammelte Schriften*, vol. III, ed. Hella Tiedemann-Bartels. Frankfurt am Main: Suhrkamp.

Carter, Angela, 1985 [1984]. *Nights at the Circus*. London: Picador.

Chaplin, Charles, 1966 [1964]. *My Autobiography*. London: Penguin.

Clair, Jean, ed, 2004. *La Grande Parade: portrait de l'artiste en clown*. Paris: Gallimard.

Dickens, Charles, 1965–2002. *The Letters of Charles Dickens*, ed. G. Storey, K. Tillotson *et al.* Pilgrim edition. 12 vols. Oxford: Clarendon Press.

Dickens, Charles, 1998 [1989]. *Hard Times*, ed. Paul Schlicke. Oxford World's Classics. Oxford: Oxford University Press.

Disher, M. Willson, 1925. *Clowns and Pantomimes*. Boston and New York: Houghton Mifflin.

Disher, M. Willson, 1937. *The Greatest Show on Earth*. London: G. Bell and Sons.

Disher, M. Willson, 1942. *Fairs, Circuses and Music Halls*. London: William Collins.

Findlater, Richard, 1955. *Grimaldi*. London: McGibbon and Kee.

Frye, Northrop, 1957. *The Anatomy of Criticism*. Princeton, New Jersey: Princeton University Press.

Green, Martin, and John Swan, 1986. *The Triumph of Pierrot*. New York: Macmillan.

Loxton, Howard, 1997. *The Golden Age of the Circus*. London: Grange Books.

MacCarthy, Desmond, 1953. *Memories*. London: MacGibbon and Kee.

Mills, Cyril Bertram, 1967. *Bertram Mills Circus: Its Story*. London: Hutchinson.

Penrose, Roland, 1985 [1958]. *Picasso: His Life and Work*. London: Granada Publishing.

Plath, Sylvia, 1981. *Collected Poems*. London: Faber and Faber.

Schlicke, Paul, 1988 [1985]. *Dickens and Popular Entertainment*. London: Unwin Hyman.

de la Serna, Ramon Gomez, 1968 [1917]. *El Circo*. Madrid: Espasa-Calpe.

de la Serna, Ramon Gomez, 1927. *Le Cirque*, trans. Adolphe Falgairolle. Paris: Simon Kra.

Shone, Richard, 1976. *Bloomsbury Portraits*. Oxford: Phaidon.

Simpson, Margaret, 1997. *The Companion to 'Hard Times'*. Robertsbridge: Helm Information.

Spalding, Frances, 1997. *Duncan Grant: A Biography*. London; Chatto and Windus.

Starobinski, Jean, 2004 [1970]. *Portrait de l'artiste en Saltimbanque*. Paris: Gallimard.

Stott, Andrew McConnell, 2009. *The Pantomime Life of Joseph Grimaldi*. Edinburgh: Canongate.

Vegh, Beatriz, 1998. '*Hard Times* Gone Modernist: The 1921 Rafael Barradas Illustrations for *Tiempos Difíciles*', *Dickens Quarterly*, 15: 3–27.

Welsford, Enid, 1968 [1935]. *The Fool: His Social and Literary History*. London: Faber and Faber.

Woolf, Virginia, 1964 [1927]. *To the Lighthouse*. Harmondsworth: Penguin.

The Oliver! *phenomenon;*
or, 'Please, sir, we want more and more!'

JOSS MARSH and CARRIE SICKMANN

ON THURSDAY 30 JUNE 1960, a hummable musical 'freely adapted' from *Oliver Twist* (though also inspired by a chocolate bar)[1] 'sizzled' onto the stage of the New Theatre, London, launching the star careers of stand-up comedian and cabaret artist Ron Moody (Fagin), night-club singer Georgia Brown (Nancy), and a string of musical Artful Dodgers, including Davy Jones (later one of the pop group the Monkees, who performed as the Dodger on 'The Ed Sullivan Show' the same night the Beatles made their American TV debut), the rock star Phil Collins ('the loudest Dodger', his child-actor-agent mother proudly recalled),[2] the Small Faces singer-guitarist Steve Marriott, and the teen actor Jack Wild (who went wild, as ex-Dodgers were wont to do). 'The curtain-calls went on and on', recalled Moody, 'there was a kind of electrical magnetism around the theatre.'[3] 'A

The authors thank the staff of the Theatre Museum, London (TM), together with Rosy Runciman and her assistant Jenny Cartwright, at the Cameron Mackintosh archive (CM), for their generous assistance in researching this essay. It builds on work by CS towards her doctoral dissertation, on adaptation as continuation, and by JM for her forthcoming book *Starring Charles Dickens* (Ashgate, 2013). Please note that some of the footnotes contain only partial bibliographic information; when working with original archival materials (including newspaper clippings and reviews sent in by generous fans, collectors, and theatre aficionados) details are not always recoverable. We have tried to include as many specifics as possible.

[1] A childhood favourite of *Oliver!* author-composer Lionel Bart. Its wrapper showed a boy asking for more (see below).
[2] Quoted in Victoria Hinton, 'A Case of Mother's Pride', unidentified cutting (CM).
[3] Ron Moody (30 June 1960). Quoted by Elaine Peake in 'A Twist in the Tale' from the 2006 programme of 'It's a Fine Life' a Hornchurch production at the Queen's Theatre.

triumph ... rush for seats' raved the *Evening Standard*; 'A magical musical', sang the *Sunday Dispatch*; 'A whopping welcome winner', proclaimed the *Daily Sketch*.[4] On 20 November 1965, on its 2,284th performance, *Oliver!* became the longest-running musical in British theatre history;[5] at its final, 2,618th performance, there were an astonishing twenty-five curtain calls. On 14 November 1964, *Oliver!* became the longest-running British musical ever seen on Broadway.[6] (Records encapsulate both the legends and the economics of theatre history.) Translated to film, at huge cost, the last of the classic screen musicals, in 1968, *Oliver!* won six Oscars. *Oliver!* would turn out to be a star-making machine, a star British export, and a populist post-modern tourist experience.

The 'avalanche' of Dickensian musicals critics feared – with titles like *Bleak!*, *David!*, *The Pickwick Capers*, and *Miss Havisham Misses a Wedding* – did not sweep across stage and screen in *Oliver!*'s wake,[7] though a trickle did follow: *Pickwick* (London, 1963), starring Harry Secombe, who scored a hit song with Pickwick's Eatanswill election manifesto, 'If I Ruled the World'; the 1970 film *Scrooge*, memorably analysed by Paul Davis in his history of *A Christmas Carol* as 'culture-text' (1990); and *The Old Curiosity Shop* (United States title *Mr. Quilp*, 1975), a limp screen vehicle for David Lean's 1948 Dodger, Anthony Newley. But *Oliver!* nevertheless marked a genuine 'revolution' in theatre history – a loaded term, to which we will return – and spur to the Dickens adaptation industry. It was thus an extraordinarily powerful iteration and renovation of Dickens's novel, and of Dickens himself, a fact this essay will keep in view. But it was also more.

It was, in the first instance, an economic force. *Oliver!* ushered in the modern era of the 'mechanised', 'monster' musical, which now dominates Broadway, the West End, and the national and international theatrical touring and licensing business. *Oliver!* itself was revived in 1977, complete with its original set, running for a further two years, and again in 1983. It returned in 1994, in a redesigned £3.5m production (grossing an estimated £6.3m in advance sales alone), on the mammoth stage of the

[4]   Reviews quoted in 1962 New Theatre *Oliver!* programme (CM).
[5]   The previous record holder was *Salad Days*.
[6]   774 performances. The Broadway production of *Oliver!* earned ten Tony nominations in 1963, winning three.
[7]   Milton Shulman, *Evening Standard* (1 July 1960); Kenneth Tynan (*Observer* 1960), quoted by Samantha Ellis, *Guardian*, 18 June 2003.

2,325-seat London Palladium; and that production came back again, to palatial Drury Lane, to rave reviews, in December 2008 (just in time for the Christmas pantomime market). All of these revivals and more radical 'resuscitations' were the work of a once lowly assistant stage manager, who had been struck with stage fright, going on as the pie man, by order, in the big production number 'Consider Yourself (at Home)', on tour in 1965 – Cameron Mackintosh, a principal 'alumnus of the *Oliver!* school of fame'.[8] His *Oliver!* revivals were a significant boost to his extraordinary career as 'The most successful, influential and powerful [theatrical] producer of our time',[9] arguably in theatre history. Four of his West End productions since his 1977 revival of *Oliver!* have broken the original show's record run: *Les Misérables* (1985, still running; conceived by composer-writer Alain Boublil during a performance of *Oliver!*),[10] *The Phantom of the Opera* (1986, still running), *Cats* (1981–2002), and *Miss Saigon* (1989–99).[11] This is an unprecedented 'industry' record, as Mackintosh's company web page reports; and the economic scale and artistic ambition of Mackintosh's (to date) over three hundred West End, Broadway and international productions have been recognised in awards that are pointers to key elements in the *Oliver!* phenomenon: the Queen's Award for Export Achievement, 1995; a knighthood for contributions to British Theatre, 1996; and the Enjoy England Award for Outstanding Contribution to Tourism, 2006.[12] There is probably no knowing how many millions have now seen touring or 'licensed' (and strictly quality-controlled) Mackintosh productions of *Oliver!* in Sweden, Estonia, Israel, the Czech Republic, Slovakia, and Japan. Book now for the United Kingdom tour, 2011–2013, urges the CM website, since 'You couldn't ask for more'.[13]

But there is always more. Any company that pours resources into a product must also protect its investment: and, in the teeth of public protest,

---

[8]   Mackintosh had also been stage-struck, aged thirteen, by the 'grittiness' and 'magic realism' of the original production (Clive Hirschhorn, 'A Twist in the tale', *Sunday Express* magazine (20 November 1994)).
[9]   *New York Times*, quoted on CM website.
[10]   Cameron Mackintosh, 'Reviewing the Situation', 1994 *Oliver!* souvenir programme (CM).
[11]   *Oliver!*'s record has been broken sixteen times since 1966.
[12]   Mackintosh owns seven West End theatres; his personal worth is estimated at more than £200m.
[13]   Cameron Mackintosh official *Oliver!* website <oliverthemusical.com>.

Cameron Mackintosh has exerted strenuous control over *Oliver!*[14] – with limited effect, however: even by 1977, as one critic put it, 'Reviewing . . . *Oliver!*' felt 'a bit like reviewing Niagara falls . . .: it is simply there'.[15] *Oliver!* remains a theatrical product, but it has also escaped company bounds, to become a *bona-fide* cultural phenomenon – a rite of childhood initiation, a focus of identity and aspiration, an apparently driven but in fact unstoppable train. Thus, lounging in her garden on a summer Sunday in 2010, one of the authors of this essay was subjected to a post-prandial full-throttle performance of the show by her intoxicated, but word-perfect, neighbours; walking round the Charles Dickens Museum, she overheard Spanish tourists singing along, lustily, to 'Consider Yourself'. (We pause here for full disclosure: Joss Marsh's father, Terence Marsh, split the design Oscar with John Box, for the 1968 film of *Oliver!*, and she has herself performed professionally as *Oliver!*'s repellent Widow Corney.) *Oliver!* investigations have turned up an LP produced in Mexico by aspiring English as a Second Language students; workhouse sequence quotations in Pink Floyd's *The Wall* (1982); and rap sampling of the ensemble thieves' song 'I'd Do Anything' (in the chorus to his 1999 song 'Anything', by Jay-Z). Revived, resuscitated, revamped, replayed in church hall after numberless church hall and school theatre after school theatre, reprised and re-rendered in song, replayed with fervour on YouTube, the *Oliver!* beat goes on.

The show's initial success was a surprise. The British musical had been theatrical poison since the days of Ivor Novello; and with no star names in the star parts, the 1960 production had no sure cards to play with the public. Twelve managements turned *Oliver!* down before Donald Albery, at the New Theatre, took a £15,000 risk;[16] the show promptly flopped in preview in Wimbledon. On West End opening night, when the massive triple revolve on which the staging depended hit a technical glitch, the author-composer sidled out of the theatre, to escape the misery, returning only to hear the thunder of cheers.

For another dimension of the *Oliver!* 'revolution' was its fulfilment and expansion of the musical as an art and entertainment form – a shift in

---

[14] See: 'West End rules force *Oliver!* off school stage', *The Independent* (31 January 1994); 'Ban is lifted on Olivers starring in school plays', *Evening Standard* (7 February 1994).

[15] *Guardian* (29 December 1977).

[16] A legendary chance-taker, Albery had previously risked *Waiting for Godot*, 'a damned dodgy play' (quoted in *Evening Standard* (17 January 1964)).

scale rather like that Dickens achieved in *Oliver Twist*. It was a 'miracu-
lous' musical 'that succeed[ed] on every level' (Kretzmer). In 1960, 'its
unbroken stream of exciting action' was directed with unprecedented
fluidity by musical newcomer Peter Coe, an artist grounded in radical
and classical theatre, with an edgy working-class background (Young).
Oliver! 'wrap[ped] up [the] complicated story of a small boy's odyssey . . .
with true economy and narrative skill' (Kretzmer 1). 'It [was] supremely
accomplished theatre music, whether it is covering crowd action to the
split second, incorporating pantomime inside a number (as in Fagin's lesson in picking pockets), or simply projecting character on a large scale'
(Wardle 5). More even than the first great 'book' musical, *Oklahoma!*
(Broadway 1943; filmed 1955), with its landmark choreography by Agnes
de Mille, *Oliver!* seamlessly integrated dialogue, dancing and action with
'a wealth of singable tunes': each song forwarded the plot, toured the
stage, enabled the spectacle, expressed the characters (Wardle 5). It was
designed with genius (see design notes below). As theatre critic Milton
Shulman put it, in 1960, the musical genre rose up to greet Dickens, in
Oliver! in part because 'The flamboyant theatricality of Dickens fits in
admirably with the florid and melodrama[tic] techniques of the musical'.
The boy who was once lifted onto a pub table to sing 'The Cat's Meat
Man' for his father's friends might not have been displeased.

The prime author of the *Oliver!* 'revolution' was a musical 'illiterate'
and Cockney Pied Piper by the name of Lionel Bart. Unable to write (or
read) a note of music, he had hummed the songs – like all his songs, an
apparently inexhaustible stream – into a tape recorder, with 'somebody
else' on hand to 'put the dots down on paper'.[17] His 'illiteracy' may have
enabled his genius, giving all his songs a vital sense of performance.

Initially trained as an artist (expelled from St Martin's School of Art
for 'mischievousness'), Bart had found work, after National Service, in
the left-wing Unity Theatre as a scene painter, poster designer and under-
study. He had also joined a skiffle group, The Cavemen, with Tommy
Steele, for whom he wrote his first pop hit, 'Rock with the Cavemen', in
1956. A string of chart climbers followed, each one packing dexterous
rhymes and lightning timing. Bart found his *métier* shortly after, when the

---

[17]   Bart interview with Kretzmer on the morning of *Oliver!* press night, 1960, as
quoted in programme notes for *It's a Fine Life!*, The Queen's Theatre, Hornchurch,
2008.

producer Joan Littlewood, a genius of the fringe, asked him to write the songs for her Stratford East show, *Fings Ain't Wot They Used T'Be*, 1959 – most of them in an intense two-week period immediately before opening, and one (which Bart himself performed, in the character of a busker) during the first-night interval. It became his first West End hit. *Oliver!* followed in 1960, and two further successes, *Blitz!*, in 1962, and *Maggie May*, set in Liverpool, in 1965. Bart's two backgrounds – commercial pop and radical theatre – had proved a heady brew.

Like Dickens, the self-made gentleman and instinctive actor who enjoyed his celebrity, and who persisted in social criticism despite the sneers of the intellectual *élite*, Bart was a walking epitome of the times in which he wrote, his life and various shortcomings the stuff of myth and mirth through the 1960s and 1970s.[18] The key theme was 'More!' (Franks 1994): more parties, more fun, more celebrities, more sex, more drugs, more drink, and more shows – including the greatest flop in British theatre history, Bart's satirical Robin Hood musical, *Twang!!*, in which he had sunk his own money, including the rights to *Oliver!* A millionaire at 30, who had filled his baroque Fulham 'Fun Palace' with up to 600 party people a night (the Beatles, the Stones, the victorious 1966 England World Cup team), with no head for business, and addicted to booze, by 1972 Bart was bankrupt. He moved to a flat in dismal Acton (conveniently positioned between two off-licences), paid in full, and kept drinking. In 1985 he was given two weeks to live, and the party finally stopped. A long, slow recovery followed, with a happy return to the limelight in 1994 at the hands of Cameron Mackintosh, who made a percentage for Bart the condition of his revival of *Oliver!* The press (especially the *Daily Mail*) revelled in every development. This was a life that incorporated all the plots: rags-to-riches, tragic humbling, comeback kid, celebrity confessional. (David Roper's so-called 'unauthorised' 1994 biography, *Bart!*, makes mean-spirited use of every one.) He died of cancer in 1999.

It is as easy to pick critical holes in Bart's *Oliver!* as it was to pillory its gifted and vulnerable creator. Like Bart, *Oliver!* lived intensely in its cultural moment. It smacks, for example, of the new consumer culture of the post-rationing, materialist generation of Britons who (as Prime Minister

---

[18] In 2006, Bart's biography was itself staged, with characters based on his mother and other 'real people' mixing with Fagin, Nancy, and Bill, in Chris Bond's Queen's Theatre production, *It's a Fine Life!*

Macmillan put it in 1957) had 'never had it so good': 'Who Will Buy (this Beautiful Morning)?' sings happy Oliver, from the balcony of Mr Brownlow's white stucco Bloomsbury townhouse. In this version of Dickens's angry novel, the hardest record of his childhood despair, everything, even an experience, can be bought: 'In this life, one thing counts: / In the bank – large amounts'. Little Oliver himself is the premium commodity – as Dickens had understood: in the film version, Mr Bumble commiserates with the boy, an unlucky slave in a slave world, as his price is pushed down, during the number 'Boy for Sale'; Mrs Sowerberry examines his teeth, like a horse, while her undertaker husband ponders the worth of his melancholy face; a carter delivers him to Covent Garden in a basket of cabbages; Dodger and Charley disguise him, during the 'Stop Thief!' sequence, as a side of Smithfield market meat.

Oliver! indulges in crime – or at least the imagining of it – with the same gusto as the Kray Brothers, 'Mad Frankie', and the Great Train Robbers – celebrity 1960s denizens, all, of Bart's native East End of London: 'You'd Better Pick a Pocket or Two'. No-one is so feared or so respected as *Oliver!*'s greatest thief, Bill Sikes, whose name is all-powerful, taboo, a kind of swear word: 'Nobody Mentions – My Name.'

Like Bart's own hit pop songs (the number one he dashed off in ten minutes for teen idol Cliff Richard, for example: 'Living Doll', 1959), *Oliver!* exults in the pop/rock era's juvenilisation of culture. In this, you might say it makes good on Graham Greene's not entirely unfair description of Dickens's novel as 'magnificent juvenilia' (427). Some of the musical's interpreters have passed beyond juvenilisation, to making hay of the paedophilic promise of Oliver's angelic face. Director Carol Reed, for example: he stages 'I'd Do Anything' around a half-naked Oliver, caught – like an instinctively good bourgeois boy – washing himself at the tub. (There are several porn versions of *Oliver!*, but we draw a veil over these.) One of the most inspired moments in the show's production history was probably the casting of the gravel-voiced pop 'child prodigy of the early 1960s' as Nancy, in 1979: Helen Shapiro, who had headlined (with the Beatles as back-up) at age fourteen, but was left behind with the 1950s by age nineteen.[19] The world *Oliver!* imagines is one where the greatest horror is not sin or crime or the Workhouse, but getting old: 'I'm reviewing the situation', sings Fagin, voice cracking with fear – 'What happens when I'm seventy?'

---

[19]   *Doncaster Evening Post* (22 November 1979).

Like Bart's own life, *Oliver!* was a performance always threatening, or pretending, to descend into a 1960s party. One of its show-stoppers thematises both the threat and the pretence, Nancy's 'Oom-Pah-Pah' – a 'happening' manufactured to allow her to abstract little Oliver from the Three Cripples pub, under Bill's very nose. (As Georgia Brown sang it in 1960, the song put *risqué* 'oomph' into the onomatopoeic brass-band sound 'oom-pah-pah'.) The London that welcomes Oliver, in the great production number 'Consider Yourself at Home', Bart's love-song to the city, may be recognisable, more or less, as Victorian. But it is also, always, the 'Swinging London' of once-*declassé*, now-hip locations like fashion-centre Carnaby Street.

Indeed, *Oliver!* was itself part of the 1960s fashion explosion: its affection for 'These trappings, these tatters, / These we can just afford' (Nancy's tarty outfit), even its liking for dirt, pronounce the fashion statement of the era: defiance of convention, modesty and class constraints. Recreating the costumes of the original production for the 1977 revival at the Haymarket, Leicester, designer Irene Wilton redrew them, with detailed notes on condition, materials, accessories and colour that reveal both how the retro-Victorian *Oliver!* look could be manufactured on a tight budget, and how invested that look always already was in the fashion mores of the show's era: 'ragged', 'filthy', 'dirty', 'blotchy', 'old'; 'cord', 'crimplene', 'vyella', 'rayon', 'paisley' and 'Liberty' prints; 'ribbons', 'reticules', 'frilly' under-skirts, 'black velvet chokers' (a 'tart' must-have, and always a part of Nancy's costume, separating maternal mind from tarty body), 'button boots' (for both 'ladies' and 'tarts'), 'hob-nailed boots' (for the heavy feet of Bill Sikes and the Dodger, who thus literally follows in his criminal footsteps), and 'elastic-sided boots' (for the subordinate men and boys); 'dusty pink', 'sage green', 'nut brown' and 'sky blue' (for Oliver's Bloomsbury sailor suit). Like Columbia Pictures' ideal child consumers, the Workhouse boys wore 'grey wool waistcoat[s] with cotton fine striped back[s]' – entirely without historical foundation, but handy for cocking your cheeky thumbs, in the style of Stanley Holloway in *My Fair Lady* (Broadway 1956, West End 1958, an evident inspiration for *Oliver!*), or (more mockney than cockney) Dick Van Dyke in the film *Mary Poppins* (1964). (Waistcoats made a big fashion comeback in the 1970s.) Bill Sikes's all-male, dirt-brown, huntsman look, as worn by Danny Sewell, the ex-boxer who originated the stage role, and by hulking Oliver Reed in the film, is still regularly referenced by fashion commentators: 'dirty tan suede breeches, with leather cuffs' and 'beige leather jerkin with 1" horn buttons (one missing)', both cut to maximise Bill's animal presence, and set off by an 'off-white silk scarf' and 'tan topper'.[20] Reimagining the show in 1994 (as what the commentator Tamasin Doe called a 'scruffian' 'fashionfest'), the designer Anthony Ward, who had worked in opera, made exuberant use of bolder colours: tart red for Nancy, with corseting that presented her breasts like 'two blancmanges on soup spoons' (Doe 36);[21] heavenly blue for Oliver (in another Fauntleroy sailor suit); magician's purple for Fagin, in a gentle- man's distressed dressing gown, a costume choice that underlined the themes of class usurpation, parody and carnival reversal expressed in Dickens's original descriptions – most famously, of Dodger's ill-fitting tenth-hand ex-gent's togs. Accessories like Fagin's pointed Moroccan slippers, and gang-members' pirate head-scarves, ponchos and amulets cemented the 1990s *Oliver!* look of eclectic diversity. On 30 June 2011, a Google search for the phrase 'clothes, glorious clothes' turned up 8,480 results.

But what an extraordinary show *Oliver!* was! It burst on to the London stage in 1960 with the full force of new freedoms behind it. The free- dom to protest, against everything. The freedom to say to life and society 'Please, sir, I want some more'.

More sexual freedom ('Oom-Pah-Pah'), especially for women: 'Let the prudes look down on us', Nancy sings; 'It's a fine, fine life!' She was, at her first creation, Dickens's greatest risk: an unspeakable character who speaks up for her own desire ('I wish to go back . . . I must go back' (Dick- ens 325)).[22] The central critical problem of the musical is its apparent embrace of her masochism: it is a punch in the face that triggers Nancy's show-stopper torch song, 'As Long as He Needs Me'. Its doormat logic was celebrated by the pop culture of the period: Shirley Bassey spent almost eight months in the United Kingdom charts with the ballad in 1960, peak- ing at number two; in America, Judy Garland (a close friend of Bart's, and his pick for the film Nancy) sang it live, with feeling, on her TV show in 1964. It enjoys continuing karaoke and YouTube popularity.

---

[20] Notes to drawings by Irene Wilton (CM).
[21] Quoting actress Sally Dexter.
[22] Nancy to Rose Maylie, *Oliver Twist*, ch. 40. In the musical: 'I've got to go back. I want to go back.'

Freedom from class oppression: *Oliver!* wears its cockney cachet with pride. Middle-class Mr Brownlow is the only character in the show who does not sing. It's the Dodger who has the keys of swinging Victorian London: 'Consider Yourself – At Home!' In musicals, nothing is so much valued as performance; in *Oliver!*, nothing else is so much valued as play. So Nancy, improvising 'Oom-pah-pah', Fagin, pantomiming the picking of pockets, and Dodger, taking the mick out of toffs, rise to the top of the musical tree. The show's other bravura production number, 'Who Will Buy?' is a choreographer's full-chorus fantasy of bottom-up social harmony. 'I read a book about Charles Dickens' life', Bart recalled in 1994,[23] 'and how he had a hard time finding love. So when I started to write the musical, I began with that. The song "Where is Love?" . . . was the premise of the whole thing'. In *Oliver!*, love is everywhere – even in Fagin's den.

When *Oliver!* demanded the creative freedom to get inside a Victorian 'classic', and recover its restless inventiveness, it demanded above all the freedom to redeem 'the Jew', to find the theatrical magic under the dirt and demonic red hair. It was always there, though Dickens's Fagin really is the child-killer of medieval prejudice. In *Oliver!*, monster becomes trickster ('Just a game, Oliver, just a game'), child-exploiter becomes caring mentor ('Be Back Soon'), social enemy becomes carnival master of ceremony ('Shut up and drink your gin').

Bart's motive was straightforward: he was born, in 1930, not Lionel Bart but Lionel Begleiter, the youngest of seven surviving children of a family who had fled the pogroms of Eastern Europe. (The new monicker was inspired by a bus-ride past St Bartholomew's ('Bart's') Hospital.) His father was a tailor, who wanted only for his son that he should grow up a 'mensch'. For Bart, Dickens's evil Fagin was 'unreal, a comic-strip character'. He 'enlarged on something that was already there in Dickens – his ability to play' (Nathan 33): *Oliver!* indeed 'derive[s] much of its energy from being a Jewish rewriting of *Oliver Twist*' (Gross). The role made a star of its brilliant Jewish originator, Ron Moody. And it demanded a search for headline star after headline star, an apostolic succession of Fagins, each of whom – as the stage demands – worked a different creation: Roy Hudd (1977), a Butlin's and TV-trained comedian, with a passion for music hall, who introduced some delightful 'business', though he over-sanitised the character, like picking his own pocket with an errant left

---

[23]   The 'book' was presumably Edgar Johnson's Freudian biography of 1952.

hand;[24] the classical actor Jonathan Pryce (1994), whose 'new age traveler of a Fagin' was a reflective figure of tragic-comedy ('I'm Reviewing the Situation') (Klein 21); the quick-silver comedian Rowan Atkinson, aka Blackadder and Mr Bean (2008), who had once played the role in a school production, and made great improvisational play with the treasure box and its contents. Fagin's face, not Oliver's, was the natural logo of the 1994 and 2008 Cameron Mackintosh revivals: the eyes, gigantic nose, and cauliflower ear spelling out the title, *Oliver!*

The theatrical 'revolution' that was Bart's *Oliver!*, had a second original instigator, however – Bart's 1960 collaborator, the visionary designer Sean Kenny. Thirty years old, he had trained as an architect, both in his native Ireland and in Arizona, under Frank Lloyd Wright, and came to theatre fresh – by chance, only two years before – with an architect's capacity to think 'in three-dimensional and kinetic terms about how to fill theatrical space' (Anon. 1973: 18).[25] Like a good revolutionist, Kenny openly nailed his manifestos to the West End's stage doors. 'Let us rebel, fight, break down, invent and reconstruct a new theatre. Let us destroy and liberate'.[26] 'The only thing to do is to go down to the basement and, with a bloody great bomb, blow the lot sky high.'[27] (For the finale of *Blitz!*, in 1962, Kenny actually dropped it – and a three-story building collapsed towards the audience. 'A great many people are simply terrified', he remarked to an interviewer, 'with apparent satisfaction' (Eichelbaum).

Kenny began work with Bart before a word was written. The result was perhaps the single most significant piece of stage design in the twentieth century, 'an integral part of the way the show worked', remembered 1994 designer Anthony Ward, 'embedded in the way it was written':[28] a revolving mass (4,000 linear feet) of wooden beams on a steel triple turntable

[24] The Music Hall qualities of the show were also recognised by 1994 choreographer Matthew Bourne, who gave Fagin and his gang some 'wonderful traditional steps' in 'Be Back Soon' (Macaulay).
[25] Kenny assisted Wright 'in the creation of the epoch-making Guggenheim Gallery' (*Daily Express* obituary (12 June 1973)). He designed 23 major shows in ten years, 1960–70, as well as the Gryoton, 'a huge thrill ride for Expo '67 in Canada' and a 'mechanised, multi-layer stage for a Las Vegas nightspot' (*Times* obituary). He died, of a heart attack, at 42.
[26] Kenny essay for Mermaid Theatre souvenir book, quoted in *Times* obituary (12 June 1973).
[27] Sean Kenny, 'Set Theatre Free!' unidentified cutting [1973] (CM).
[28] Anthony Ward, quoted in section 'The Design Challenge', 1994 souvenir Brochure (CM).

that, like a mobile jigsaw (a 'uniquely suggestive geometric abstraction' (Eichelbaum) of 'kaleidoscopic ingenuity' (Billington)), came apart, swung together and turned to create, before the audience's eyes, as part of the spectacle: the miserable Workhouse, with staircases to left and right, down which marched the regiment of pauper children (the action taken, literally, to multiple levels); the undertaker's shop ('Coffins In', reads the stage manager's cue sheet);[29] the streets of London, alive with pie men, peelers, hawkers, laundry-women, street performers; the Thieves' Kitchen, Fagin's anarchic empire, with sly visual suggestions of portcullis and scaffold; an airy Bloomsbury square; the Three Cripples pub and song cellar; and (most impressively) London Bridge by night, complete with dry-ice fog and the suggestion of night skies and gas light (one of the features that made *Oliver!*'s lighting plot exceptionally 'tricky').[30] (The plot also required follow-spots with delicate dimmer settings, to help audiences pick the show's stars from the settings into which they were so organically integrated, without quite knowing how they were doing it.) 'Trucks', wheeled in from left and right, supplied other elements of the set: Kenny called their movement 'choreography' (Smith). A drear perspective of London rooftops was painted directly onto the stage's back wall. Kenny's design supplied and created the darkness lacking in Bart's adaptation. It was 'so spectacular', one critic remarked, 'You come out humming the sets'.[31]

Kenny was the architect as designer, unshackled by theatrical tradition. But he was also a child of cinema, the ubiquitous art form of the twentieth century. Audiences want 'spectacle on a continuous level. They are no longer content to sit through obviously devised sequences before a drop curtain while hordes of people rush about building a new set behind it'(Smith). A theatrical spectacle 'should run through' without break, '[like] a film'.[32] Peter Coe, *Oliver!*'s original director, who grew up with no access to theatre, 'inspired' rather by cinema,[33] directed *Oliver!*, as Bart had written it, 'with the sort of fluidity and elisions familiar in the

[29] 'Flying Cues' sheet, Haymarket Leicester production, 1977 (CM).
[30] Donald Albery, interview in *TABS* (September 1973), p. 92.
[31] Obituary, *Daily Express* (12 June 1973).
[32] Kenny manifesto, quoted in programme notes for *It's a Fine Life!* His later work included a remarkable 1968 Mermaid Theatre version of *Gulliver's Travels* that using film projections to create giant illusions of scale.
[33] 1960 programme note (CM).

cinema, rare on the stage'.[34] Anthony Ward and Sam Mendes followed cinematic suit in 1994, producing (for example) a chase sequence during which Oliver ran on the spot (courtesy of a roller), while London apparently revolved around him, like a concrete realisation of back projection. 'Forever changing perspective', wrote one critic, Ward's sets 'move[d] with the fluidity of mercury' – or film.[35]

If *Oliver!*'s first creators were in formal terms most influenced by cinema, they were also inspired by a particular film: David Lean's 1948 *Oliver Twist*, one of the masterworks of the decade *mirabilis* of British cinema, the 1940s, an anti-Semitic failure in historical tact, but a marvel of immersive design by the brilliant John Bryan, who had won the Oscar for his work on Lean's 1946 *Great Expectations*. (We use the word 'inspired' advisedly. The film's scene of the 'curious' pick-pocketing 'game', directed by Lean as a 'ballet', the only scene in which Alec Guinness's Fagin is purely and joyfully playful, addresses itself directly to the audience, in performative musical style: it was surely an invitation to Bart's adaptation, and thus to the modern phenomenon of the stage musical based on a film – from Lloyd Webber's *Sunset Boulevard* to *Shrek the Musical*, which moved into Drury Lane when *Oliver!* closed on 8 January 2011.)

Bryan created the 1948 film's ultra-realistic illusion of entrapment in a nightmare city through trick perspective, low-ceilinged sets and intensely researched detail, right down to the *minutiae* of 'How the Dodger strikes a light' for his clay pipe.[36] The 1948 *Oliver Twist* announces itself in *Oliver!* in such bravura touches as the cynical notice that dominates the Workhouse hall, 'God is Love', based on an image in the *Illustrated London News*, and the bridge between crumbling warehouses that Oliver crosses, like a bridge between worlds, while St Paul's looms behind, to reach Fagin's den, derived by Bryan from a haunting image in the black-and-white artist Gustave Doré's *London: A Pilgrimage* (1872). The 1968 film design team did not exactly replicate the Doré bridge (though they kept the concept), but turned to him explicitly in their re-creation of Holborn Viaduct and the steam train by which Oliver is nearly mown down (*Oliver Twist* meeting *Perils of Pauline*) – while St Paul's sits atop the film's very opening

---

[34]   *London Life* (9 December 1966).
[35]   Clive Hirschhorn, 'Oliver leaves you wanting much more', unidentified cutting (CM).
[36]   Bryan team research notes, Joss Marsh collection.

titles, like a crown.[37] In 1994, in their turn, perhaps in an effort to duck the shadow of the 1968 film, Ward and Mendes soaked themselves in Lean and Bryan's 'brilliantly atmospheric' and 'magical' 1948 creation.[38] The soaking redoubled *Oliver!*'s emphasis on London, epitomised by St Paul's: while the crowded, kinetic drawings of Dickens's contemporary, George Scharf, were another Ward inspiration to realising 'the most detailed depiction of early 19th-century London that you are ever likely to see on stage' (Paton 45),[39] the depiction was repeatedly capped by con-crete moving images of St Paul's. So the cycle of Twisted influence comes round: no 'new version' either of *Oliver Twist* or of *Oliver!* can step fully aside from the vibrant and complex tradition of Dickensian adaptation. And all versions contribute to the building, in the minds of audiences, of an ever more detailed sense of the 'real' Dickens 'world' of *Oliver Twist*, in which they might like 'really' to wander. And thus key dimensions of the *Oliver!* phenomenon: its invitation to tourism, its celebration of British-ness and its remembrance of the Second World War.

Bart's 'greatest ambition', he declared in 1961, was to write 'a full scale English Folk Opera based on the life of London's East End during the air raids of World War II'.[40] *Blitz!* was the result, in 1962. But *Oliver!*, as much as *Blitz!*, grew out of Bart's childhood experience of wartime Lon-don: the dangers (exemplified by Kenny's 'bomb' and the violent climax of *Oliver!*), but also the relaxing of old social rules, the spirit of endurance ('London Can Take It!', as the title of Humphrey Jennings's documentary exclaimed in 1940), indelibly symbolised by St Paul's cathedral (which survived the bombs, while the buildings around it perished), and the extraordinary sense of community: 'Consider Yourself One of the Fam-ily!' Bart's up-to-date sixties *Oliver!* was also a classic product of British nostalgia.

It was also a prime instance of that modern semantic slippage whereby Dickens = London = Victorian = England. (The film version spiked up the theme, stringing Fagin's den with Union Jacks – and saluting them.) *Oklahoma!* had gained its status as America's best-loved musical not only for its memorable songs, brisk narration and ground-breaking

---

[37]   Information supplied by Terence Marsh.
[38]   Ward and Mendes, quoted in 1994 programme notes.
[39]   Scharf was the major design source for Christine Edzard's 1987 film *Little Dorrit*.
[40]   1961 *Oliver!* programme note (CM).

choreography, but because it wrapped up key elements in national mythology: the cowboy figure, the movement West, the pioneer spirit. *Oliver!* offered a similarly seductive mix, and its original audiences understood the gift. 'A British musical at last that will and must charm audiences all over the world', proclaimed the *Daily Mail*; 'Resounding uproarious cheers for a British musical' roared the *Daily Sketch*.[41] *Oliver!* 'conquered' Broadway in 1963, and its British spirit has gone on (in warlike theatrical metaphor) 'triumphantly' ever since (Kretzmer). What it projects abroad (most recently in China) is not so much the vulgarity, violence and thieving propensities of its characters as a condensation of British national mythology: it is a formidable economic and cultural export. And the 'mechanised', 'monster' – and *British* musical – to which it gave birth is 'the most formidable commercial force in world theatre' – as exportable, 'cloned and franchised', as 'a McDonald's hamburger', as 'formidable' as a corp of 'panzers' parked on America's theatrical lawns: 'the occupation is total'.[42]

Dickens, Bart, Lean, Bryan, Kenny and Ward all realised *Oliver!* as a 'love song to London', and the show has proved (as one journalist remarked in 1994) literally a 'gift' to the city's extended 'tourist trade' (Macaulay):[43] *Oliver!* exists now not only as an export, but off-stage, off-screen, as a British tourist attraction. Inside 'Dickens World', a monstrosity manufactured in a suburban shopping centre in Chatham, Kent (the management of which the editor of this volume inadvertently offended by her 'Reflections' in the *Dickensian*) fans can indeed wander *Oliver!*'s dark and winding streets. While they are there, they can eat sausages in the Six Jolly Fellowship Porters pub, empty their purses in Peerybingle's Pawnbrokers, take the *Great Expectations* boat ride, and perform in *Oliver Twist* – a twice-daily interactive 'show' derived from *Oliver!* (carefully, with an eye on copyright). In Dickens World's Britannia Theatre they meet a robotic Dickens, who coexists there in the same space and time as his characters Sam Weller, Samuel Pickwick, Fagin and the Artful Dodger (who is heard, periodically, picking an i-phone in the dress circle). The Dickens World idea is not original: it

[41] Original 1960 New Theatre production reviews, quoted in 1962 programme (CM).
[42] 'Last week more than 40% of theatre income in America came from Lloyd Webber works' (Fowler).
[43] The *Daily Telegraph* described the show on 9 October 1995 as 'more of a tourist attraction than a musical'. Exactly so.

dates back to nineteenth-century stage adaptations, which revelled in the London settings and sought actively to realise Cruikshank's illustrations in theatrical three dimensions, to Charley Dickens Jnr's *Dictionary of London* (1879), to the 'Dickensland' constructed (long before there was Disneyland) in guidebooks, illustrations, photographs and magic-lantern slides in the decades just after Dickens's death. In the new 'Spirit of London' exhibit in Madame Tussaud's tourists can similarly have their pictures taken with the four most recognisable Victorian celebrities – Queen Victoria, Charles Dickens, the Dodger and Fagin, against a three-dimensional backdrop: a souvenir that combines the past and present, fiction and history. In 2009, the Cameron Mackintosh website invited fans to take the 'Oliver London Walking Tour', with headset commentary by Fagin (Russ Abbot) and Dodger (Archie Duffy) to transform the One Tun Pub into 'The Three Cripples' and make listeners' flesh creep with fear of pickpockets as they reached Saffron Hill.

These are 'family' attractions. *Oliver!* began life as a revolutionary show with sexual and social 'attitude', along with troops of crowd-pleasing kids (and a performing dog). In 1977, it returned as pantomime – a childhood Christmas treat. In the 1990s and 2000s, as it sought out new and thus necessarily always younger audiences, it morphed into a show pitched directly to children, in which the numbers of children proliferated – most notably the tiny new character 'Nipper', a sub-Oliver-sized little chappie who 'shadows' Fagin. This was 'juvenilisation' become 'infantilisation', though the child-centred *Oliver!* does ravel out a true Dickensian thread: Oliver may not always feature very brightly in *Oliver Twist*, but it was the first significant novel to feature a child at its centre.

New Theatre casting criteria had always stipulated that Oliver should be diminutive, blonde, innocent-looking and soprano, and successive Olivers through the 1960s had got smaller and smaller ('Oliver No. 9', reported the *Daily Mail* on 9 February 1965: 'Heading for the pint-size record!'): Nipper's addition was perhaps inevitable. All child actors are restricted to a total of eighty-five performances (forty, in the Greater London Council area in the 1960s), with a maximum of two performances a week, and 'child artists age quickly in terms of vocal suitability for *Oliver!*' (Albery 88),[44] so that it was also inevitable that *Oliver!* should develop a child production line: 700 Olivers performed during the New Theatre

---

[44]   Donald Albery, interviewed at the time of the 1973 Tokyo production.

run; about 3,000 children auditioned for roles in 1994. The auditions were open and public – often, claims David Roper, held 'for the exclusive benefit of press photographers' (41). They created excitement, but also a haphazard tradition which harks back to the melodramatic and fairy-tale logic of *Oliver Twist* itself: Who is the chosen child? Who will be the gentleman – or the star? Middle-brow newspaper readers heard lines of hopeful children pleading 'Please sir, can I play the lead in *Oliver!*', and lost their hearts to the 'Stars in their eyes'.[45] Local papers congratulated every hometown boy who nabbed a part.[46] (There was a recurrent sub-theme: local boy hits West End big-time 'just months after being thrown out of the parish choir'.)[47] Some papers even commiserated with those who failed to make the cut.[48] The auditions were an integral part of the off-stage *Oliver!* show. Sean Kenny's triple revolve had turned invisible hands into active performers, and made the hidden work of theatre part of the performance. But turning auditions into public spectacle most dra-matically extended the audience's engagement with the show. It is no wonder, then, that in 2008 Cameron Mackintosh allowed the BBC to turn it into – what it had always been – a TV talent and reality show. It was a highly profitable post-modern twist.[49]

I'd Do Anything was commissioned after the success of *How Do You Solve a Problem like Maria?* (in casting the Mackintosh stage production of *The Sound of Music*, 2006) and *Any Dream Will Do* (which found the Joseph of the 2007 *Joseph and the Amazing Technicolor Dreamcoat*). Its judging panel consisted of John Barrowman, 'an Entertainer with a capital

[45]   Headlines, *Daily Express* (8 April 1994) and *The Voice* (23 August 1994).
[46]   'Theatre-mad schoolboy Steven Milton', a former Charlie Bates, 'considers himself very artful in getting picked for a star part' (the Dodger) reported the *South East London and Kentish Mercury* on 7 September 1978; 'A review of the situation and it was decided a fellow can't be a minor villain all his life'. 'Consider yourself a star Tom Bryden', crowed the *Hastings and St. Leonards Observer* (23 September 1994). 'I watched the film Oliver! when I was six', Gregory, of Eign Road, Hereford, told the *Western Daily Press*, 'and that was when I knew I wanted to be an actor' (undated cutting (CM)).
[47]   'Why?' the *Surrey Daily Advertiser* asked Paul Hawkins, ten on 18 September 1978. 'I was purposely singing the wrong words'.
[48]   See, for example, an *Essex Evening Gazette* piece on 'unlucky' Tommy Bartlett (16 September 1994).
[49]   There were a large number of talent-show winners among earlier stars, among them the first Oliver, Keith Hamshere (1960 programme note), and Gillian Burns, the Nancy of 1977, who was an ATV *New Faces* winner.

E' ('He sings, he dances, he acts, he presents, he judges');[50] actress and
TV presenter Denise Van Outen; 'Oz' comedian Barry Humphries, aka
Dame Edna, a former Fagin (1967, promoted from Mr Sowerberry, the
role he originated in 1960);[51] and 'monster'-musical overlord Andrew
Lloyd Webber, who presided as chairman. Their mission was not only to
evaluate but also to devise 'missions' and 'tasks' for the potential Nancys
and Olivers. The final vote on who should play Nancy, however, went
to the audience. By turning audiences into director-producers, privileged
to make production decisions and go behind the scenes (the watching
and voting audience) and into actors who could become characters (the
talent-show candidates), *I'd Do Anything* created a performance phenomenon that blended consumption and production, fiction and reality,
stage and street.

Lloyd Webber wanted a 'gritty' Nancy who 'is a girl of the street and
yet . . . ha[s] a heart of gold underneath it all' (Mackintosh). He urged
women who had 'lived a little bit', from diverse and working-class backgrounds, to compete in the show: debt collectors, newspaper saleswomen,
telephone operators (*I'd Do Anything*, 2008). These became – probably
already were – the audience's criteria in voting. Each week, Graham Norton, as host, revealed which candidate they had eliminated, by telling her:
'You're not Nancy.' The dismissal was not necessarily a judgement on her
acting or singing ability; it was a comment on her identity. The 'missions'
and 'tasks' also reflected the show's blurred distinction between performer
and character. The Olivers had to prove they had his 'character of steel'
by playing soccer and abseiling (Mackintosh) . The Nancys not only had
to demonstrate the strength to 'sustain the performance' by rowing and
handling rats, but had to plunge into the work of an East End market, and
to negotiate an 'authentic' Victorian house (Mackintosh).

Music dominated the show, of course. Every week the Olivers and
Nancys performed at least one of Bart's songs, usually as a group. As indi-
vidual challenges the Nancys belted out pop hits like 'Respect', 'I'm Every
Woman', 'Killing Me Softly with his Song', and 'The Lady is a Tramp'.
The combination highlighted the continuing relevance of Bart's songs, a
reason for their phenomenal popularity. They were always both of their

[50]   John Barrowman official website <http://www.johnbarrowman.com>.
[51]   Humphries was so effective in rehearsal Bart added his creepy number,
'That's Your Funeral'.

time and out of time, a mix of Yiddish patter, 'old melodies . . . heard at
bar mitzvahs' (Franks), English folk music, renaissance madrigal ('Boy for
Sale'), Viennese waltzes and brass-band marches, music hall, public-house
floor song, Tin Pan Alley, Broadway show tune and pop music. The singing challenges recognised the melting-pot quality of his music, as had fifty
years of *Oliver!* newspaper headlines: 'You Can't Ask for Anything More'
(recalling Gershwin's 'I've Got Rhythm), 'Let's Twist Again' (invoking
Chubby Checker's hit single), et cetera.[52]

I'd Do Anything also reimagined Bart's lyrics as direct communications
between contestants and audience. The title of the show dropped the
explanatory tag phrase in the song's title – 'I'd Do Anything *(for You,
Dear)*', turning a sentimental declaration into an expression of commit-
ment to win: the song played during the opening credits, while a pride
of Nancys fought to grab the locket that would identify the true Nancy
(a strange but apt theatrical transmogrification of Agnes's locket, which
once identified Oliver). The closing of each show created conciliatory
goodbyes between the survivors and the week's defeated contestant.
'Cheerio, but be back soon: / Give me one long last look, / God bless you!
/ Remember our old tune, / Be Back Soon!': the lines assured the unlucky
non-Nancy she would have a future on stage. Then she sang: 'As long as
he needs me, / Oh yes, he does need me, / In spite of what you see, / I'm
sure that he needs me'. The pronouns often took on defiant resonance:
'he' was Cameron Mackintosh, and 'you' the voting audience, who had
made the wrong choice.

Just as the 'Sparkler of Albion' once redefined celebrity for the Victorian era, and the characters he created provided 'cast-iron' roles for
star after star – Irving as Jingle, Martin-Harvey as Sydney Carton, Harry
Secombe as Pickwick – so the new-born stars of this new iteration of *Oliver!*
instigated a new expression of fame and fan investment. The *Telegraph*
reported from the West End in 2009 that 'it was Jodie Prenger, the winner
of the BBC talent show *I'd Do Anything* who was exciting most interest
among the first night audience'.[53] Everyone wanted to see 'the people's
Nancy'; her character took on new significance, even overshadowing

---

[52] Georgia Brown, the original Nancy, included a 'straight' recording of 'As
Long as He Needs Me' on her solo album of 1963, mixing it in with standard hits.
[53] *Telegraph* 15 January 2009.

Fagin.[54] The TV show turned the 2008 production into a still more massive commercial success than it might otherwise have been.

Oliver! survives also, however, as a Dickensian gift of pleasure to amateurs and regular folks. 'Half the people in Britain have either seen it or been in it', said Mackintosh in 1994 (Gritten). On the first day of rehearsals for his production for that year, Bart was surprised when 'the entire company, the kids, the musicians, assistants, technicians and production staff' launched into a sing-along: 'And everyone knew all the songs!' (Bart). The lyrics have become English vocabulary, the tunes hardwired into consciousness: when Carrie Sickmann shouted 'Be Back Soon' to a friend one afternoon, she heard 'Bye Dodger!' in response; humming 'Consider Yourself', at a market, Joss Marsh startled a local horticulturist into memories of playing Oliver, aged twelve, in a high-school production, terrified of the big boys ('Like Dodger?' 'Oh yes – he went wild'). Every friend, acquaintance, and total stranger we have told about our *Oliver!* research has immediately launched into song (usually 'Food, Glorious Food'). It has all given us more fodder for this critical 'love-song' to *Oliver!*

Works cited

Albery, Donald, 1973. *TABS* (September): 88–93.

[Anon.], 1973. 'Obituary: Sean Kenny', *Times* (12 June): 18.

Bart, Lionel, 1994. 'One of the Worldwide Family', Cameron Mackintosh Souvenir Brochure. London: Dewynters.

Billington, Michael, 1977. 'Oliver', *Guardian* (29 December): 29.

Brownlow, Kevin, 1996. *David Lean: A Biography*. New York: St. Martin's Press.

Davis, Paul, 1990. *The Lives and Times of Ebenezer Scrooge*. New Haven: Yale University Press.

Dickens, Charles, 1999. *Oliver Twist*. ed. Kathleen Tillotson. Oxford: Oxford University Press. Originally published in Bentley's Miscellany, 1837–9.

Doe, Tamasin, 1994. 'Dressed up for Dirty Dancing' , *Evening Standard* (22 December): 36.

Eichelbaum, Stanley, 1962. 'Sean Kenny Sets the Stage', *Theatre Arts* (USA) (December): 19–20.

---

[54]   Prenger shared the role with Australian Tamsin Carroll, who performed twice a week; she was built up, before her debut, by a stretch in *Les Misérables*. Nancy was understudied by a runner-up on *I'd do Anything*, Sarah Lark.

Fowler, Rebecca, 1994. 'Begging for More', *Sunday Times* (11 December): 14.

Franks, Alan, 1994. 'The Man Who Asked for More', *The Times Magazine* (10 December): 32–5.

Greene, Graham, 1992. 'The Young Dickens', in *Oliver Twist*, ed. Fred Kaplan. New York: Norton & Co., pp. 426–32.

Gritten, David, 1994. 'The Return of *Oliver!*', *Daily Telegraph* magazine (3 December): 32–7.

Gross, John, 1994. 'The Dickens of a Christmas', *Sunday Telegraph* Review (11 December): 6.

I'd Do Anything, 2008. Episode no. 1, first broadcast 29 March by BBC. Presented by Graham Norton and Andrew Lloyd Webber.

John, Juliet, 2008. '"People mutht be amuthed?" Reflections on Chatham's 'Dickens World', *Dickensian*, 104 (2008): 5–21.

John, Juliet, 2010. *Dickens and Mass Culture*. Oxford: Oxford University Press.

Johnson, Edgar, 1952. *Charles Dickens: His Tragedy and Triumph*. New York: Simon and Schuster.

Klein, Reva, 1994. *Times Educational Supplement* (25 December): 21.

Kretzmer, Herbert, 1977. 'Oliver asks for more full houses', *Daily Express* (31 December): 20.

Macaulay, Alastair, 1994. 'An Oliver! for the Nineties', *Financial Times* (10 December): xix.

Mackintosh, Cameron, 2007. 'About the Show' (October), *I'd Do Anything*. BBC One. <http://www.bbc.co.uk/oliver/about>.

Nathan, David, 1994. 'The Devil in Dickens', *Jewish Chronicle* (2 December): 33.

Paton, Maureen, 1994 'Cameron's £3.5 m Gamble is a Dickens of a Big Hit', *Daily Express* (9 December): 45.

Roper, David, 1994. *Bart! The Unauthorized Life and Times, Ins and Outs, Ups and Downs of Lionel Bart.* London: Pavilion Books.

Shulman, Milton. 1960. 'This one could start an avalanche!', *Evening Standard* (1 July): 12.

Smith, Lisa Gordon, 1962. 'Further Thought on "Blitz!"', *Stage and Television Today* (31 May): 15.

Wardle, Irving, 1977. 'Oliver!' *The Times* (29 December): 5.

Young, B.A., 1977. 'Oliver!', *Financial Times* (30 December): 3.

'Wow! She's a lesbian. Got to be!': re-reading/ re-viewing Dickens and neo-Victorianism on the BBC

KIM EDWARDS KEATES

> Then there are the lesbians. What, you don't remember them in
> Dickens? You weren't paying enough attention. (Moreton, 2008)[1]

'I'M A BIG DICKENS FAN', confessed Sarah Waters in an interview; 'His pre-
occupations [. . .] with class, with desire, with guilt, and with the gothic
traumas of maturation and love – still seem enormously resonant to me'
(Waters, quoted by Pete Bailey). Speaking as a neo-Victorian novelist,
the 'resonance' that Waters has in mind invokes a reverberating movement, a conceptual shifting backwards and forwards between Victorian
and post-modern periods and values that engenders a proximity of feeling
to the frustrated and unresolved intimacies of Dickens's fiction. It has
been in her re-readings of Dickens and rewritings of the Victorian past
that Waters has taken the focus of a queer, revisionist lens through which
to reconsider the sexually subversive tensions and suppressed homosexual
identities that discreetly exist within the nineteenth-century literary text,
popularly recasting Waters as the 'lesbian Charles Dickens', in the phrase
of *Kirkus Reviews* ([Anon.]). This process of (re)presenting thwarted
lesbian desire has proved to be hugely popular as well as radical, having
succeeded, according to Kate Mitchell, in 'silently' inserting 'nineteenth-
century female homosexuality into our cultural memory of Victorian
fiction' (118). If this is so, then Waters's fiction has opened up an important, transitional interpretative space, through which understandings of
homosexuality in the Victorian era can be interrogated and explored, new

---

[1] The quotation in my title is from Andrew Davies in the interview with Cole
Moreton (2008): '"You come across Miss Wade," insists Davies, "and say, 'Wow!
She's a lesbian. Got to be!'"

interpretations may be conceptualised and competing cross-currents of similarity and difference brought into sharp relief. Her form of neo-Victorianism has, then, produced a creative but also analytical and theoretical matrix through which to reinterpret the overlap of contemporary feeling and historical understanding.

Mark Llewellyn has referred to this interplay between concurrent sensibilities as a defining feature of 'neo-Victorianism', as the 'blurring between criticism and creativity' – resulting in what he terms 'critical f(r)iction' (170). The competing understandings of simultaneity within 'criticism and creativity' that formulate much of neo-Victorian studies will inform the theoretical focus of this essay. By combining these developments in our understanding of 'neo-Victorianism' with figurations of normative and non-normative narratives of time, this essay seeks to interrogate an emerging area of Dickens and adaptation studies, which extends and challenges contemporary perceptions of female homoerotic desire. Through an examination of the BBC's adaptations and televised series *Bleak House* (2005) and *Little Dorrit* (2008), and building upon Holly Furneaux's recent work in this area, I propose an alternative interpretative approach to the twenty-first century's imaginative response to Dickens that teases out a specifically 'queer' genre of neo-Victorian adaptation.

Dickens, adaptation and queer television

Dickens's creative legacy has long enjoyed a unique association with film and cinema adaptation; as Joss Marsh observes, 'more films have been made of works of Dickens than any other authors' (204). Until recently, however, in the conversion from page to screen these adaptations have missed or denied the female homoerotic impulses that are central to Dickens's novels. Christine Edzard's critically acclaimed 1987 adaptation of *Little Dorrit*, for instance, deleted the lesbian possibilities of the novel entirely with the complete removal of the characters Miss Wade and Tattycoram from the screenplay. But with the recent work of Andrew Davies, the politics of adapting the Victorian novel onto the television screen have been transformed from a project concerned with presenting the Victorians as occupying a secure and knowable nineteenth-century past to one that begins to destabilise and challenge popular contemporary understandings of 'normative' sexuality and desire.[2] And indeed, Davies

---

[2]   See Heilmann and Llewellyn for more on the significance of Davies's work

has developed a reputation as a television screenwriter whose expertise lies in sensationalising and teasing out the sexual subtext of nineteenth-century fiction. However, this reputation has led to accusations of Davies being 'obsessed with sex', of slipping sex into the neo-Victorian adaptation 'where it has no place' (Moreton).

This interpretative tension raises one of the central issues within the intersecting fields of Dickens, sex and adaptation studies: the question of 'fidelity' to the 'original' text and the matter of imaginative licence. The idea of faithfulness to the 'original' has come under critical fire in the last decade for allowing nothing more than an analytical 'dead-end', raising only the most 'hackneyed questions' (Furneaux 2009b: 244; Hankin 121), which has led to a more interesting and fruitful discussion of the fluidity and variability of adaptation. As John Glavin states in *Dickens on Screen*, 'Film adaptation disrupts, rather than copies, fiction' (4). It is this point of disruption, 'the space of disjunction between texts and media', as Christa Albrecht-Crane and Dennis Cutchins suggest, that generates the possibilities for questioning how far 'that space, that necessary difference' (20) (and similarity) may have an enabling interpretative effect in 'adaptation studies' (20), particularly when considering Dickens and adaptation in the context of neo-Victorianism by way of a specifically queer lens. Through this disjunctive approach to the study of creative fluidity and adaptation, this essay seeks to consider the somewhat unexplored area of Dickens and the representation of female homoerotic desire on the television screen.[3] It therefore repositions Dickens's fiction within the theoretical framework of 'queer television studies'.

Broadly construed, 'queer television studies', as understood by Glyn Davis and Gary Needham, compellingly brings together the study of 'the medium of television and its distinctive characteristics' with queer theory – 'queerness, that is, as a location of sexual alterity, as desire, and as a praxis of dissidence and political abrasion' (1). This approach focuses on the queer potentialities of the embodied television experience, including the

in the twenty-first century (237–44; for an examination of Davies's treatment of sexuality, see 243), and particularly Furneaux's discussion of Davies's queer Dickens adaptation (2009b: 251–3). There has, however, also been other interesting work before Davies's adaptation of Dickens, such as Alan Bleasdale's *Oliver Twist* (ITV, 1999), as noted by John (234–5).

[3] See Furneaux, *Queer Dickens*, for a queer reading of male desire and masculinity in adaptations of Dickens (2009b: 243–53).

reception of its images and sounds, in a particular environment; the other embodied audience members with whom viewing occurs; the phenomenology of interactions with screen [. . .]; (mis)readings, appropriations, and re-encounters with individual texts; inflections of, or confrontations with, particular components of the televisual landscape, from 'liveness' to 'intimacy', from the cancelled television series to the regulated timescape of the ordered schedule. (Davis and Needham 3)

Such theoretical attention devoted to the multiple phenomenological experiences that influence televisual interpretation is particularly significant for its relationship to the extra-textual interpretations and perceptions of Dickens's fiction that viewers inevitably bring to the screen. In other words, the manifold meanings of the Dickens adaptation will be uniquely informed by the interplay and cross-fertilisation of various con(texts) – those of the spectators, the creators and the actors – their various engagements with the screen and text(s), and the cultural milieu in which this interpretation is received. Significantly, for the purposes of this essay, I am interested in the way in which the screenwriter's understanding of, or confrontation with, Dickens's textual rendering of inter-female intimacy is refracted back onto the screen, how this can be conceptualised, and to what extent the neo-Victorian adaptation operates as a filtering mechanism through which to subtly contemplate Dickens's negotiation of same-sex desire.

The case of Esther Summerson and Ada Clare

To put some of these ideas into practice, I will begin by following up on the tantalising question posed by Davis and Needham: 'Might it be that the queerest programmes on television are not necessarily those that centrally feature queer characters and storylines?' (5). Davies's extensive *Bleak House* adaptation (BBC One, 2005), aired twice weekly over a period of eight weeks, provided ample televisual space through which to explore the queer potentialities of Dickens's novel (see Furneaux 2009b: 251). Yet Davies's creative negotiation of arguably the 'queerest' female relationship in *Bleak House*, that between Esther Summerson and Ada Clare, who enjoy an intensely passionate bond throughout the novel, is remarkable for the complete negation of their excessive intimacy. Literary criticism examining the representation of inter-female intimacies in Dickens's *Bleak House* has largely centred on the relationship between Esther

Summerson and Ada Clare, with Patricia Ingham and Holly Furneaux among others commenting on the ardent expression of Esther's desire for Ada and the potential homoeroticism of their bond.[4] Despite such recognition in academe, though, Davies's adaptation presents their relationship in a much more restrained way.

This moderation is initially apparent through Esther's (Anna Maxwell Martin's) onscreen verbal restraint. The effusive linguistic register of romantic female friendship as expressed by Esther Summerson in Dickens's original text, for example, is muted in the adaptation as her affectionate and exclusively possessive references to Ada as 'my love', 'my dear', 'my pet' and 'my darling', which so characterise their relationship in the novel are removed from the script entirely. Additionally, while Esther's (Maxwell Martin's) vocal tone affects kindness and sympathy, it is distanced by an air of maturity which is without the fervour of feeling or enthusiasm that is present in the novel. In fact, this restraint is also visually reinforced. In one of the first onscreen moments of secluded intimacy between Esther and Ada, the viewer is presented with a highly *controlled* display of regard when sitting beside Ada (Carey Mulligan); Esther mildly reassures her with a slight squeeze of the hand that they shall become 'good friends'. This is in stark contrast to the corresponding scene in the novel when the passionate and romantic nature of their relationship is first properly established:

> Ada laughed; and put her arm about my neck, as I stood looking at the fire; and told me I was a quiet, dear, good creature, and had *won her heart.* 'You are so thoughtful, Esther,' she said, 'and yet so cheerful! and you do so much, so unpretendingly! You would make a home out of even this house.'
> My simple darling! She was quite unconscious that she only praised herself, and that it was in the goodness of her own heart that she made so much of me! (Dickens 2008a, ch. 4: 52; emphasis mine)

Here, the reader views Ada through Esther's narrative gaze, and as Furneaux observes, 'Esther is immediately drawn to Ada's beauty' in the novel (2009a: 26); indeed, it 'is difficult' suggests Kimberle L. Brown's examination of Esther's homoerotic gaze, 'to ignore such a burst of enflamed desire coming from' her (22).[5] Esther, for instance, effusively

---

[4]   See Ingham 127, Oulton 88–93, Furneaux (2009a) and Brown.
[5]   Carolyn Oulton alternatively observes that this moment of instant attraction

describes the moment she first sees Ada: 'They both looked up when I came in, and I saw in the young lady, with the fire shining upon her, such a beautiful girl! With such rich golden hair, such soft blue eyes' (ch. 3: 38; quoted in Brown 22), and again later, when 'Shaking back her golden hair, Ada turned her eyes upon me with such laughing wonder, that I was full of wonder too – partly at her beauty' (ch. 4: 52–5).

Read through Laura Mulvey's seminal essay on 'visual pleasure' and the male gaze of the cinema screen, which Brown's study relies on, Mulvey conceptualises 'man as bearer of the look' and woman as 'simultaneously looked at and displayed, with [her] appearance coded for strong visual and erotic impact' (11), Dickens's representation of Esther's narrative gaze and her eroticisation of Ada's body can be understood as an alternative to this theory. According to Brown, Dickens instead textually repositions the 'gaze' through the eyes of women (Esther and the female reader), constructing, 'a male gaze through female eyes as an agency of rebellion' (17) – thus arguably empowering the female gaze and the female spectator. For it is Dickens's deliberate textual positioning of the empowering female gaze through Esther's eyes that results in the notable scenes of her homoerotic attraction to Ada which serve to heighten the subsequent representations of intimacy and attachment between the women (see Brown 11-12 and 23). Yet, while it is possible to negate the power of the female gaze by suggesting that Dickens simply utilised Esther's first-person narrative to initially supplant, and then simultaneously function for the male gaze (of the reader and of Dickens), the complexities of always reading desire through notions of masculinity and heterosexual masculine desire are problematic and point towards a need for a readjustment of Mulvey's theory of the eroticised female body.[6]

In the transposition of the novel onto the screen, Davies notably *removes* this problematic by eliminating the narrative's *focus* on Esther's gaze and the consequent eroticisation of Ada's figure (connoting her '*tobe-looked-at-ness*' appearance), which, in this instance, disrupts Mulvey's thesis of the neatly 'combined [female] spectacle and narrative' (11). Thus the spectator is denied both the presentation of Esther's active and

is mutually felt between Esther and Ada (88). See Kimberle L. Brown for a detailed discussion of the homoerotics of Esther's gaze (17–24).

[6] See Jackie Stacey, who further conceptualises this same issue in *Star Gazing: Hollywood Cinema and Female Spectacle* (25–9).

powerful gaze which would signal to the spectator that Ada is an object of desire, and additionally, the close-up first-person shot/reverse shots which would reinforce Esther's eroticised view of Ada; such possibilities remain unexplored.[7] Instead, the adaptation frequently frames the female dyad in the same screen shot, so that quite often neither Ada nor Esther's narrative gaze is given precedence. While this framing of the women together creates a sense of their shared bond, the exclusion of their gaze and the systematic deletion of the subsequent scenes of intense intimacy, physical admiration and expressions of desire (such as the numerous kisses and embraces between the women that occur in the novel) removes the rich possibilities for a homoerotic interpretation of their intimacy on the television screen and places their relationship firmly within the realms of platonic female friendship.

Yet, ironically, this disjunction between page and screen can be understood as Davies's complex negotiation with, rather than his denial of, Dickens's representation of Esther's desire and intimacy with Ada. In purposely selecting to remove the intensity of their relationship, Davies tacitly engages with and acknowledges the problematics surrounding the issue of how to present Dickens's textual negotiation of romantic female friendship in the adaptation, although this would of course not be obvious to those readers who have not read the novel.

Carolyn Oulton has demonstrated that the form of romantic female friendship enjoyed by Dickens's Esther and Ada was fraught with anxiety in the mid-nineteenth century and was recognised by Victorian popular novelists to be problematically excessive. According to Dinah Mulock Craik's *A Woman's Thoughts about Women* (1857) such bonds were short-lived but as 'delicious' and 'as passionate as first love', and as

> self-forgetful and self-denying [. . .] the nearest approximation to that feeling called love [. . .]. This girlish friendship, however fleeting in its character, and romantic, even silly, in its manifestations [. . .] as jealous, as exacting, as unreasoning – as wildly happy and supremely

---

[7]   Mulvey explores the various methods of presenting a desiring gaze to the cinema audience, and Jackie Stacey provides this useful gloss on Mulvey's theory: 'The spectator identifies with the powerful look of the male character on the screen, and his position in relation to it is produced by the camera(man)'s/director's look. In popular cinema point-of-view shots and shot/reverse-shot editing techniques are used to achieve the effect of seeing the female characters as objects of desire through the eyes of male characters' (Stacey 21).

miserable; *ridiculously so to a looker-on*, but to the parties concerned, as vivid and sincere as any after-passion into which the girl may fall; for the time being, perhaps long after, colouring all her world. (Craik 154, also quoted in Oulton 10; emphasis mine)

Viewed in this context, the difficulty with presenting such an intimate bond to the twenty-first-century audience becomes apparent: Davies faces an interpretative choice between representing a complex negotiation of Victorian structures of emotion and (homo)eroticism, or alternatively, representing their intimacy in such a way as to subtly construct an extremely muted engagement with that tension to avoid destabilising or aesthetically disrupting the adaptation's narrative focus on the story of Esther's origins. By reducing and regulating their onscreen intimacy, then, Davies arguably begins to make this latter step. This motion, however, surprisingly achieves a latent connection with Dickens's aesthetic negotiation of female–female desire in *Bleak House*.

Through a close examination of the source text, it is possible to see that Dickens's textual rendering of Esther's and Ada's relationship was vexed with creative tensions and uncertainty. This is most clearly apparent in Dickens's deleted passages. At 'proof stage', for example, Dickens deleted a passage deemed superfluous (or problematic) to the novel in which Ada 'rhapsodises' about a shared future life with Esther (through an emotional marriage of sorts) if the 'Chancery judgement' is unfavourable to their case (Oulton 88).[8] Ada blushes at the thought of their shared life together as she asks 'how much could you and I live upon Esther?' (Dickens 1977: 821; also quoted in Furneaux 2009a: 32). Such deleted scenes and textual modifications certainly manipulate the reader's interpretation of their intimacy as the removal of Ada's imaginative lens subsumes the full reciprocity of their desire at the margins of the text. Indeed, Dickens's representation of Ada's reciprocity would have risked rendering their intimacy doubly transgressive through its affirmative effect and legitimisation of Esther's desire. It is perhaps this possibility that persuaded Dickens to remove that particular passage. The disruptive potential of their relationship is therefore contained within Esther's narrative gaze.

Yet despite this, the 'youthful', emotional indulgence of Esther's narrative is removed from the adaptation, which is particularly significant for the central role she plays. Davies's curtailment of Esther's expressivity has

[8]   See Furneaux (2009a: 32), who also takes note of this deleted scene.

the effect of constructing her as a reliable, mature and identifiable figure
– a character with whom the mainstream audience are likely to connect,
someone who Maxwell Martin describes as 'savvy, and interesting, very
intelligent and very "switched on"'.[9] Certainly not the type who, upon
ascertaining Ada's marriage to Richard Carstone, would 'steal up-stairs' to
their marital bedroom, surreptitiously listen in at the door to the 'murmur
of their young voices', and longing 'to be near' Ada, impart a kiss upon the
door in an attempt to diminish her feeling of 'separation' (Dickens 2008a,
ch. 51: 730–1; see Furneaux 2009a: 29).

The alternative portrayal of Esther by Davies, then, provides a
'grounded' version of her character, and builds upon Arthur Hopcraft's
1985 BBC dramatisation of *Bleak House*, which Jefferson Hunter has
described as 'substitut[ing] a more modern aesthetic, of controlled feelings
and expressive simplicity' over the 'emotionally and verbally indulgent'
original text (Hunter 175). In supplanting Esther's emotional excess with
reserve, then, the 2005 adaptation also functions as an extended intertextual engagement with the 1985 *Bleak House*, which Hunter observes to
be 'especially non-verbal' (174). Hunter reads this as an indicator of the
'modern', aesthetically styled impetus to present Esther as a 'stable, secure'
and knowable character type, owing to her central positioning within the
adaptation (174). But, one is surely left to wonder, why is it that Davies
presented their relationship in such a conservative way if he is such an
innovative screenwriter and adapter of nineteenth-century fiction?

It is my contention that the adaptation's 'straightening' of Esther's and
Ada's relationship creates and allows space for alternative queer possibilities. It is precisely through Davies's *straight* rendering of Esther's and Ada's
intimacy that other, less visible and 'marginalised' female homoerotic
desires in Dickens's novel emerge in a comparatively highly visualised
form on the television screen. Although these 'secondary' intimacies are
not openly queer, the contrasting intensity of the attachment generates
a residual tension for the viewer, who recognises a textual incongruity
in the adaptation's alternative positioning of these desires; or in other
words, the marginalised relationships and desires seem comparatively
intensified, and therefore out-of-sync in contrast to the central platonic
friendship between Esther and Ada. In this way, Davies's adaptation

---

[9]   See online audio clip, 'Interviews: Anna Maxwell Martin and Burn Gorman',
<http://www.bbc.co.uk/drama/bleakhouse/welcome.shtml>.

invites the viewer to question the construction of normative and non-normative intimacies, which, to use Alexander Doty's phrase, function as an 'oppositional practice' of 'unconventional production and narrative models' (26). Davies's adaptation, then, engages with a potentially radical approach. By denying the homoeroticism of Esther's and Ada's relationship through the removal of their effusive linguistic register and intimacy, synonymous with romantic female friendship, he is obliquely revealing the homoeroticism of inter-female desires elsewhere.

Cross-class intimacies and the queer temporalities of Lady Dedlock

Where Davies's representation of female intimacy between socio-economic equals (Ada and Esther) diminishes the full erotic possibilities of *Bleak House*, the introduction of a power hierarchy through socio-economic difference conversely serves to intensify the apparent desire between women on the television screen. This is visible in the first episode with Caddy Jellyby's (Natalie Press's) introductory scene and her encounter with Esther.[10] Following Esther's and Ada's arrival at the Jellybys', Caddy visits Esther at night in a temporary bedroom Esther is to share with Ada (who lies sleeping in the background). Entering the candlelit bedroom in a state of emotional discomposure, Caddy presents a fragile yet refractory affective appeal to Esther's sympathy, as she confesses to the frustration she feels as Mrs Jellyby's daughter and assistant in the 'Africa cause'. Sitting away from Caddy, Esther rises and approaches her. The camera follows Esther's gaze and provides an up-close shot of Caddy's face as a single tear runs down her cheek, generating a sense of Caddy's self-exposure and an aura of intimacy. As the camera signifies their physical proximity to each other, Caddy goes on to lament (with a softly spoken vocal tone): 'I know I'm a disgrace Miss Summerson. I wish I'd had you to teach me better manners [. . .] I wish, well, never-mind', which is swiftly followed by a kiss imparted upon Esther's cheek, ending the scene.

The high degree of Caddy's emotional intensity and her immediate desire to approach Esther, as presented in this scene, then, offers an alternative level of intimacy to that enjoyed by Esther and Ada in the adaptation. Importantly, the kiss, which momentarily connects Caddy and Esther, is inserted into the scene on the television screen but is absent from the source text. This does not serve to exaggerate the emotional

[10]   See Furneaux (2009b: 220) for a discussion of Caddy and Esther's intimacy.

intimacy as originally described in *Bleak House*, however, but instead renders it *visible* for the twenty-first-century audience.

The most affective delineation of homoerotic desire to cross class barriers, however, emerges through the figure of Lady Dedlock (Gillian Anderson) and her intense attraction to the young maid, Rosa (Emma Williams). Although traditionally read as a surrogate mother–daughter relationship, Mary A. Armstrong has instead convincingly argued that Dickens presents their intimacy as 'an articulation of female homoerotic desire that is dangerously welded to (specifically) aristocratic power' (131).[11] And Davies's expansive adaptation picks up on this, blurring the lines 'between criticism and creativity' (Llewellyn 170), through a notably sensitive queer rendering of Lady Dedlock.

In the special commentary accompanying Episode 1, the producer, Nigel Stafford-Clark, remarks of Lady Dedlock's introductory scene at Chesney Wold as the moment when 'the audience begins to realise that this isn't going to be a normal classic adaptation'.[12] That this marks a departure from other approaches, suggests Stafford-Clark, is in part due to an alternative but deliberately claustrophobic positioning of Lady Dedlock in her first scene; shot with 'three separate angles on Gillian (as Lady Dedlock). It's like she's surrounded by boredom',[13] as she bemoans, 'bored to death with this place, bored to death with my life, bored to death with myself'. Attending this sense of incarcerating boredom and stasis is an unsettling and melancholic tone, made palpable through the dull, sterile *mise-en-scène* that is synonymous with Lady Dedlock's particularly aloof composure and perceived marital discontent. As such, this introductory scene generates, I argue, an almost indefinably queer register that resonates with Dickens's initial configuration of Lady Dedlock's deathly boredom, as, to use Lee Edelman's phrase, 'future-negating' and definitively queer (26). Edelman's *No Future: Queer Theory and the Death Drive*, suggests that a 'future-negating' identity is distinctly queer for its *separateness* from the institutions of *family* and *reproduction*, or 'reproductive futurism', which is placed centrally within the logic of (hetero) normative narratives of time and space (26). This queer formulation

[11]   See Schor (109) for a mother–daughter reading of Lady Dedlock and Rosa's attachment, for example.
[12]   Stafford-Clark's comments are taken from 'Episode 1 Commentary', *Bleak House* (2005, three-disc special-edition DVD, 2006).
[13]   Ibid.

of a 'future-negating' time necessarily draws attention to the 'powerful structuring continuities between the past, present and future' of the heterosexual reproductive narrative (Needham 151), while simultaneously alerting the reader to any resistance of such narrative structures. Significantly, it is through the subtle invocation of 'normative' temporalities and her implicit rejection of this sequence of events that Dickens first introduces Lady Dedlock:

> On Sundays, the little church in the park is mouldy; the oaken pulpit breaks out into a cold sweat; and there is a general smell and taste as of the ancient Dedlocks in their graves. My Lady Dedlock (who is childless), looking out in the early twilight from her boudoir at a keeper's lodge, and seeing [. . .] a child chased by a woman, running out into the rain to meet the shining figure of a wrapped-up man coming through the gate, has been put quite out of temper. My Lady Dedlock says she has been 'bored to death.' (Dickens 2008a, ch. 2: 18)

Lady Dedlock's boredom, here, initially signals her potentially disruptive and improper femininity through her disassociation and disconnectedness (according to the unreliable narrator) with the defining characteristics of proper womanhood, – inclusive of familial heritage, legacy, childbirth, parenting and the family unit (Armstrong 130; Halberstam 1; Needham 151). Indeed, what becomes manifest in her boredom is a temporal disruption that places her on the 'outside' and out-of-sync with the heteropatriarchal logic of time, producing a distancing effect, which invokes her frustrated observation of 'normative time' and suggested longing for an alternative existence, however unlikely, that lies beyond these 'paradigmatic markers of life experience' (Halberstam 2).[14] It is arguably through a negotiation of this experiential disruption, boredom, that Dickens's text radically proposes a temporary, but alternative affective connection for Lady Dedlock that emerges through a reorganisation of her relationships with women, that 'evolves into an articulation of female homoerotic desire' (Armstrong 131).

---

[14]   Armstrong makes similar note of Lady Dedlock's boredom in this opening scene, suggesting that 'Lady Dedlock's "boredom" and her bad temper are related to her emotional isolation. This isolation is somehow tied to her family [...] she can never be part of that [family] structure' (130). See Needham for more on the conceptualisation of non-normative time as being 'outside' or exterior to 'normative' understandings of time (151).

On Rosa's first appearance as maid, in both the source text and the adaptation, an unusual degree of attention and interest is placed on the young woman by Lady Dedlock (as Armstrong's study of female–female desire in Dickens has adroitly demonstrated), rendering Rosa a significant distraction from her hitherto character-defining boredom (131). In this way, Rosa's arresting physical presence and prettiness, for Lady Dedlock, interrupts her anticipated temporal experience, which is notably regarded as an indiscretion by Dickens's narrator for her failure to 'subdue the quickness of her observation' (Armstrong 132; Dickens 2008a, ch. 12: 169). The possible transgressiveness of this attraction is tantalisingly hinted at by Dickens, moving from one temporal extreme (boredom) to another (intense interest), but Davies's neo-Victorian work revisits and reopens this initial moment and places added emphasis on the intimacy, touch and affect of this first meeting. As Lady Dedlock is drawn to Rosa, Davies mobilises the queer potentialities of Lady Dedlock's desire by verbally and visually reducing the hierarchies of difference present in their relationship.

Approaching Rosa, gazing intently at her and admiring her beauty, Lady Dedlock (Gillian Anderson) softly strokes (rather than taps) Rosa's face with a significantly un-gloved hand that enables a sensual skin-to-skin contact, observing 'Why, do you know how pretty you are?'; as suggested by Armstrong's observation, 'Lady Dedlock is interested, primarily, in Rosa's beauty' (133). The intimacy and subtle eroticism of this scene is evocative of Dickens's novel, but is heightened by the adaptation's removal of Lady Dedlock's gloves and gloved touch – indicative of her class and social-status difference. In attempting to momentarily reduce such differences within the female dyad, Davies's script also removes Lady Dedlock's concluding noun, 'child', from her original observation, (which appeared in the text as: '"Why, do you know how pretty you are, child?"' (Dickens 2008a, ch. 12: 169)). This term is significant, for it suggestively positioned Lady Dedlock's interest in Rosa as maternal in nature. But with Davies's removal of this specific clue to her desire, which implicitly resituated Lady Dedlock within the hetero-patriarchal linear temporal logic of a mother–daughter connection, the queer possibilities of their bond are magnified.

Following this encounter, as in the novel and adaptation, Lady Dedlock restructures her relationships with her maids, dismissing Hortense and promoting Rosa to become her personal maid. The camera notably

lingers on subsequent moments of touch between Lady Dedlock and
Rosa, with Lady Dedlock's ringed fingers caressing Rosa's hand, which
she later holds to her face and kisses, accompanied by verbal expressions
of affection for Rosa. This effectively presents a subtle eroticism to their
bond that is notably absent from Lady Dedlock's relationship with Hortense. The queer significance of Rosa's and Lady Dedlock's attachment,
however, becomes most notable in the adaptation when their intimacy
is interrupted by the tall and imposing presence of Tulkinghorn (Charles
Dance), and particularly later, when Rosa's and Lady Dedlock's separation scene captures the pain and sorrow at their parting (see Armstrong
155-7). I see Davies's presentation of this scene, which renders their
distress palpable, partly heightened by the denial of any final intimacy
between the women, and for the cold, onlooking observation from the
men standing by, as a tacit acknowledgment of the psychological, emotional and erotic significance of their intimacy.

   Indeed, the queer appeal of Gillian Anderson's performance has
been enthusiastically appreciated by viewers on *YouTube*, with one keen
observer splicing scenes of Lady Dedlock and Rosa's intimacies together
with shots of Tulkinghorn threatening to expose his knowledge of her past,
dedicating the clip 'Lady Dedlock's Secret' (21 June 2010). This raises
two issues. Firstly it recognises an epistemological problematic, present in
the novel, but further developed in the adaptation, regarding tensions of
secrecy surrounding Lady Dedlock and the relationship of her 'secret' to
her intimacy with her maid. As Davis and Needham point out, the 'tension
between secrecy and disclosure' as a 'key narrative organisational strategy
[. . .] has strong resonances with Sedgwick's discussion of the concept
of the closet, and with other theorists' interrogations of the narrativiza-
tion of queer experience, making possible a queer understanding of the
series despite their absence of non-hetero characters' (5-6). Utilising this
queer narrative structure, the *YouTube* clip re-edits their female–female
intimacy, including scenes of their mutual distress at separating, to bring
the sub-textual homoerotic narrative to the forefront, subverting the heteronormative narrative structure of time and space.[15] In doing so, this fan
posting presents a substitutional (his)story for Rosa and Lady Dedlock that

---

[15]   See Dhaenens for more on queer cuttings on *YouTube* and the resistance to
heteronormative television productions in fan postings, redirecting 'the queer to
the centre' of the narrative and 'non-queer to the margins'.

affirms their desire and embraces an alternative scheduling of time, priori-
tising their relationship. But the radical potentialities of this *YouTube* clip,
as an offering of a sub-cultural or counter-cultural response to Dickens's
Bleak House and the BBC's adaptation, falls short for its failure to restruc-
ture the logic of heteronormative time. Instead, their bond is presented
in a 'future-negating' format, ending with a split-scene presentation of
their separation. What is significant about this fan clip, however, emerges
through the mini-discussion thread that ensues, revealing the distinctly
queer pleasure felt, for some viewers, watching Anderson play Lady Dedlock. With online posts admiringly remarking 'Gillian plays it VERY gay',
the specific character casting of Anderson occupies a significant role in a
lesbian reading of the adaptation.[16]

Initially rising to fame as the tough and independent Special Agent
Dana Scully in the hit television sci-fi series, The X-Files (1993–2002),
Anderson quickly earned a cult following that gained her 'quite a lesbian
fan club' (Rosenblum 2001). There was some speculation that her character, Scully, was a lesbian, with Anderson remarking in an interview with
Lesbian News, that it would be no surprise if Scully 'came out' (Rosenblum
2001). As Furneaux has suggested, the 'actors own sexualities and histories' and the casting of 'gay identified actors' offers a provocative subtext
to queer interpretations of Dickens adaptations (2009b; 248, 249), so for
those viewers who understood Scully as a lesbian, this led to a viewer
identification with Anderson that meant for some members of the audience that she personally became the focus of, and synonymous with, queer
desire. It was through the formation of the Gillian Anderson Estrogen
Brigade (GAEB), an online 'safe space exclusively for lesbian and bisexual
women' (Bury 33), that her public but off-screen support and involvement
with lesbian, gay, bisexual and transgender (LGBT) groups has come to
provide a discursive subtext surrounding Anderson as role-model for
contra- or non-normative sexuality. In this way, the adaptation's use of
character-casting (Gillian Anderson, specifically) functions as a cross-
textual gesture subtly promoting a queer, non-normative interpretation
of female desire within Davies's screenplay.

---

[16] See *YouTube* clip and comments page, 'Bleak House – Lady Dedlock's Secret'
(21 June 2010). <http://www.youtube.com/watch?v=2eRKQ6azhpw>.

'Were there really lesbians in *Little Dorrit?*':[17] character-casting Tattycoram and Miss Wade

The role of character casting in a lesbian interpretation of Dickens is particularly important in Davies's subsequent Dickens adaptation, *Little Dorrit* (BBC One, 2008). Indeed, it is interestingly through cross-racial character casting that Davies's screenplay, *Little Dorrit*, begins to subtly address the issue of visibility and lesbianism. Seduced away from the Meagles family by Miss Wade, Dickens's Tattycoram is a vulnerable, and yet passionate, rebellious and 'handsome girl with lustrous dark hair and eyes' (Dickens 2008b, ch. 2: 20). Played in the adaptation by the black actress, Freema Agyeman, whose physical appearance partly signals back to Tattycoram's dark features, the BBC's casting decision produced a deal of speculation in the media. An article in *The Guardian* (7 May 2008), for example, read: 'Why the Dickens Shouldn't Costume Dramas be Diverse?' The article went on to assume, however, that Agyeman's casting was 'colour blind', and speculated the possibility that the BBC was simply concerned with

> ticking boxes and fulfilling diversity quotas without genuinely undertaking to represent a section of the audience? Are such measures actually inadvertent indictments of how few black characters there are on television? Should we be concerned that a black Nancy or Tattycoram are simply fig-leaves hiding a bigger problem? That there isn't sufficient representation of Britain's ethnic minorities on TV. (McLean)

The issues raised in this article prioritise the socio-cultural context in which the adaptation was aired, referring to the present extra-textual concerns, but in doing so, it underestimates the textual roots of the BBC's character-casting. A debate on the BBC's *Newsnight Review* (28 October 2008) again discussed the issue, in which Sarah Churchwell argued that Dickens's Tattycoram is understood as a moral test to the Meagles family, with Tattycoram operating as a barometer to figure their tolerance or intolerance, and that understood in the context of the racism and racial politics of mid-Victorian England, the casting of Freema Agyeman was not 'colour-blind' but very specific.[18] Indeed, in an interview for the BBC

---

[17]   Quoted from the subheading of Moreton's article.
[18]   BBC Two's *Newsnight Review* (28 October 2008), <http://news.bbc.co.uk/1/hi/programmes/newsnight/review/7695488.stm>.

One Press Office website, Agyeman also recognises the colour-specificity of her casting, and similarly interprets this as a signal to the audience that her character occupies a subordinate position in mid-Victorian society; as she states: 'I was equally delighted because Tattycoram is not written as a black part. She's an orphan, and in the 1820s there was a general prejudice against anyone who wasn't from an upper-class background. So the idea transposed well to a black character' (Agyeman).

While the introduction of Tattycoram, as a black girl, alters the narrative lens and produces a post-colonial interpretation of *Little Dorrit*, the colour-specificity of Agyeman's casting also significantly gestures towards the double 'taboo' of her potential lesbian tendencies. This is significant since elsewhere in Dickens's fiction, in *Dombey and Son*, for example, Dickens makes an intertextual reference to *Othello* when attempting to articulate the intense desire Edith Skewton Granger feels for her step-daughter, Florence Dombey. As the narrator gestures towards Edith and Florence's pending separation, the narrator states: 'Oh dear Edith! it were well to die, indeed, at such a time! Better and happier far, perhaps, to die so, Edith, than to live on to the end!' (Dickens 2001, ch. 30: 449), which echoes William Shakespeare's Othello when he is most erotically attracted to Desdemona. Othello declares 'If it were now to die/ 'Twere now to be most happy' (Shakespeare 2006: 252; II.i, 184–5), and clearly resonates in the narrator's 'happier far, perhaps, to die so, Edith'.[19] The significance of this reference rests on the fact that Shakespeare's *Othello* was regarded with much controversy during the mid-nineteenth century owing to the black casting sometimes involved in the production, with actors such as the African-American Ira Aldridge, who made his name in London at this time (Finnerty 164–7). As such, Edith's erotic transgression is signalled by the reference both to Othello's passion, and to Othello as a figure of the racial Other. In this way, Tattycoram's racial Otherness perhaps operates as textual reference back to Dickens and as a visual reference to the audience of both her vulnerability and her potential sexual otherness. It is in this way, as Tamsin Wilton has equally suggested, that 'the codes of "orientalism"' emphasise 'lesbianism by further overheating [. . .] feminine sexuality' (140). The visibility of Tattycoram as a black woman, therefore,

---

[19] For more on Shakespeare's influence on Dickens, see Gager (212–22) who illustrates the striking similarity between *Dombey and Son* and *Macbeth*, but in doing so, does not refer to the influence of *Othello* in this scene.

doubly renders the visibility of their relationship as they occupy the position of homosexual lovers and inter-racial companions.

Importantly, the multi-laminated possibilities of neo-Victorian television adaptations are also pertinent to the character casting of Maxine
Peake who played Miss Wade in *Little Dorrit* (2008), and later appeared as
the lesbian figure Anne Lister in the BBC drama *The Secret Diaries of Miss
Anne Lister* (2010). The potential cross-over of Lister with Miss Wade
was implicitly picked up on by John Preston in *The Daily Telegraph*, who
described Peake's performance of Lister as 'wonderfully well-cast', 'veer-
ing between predatory seductiveness and agonised self-pity' (Preston).
It is worthy to note that this description strikingly resonates with later
critical interpretations of Dickens's Miss Wade and her relationship with
Tattycoram, reaffirming the cross-textual and concurrent conceptualisa-
tions of lesbian identity.

Conclusion

Davies's recent neo-Victorian engagements with Dickens's writing have
operated, then, to rework and re-read the representation of female–female
intimacies and the legacy of the nineteenth-century past. Davies's inflec-
tion of Dickens's complex representation of inter-female relationships,
therefore, negotiates the tensions and contradictions of the source text,
which are then re-visioned to unveil and re-present the alternative female
homoerotic impulses that are central to Dickens's *Bleak House* and *Little
Dorrit*. Indeed, Davies, as an adapter of Sarah Waters's *Tipping the Velvet*
(BBC Two, 2002) and *Affinity* (ITV, 2008), presents a particularly keen
interpretation of Dickens's representation of female homoerotic desire,
necessarily influenced by the intertextual and cross-generic fertilisation
of Waters's fiction and the adaptations.[20] But one wonders, was the intertextual nature of these adaptations recognised in the traditional family
living-room space?

Despite the tacit and fleetingly intertextual connections, the problematics of providing a queer reading of Dickens on screen are heightened
by the screenwriter's (Davies's) own apparent confusion surrounding

---

[20]   See Heilmann and Llewellyn (243–4), who recognise the potential cross-
textual reference through the prison setting motif in Davies's BBC *Little Dorrit*
(2008) and ITV's *Affinity* (2008).

Dickens and lesbianism; he is torn between both liberal and less liberal-minded possibilities (see Furneaux 2009b: 20). 'Dickens didn't write her [Miss Wade] as a lesbian – but she just is', Davies reportedly observed to the *Telegraph Review*, 'There are all sorts of things Dickens didn't realise about his characters' (Serena Davies). While Furneaux argues that this comment represents a continuation of 'the powerful stereotypes of Victorian and Dickensian prudery' (2009b: 20), it is perhaps also indicative of Davies's balancing act between the competing sensibilities of twenty-first century perceptions of the Victorian past and his own nuanced recognition of Dickens's vexed textual negotiation of inter-female intimacies. This seems to be particularly likely when we consider that there is some slippage in Davies's stance. Just one week after Serena Davies's *Telegraph* piece, Davies remarked to the *Independent*: 'You come across Miss Wade, [. . .] and say, "Wow! She's a lesbian. Got to be!" [. . .] Dickens doesn't say that, but he is probably implying it' (Moreton). Davies's comments, therefore, betray an anxiety of anachronism between what was 'realised' or understood by Dickens, and what Dickens may have knowingly 'implied'. It is through a careful engagement with Dickens's textual representation of intense and passionate desire between women, then, juxtaposed with a reflection and rewriting of the source text, that Davies attempts to provide an implicitly 'critical' but also 'creative' interrogation (Llewellyn 2008: 170) of Victorian inter-female intimacies. The simultaneity of these apparently divergent sensibilities, therefore, works to tease out a sophisticated and refractory element of the original text and the radical potentialities of Dickens's fiction are momentarily legible on screen.

Works cited

Agyeman, Freema, 2008. '*Little Dorrit* a Major BBC One Dickens Adaptation' (13 October), <http://www.bbc.co.uk/pressoffice/pressreleases/stories/2008/10_october/13/dorrit11.shtml>.

Albrecht-Crane, Christa, and Dennis Cutchins, 2010. 'Introduction: New Beginnings for Adaptation Studies', in *Adaptation Studies: New Approaches*, ed. Christa Albrecht-Crane and Dennis Cutchins. Cranbury, New Jersey: Rosemont Publishing, pp. 11–24.

[Anon.], 2001. 'Fingersmith', *Kirkus Reviews* (15 December), <http://www.kirkusreviews.com/book-reviews/fiction/sarah-waters/fingersmith/#review>.

190 KIM EDWARDS KEATES

Armstrong, Mary A., 1995. '"What Can You Two Be Together?":
Charles Dickens, Female Homoerotic Desire and the Work of
Heterosexual Recovery' (unpublished doctoral dissertation, Duke
University).

Bailey, Pete, 2007. 'Fingersmith', (20 May) <http://www.sapl.ab.ca/blog/
petes-picks/2007-05/fingersmith>.

Brown, Kimberle L., 2005. '"When I Kissed her Cheek": Theatrics of
Sexuality and the Framed Gaze in Esther's Narration of *Bleak House*'
(unpublished master's thesis, University of North Carolina, Wilmington).

Bury, Rhiannon, 2005. *Cyberspaces of their Own: Female Fandoms Online*.
New York: Peter Lang.

Craik, Dinah Mulock, 1858 [1857]. *A Woman's Thoughts About Women*.
New York: Rudd & Carleton.

Davies, Serena, 2008. 'Little Dorrit: Life and Debt', *The Telegraph* (18
October), <http://www.telegraph.co.uk/culture/tvandradio/3562235/
Little-Dorrit-Life-and-debt.html>.

Davis, Glyn, and Gary Needham, 2009. 'Introduction: The Pleasures of
the Tube', in *Queer TV: Theories, Histories, Politics*, eds. Glyn Davis and
Gary Needham. Abingdon: Routledge, pp. 1–12.

Dhaenens, Frederik [in press]. 'Queer Cuttings on YouTube: Re-editing
Soaps as a Form of Fan-Produced Queer Resistance', *European Journal
of Cultural Studies*. <https://biblio.ugent.be/publication/1182486>
(accessed 1 May 2012)

Dickens, Charles, 2001 [1846–8]. *Dombey and Son*. Oxford: Oxford
University Press.

Dickens, Charles, 1977 [1852–3]. *Bleak House*, eds. George Ford and
Sylvere Monod. London: Norton.

Dickens, Charles, 2008a [1852–3]. *Bleak House*. Oxford: Oxford
University Press.

Dickens, Charles, 2008b [1855–7]. *Little Dorrit*. Oxford: Oxford
University Press.

Doty, Alexander, 1993. *Making Things Perfectly Queer: Interpreting Mass
Culture*. Minneapolis: University of Minnesota Press.

Edelman, Lee, 2004. *No Future: Queer Theory and the Death Drive*.
Durham, North Carolina: Duke University Press.

Finnerty, Páraic, 2006. *Emily Dickinson's Shakespeare*. Amherst: University
of Massachusetts Press.

Furneaux, Holly, 2009a. 'Emotional Intertexts: Female Romantic
Friendship and the Anguish of Marriage', *Australasian Journal of
Victorian Studies*, 14: 15–37.

Furneaux, Holly, 2009b. *Queer Dickens*. Oxford: Oxford University Press.

Gager, Valerie L, 1996. *Shakespeare and Dickens: The Dynamics of Influence.* Cambridge: Cambridge University Press.

Glavin, John, 2003. 'Introduction' in *Dickens on Screen*, ed. John Glavin. Cambridge: Cambridge University Press, pp. 1–10.

Halberstam, Judith, 2005. *In a Queer Time and Place: Transgender Bodies, Subcultural Lives.* London: New York University Press.

Hankin, Kelly, 2009. 'Adapting Lesbians: Maria Maggenti and the Practice of Lesbian Screenwriting', *Adaptation*, 2: 110–24.

Heilmann, Ann, and Mark Llewellyn, 2010. *Neo-Victorianism: The Victorians in the Twenty-First Century.* Basingstoke: Palgrave Macmillan.

Hunter, Jefferson, 2010. *English Filming, English Writing.* Bloomington: Indiana University Press.

Ingham, Patricia, 1992. *Dickens, Women and Language.* Hemel Hempstead: Harvester Wheatsheaf.

John, Juliet, 2010. *Dickens and Mass Culture.* Oxford: Oxford University Press.

Llewellyn, Mark, 2008. 'What is Neo-Victorian Studies?', *Neo-Victorian Studies*, 1: 164–86.

Marsh, Joss, 2001. 'Dickens and Film', in *The Cambridge Companion to Charles Dickens*, ed. John O. Jordon. Cambridge: Cambridge University Press, pp. 204–23.

McLean, Gareth, 2008. 'Why the Dickens Shouldn't Costume Dramas be Ethnically Diverse?' *Guardian* (7 May), <http://www.guardian.co.uk/culture/garethmcleanblog/2008/may/07/anotherautumnanotherallstar/>.

Mitchell, Kate, 2010. *History and Cultural Memory in Neo-Victorian Fiction: Victorian Afterimages.* Basingstoke: Palgrave Macmillan.

Moreton, Cole, 2008. 'Andrew Davies: What the Dickens?' *Independent* (26 October), <http://www.independent.co.uk/news/people/profiles/andrew-davies-what-the-dickens-973829.html>.

Mulvey, Laura, 1975. 'Visual Pleasure and Narrative Cinema', *Screen*, 16: 6–18.

Needham, Gary, 2009. 'Scheduling Normativity: Television, the Family, and Queer Temporality', in *Queer TV: Theories, Histories, Politics.* Abingdon: Routledge, pp. 143–58.

Oulton, Carolyn W. de la L., 2007. *Romantic Friendship in Victorian Literature.* Aldershot: Ashgate.

Preston, John, 2010. 'The Secret Diaries of Miss Anne Lister, BBC Two, Review', *The Telegraph* (4 June), <http://www.telegraph.co.uk/culture/tvandradio/7803753/The-Secret-Diaries-of-Miss-Anne-Lister-BBC-Two-review.html>.

Rosenblum, Nancy, 2001. 'Lesbian News', *The Official Gillian Anderson Website* (February 2001), <http://www.gilliananderson.ws/transcripts/01_04/01lesnews.shtml>.

Schor, Hilary M., 1999. *Dickens and the Daughter of the House*. Cambridge: Cambridge University Press.

Shakespeare, William, 2006 [1604]. *Othello*. Oxford: Oxford University Press.

Stacey, Jackie, 1994. *Star Gazing: Hollywood Cinema and Female Spectacle*. London: Routledge.

Wilton, Tamsin, 1995. *Immortal, Invisible: Lesbians and the Moving Image*. London: Routledge.

Online Resources

BBC Two's *Newsnight Review*, 28 October 2008. <http://news.bbc.co.uk/1/hi/programmes/newsnight/review/7695488.stm>

'Bleak House – Lady Dedlock's Secret', 21 June 2010. *YouTube*, <http://www.youtube.com/watch?v=2eRKQ6azhpw>

'Interviews: Anna Maxwell Martin and Burn Gorman', January 2009. <http://www.bbc.co.uk/bleakhouse/welcome.shtml>

Television Series

Chadwick, Justin and Susanna White, dirs., 2005. *Bleak House*, screenplay by Andrew Davies, BBC.

Walsh, Dearbhla, Adam Smith and Diarmuid Lawrence, dirs., 2008. *Little Dorrit*, screenplay by Andrew Davies, BBC.

Out of place: David Copperfield's irresolvable geographies

DOMINIC RAINSFORD

Centredness, presence, being – these elusive categories are always at risk in Dickens. They may be threatened by self-doubt; insanity; the burden of the past (expressed as guilt or debt); foreignness and savagery; vanity and deceit; even metaphysics. A proverbial celebrant of domesticity and tradition who nevertheless needed to be perpetually in motion, both mentally and physically, Dickens was acutely aware of the difference it may make to live on one spot on the earth's surface rather than another, and the problems involved in conforming our ideas of self and duty to geographical space. Do we try to extend our sympathies, like Mrs Jellyby, to far-off places? Can we afford to do so? Is the world on our own doorstop not already exotic and shockingly alien?

We are isolated not just in space, but also in time. Dickens consistently represents the present as an island between a dreadful past and an unknowable future. The oft-mentioned titles of the false books at Gad's Hill – 'The Wisdom of Our Ancestors – I. Ignorance. II. Superstition. III. The Block. IV. The Stake. . . .' (House 35) – are fairly symptomatic of his view of a world of horrors which we are so lucky as to have left (he thought), very recently, behind. On a more speculative level, despite Dickens's professions of religious faith, where we come from and where we are going to is, in most of his writing, deeply mysterious: to adopt some pregnant phrases from *Our Mutual Friend*, we have emerged from 'the vast dark ante-chambers of the present world', find ourselves in a brief passage of consciousness and action, and may soon be 'wandering' in the 'endless places . . . at an immense distance' of a hypothetical afterlife.[1]

---

[1] Dickens 1997: 266 (book 2, ch. 5) and 719 (book 4, ch. 10). I discuss these passages in Rainsford 2010: 284.

Also in terms of how we define ourselves, here and now, alongside other humans, Dickens returns again and again to the image of a small and fragile territory. At best, there are tiny communities with the potential to renew themselves: from the families in which each generation honours and replicates its predecessor (as at the end of *Nicholas Nickleby* or *Dombey and Son*), to the slightly more institutional model of Bleak House (the building), where the individual home becomes a kind of franchise. In the most autobiographical novels, *David Copperfield* and *Great Expectations*, it is a sufficiently hard undertaking just to construct and hang on to a single workable self, and doing so requires the renunciation of many contacts with the world at large, and of many bright notions of who one might, oneself, have been.

This essay seeks to bring these various elements together, linking them to Dickens scholarship's growing concern, in recent years, with 'global Dickens'; that is, his awareness of, relations with, and posthumous presence in lands beyond his own.[2] I would argue that Dickens, the would-be 'Manager of the House' (Bodenheimer 126–69) was acutely conscious of ways in which the world beyond his doorstep resisted management, and that this consciousness permeates the concern with psychological grounding, social placement and metaphysical validity that marks his explorations of human character and identity – whether the humans in question be foreigners, locals, or even ourselves. I shall concentrate on *David Copperfield*, Dickens's most sustained study of the placement of the individual within both the real and the imagined world – perhaps Dickens's greatest theme.

In some ways, David Copperfield has an unusually self-contained and uncomplicated life. His family background, although sad, has little narrative depth. His future seems similarly simple: married and yet monk-like, under Agnes's ascetic tutelage. His great roles will have been to absorb the experiences recounted in *David Copperfield*, and then to make *David Copperfield* out of those experiences. When we have read the final chapter, all of that has been accomplished. In other respects, however, he is less contained. From the start, he transcends conventional boundaries by being 'privileged' – despite his own mockery of this notion – 'to see ghosts and spirits' (Dickens 1981, ch. 1:1). Although he never met his father, he is

[2]   See Jordan 2009 for a recent survey of this field. Also Moore, Clemm, and Jacobson.

haunted by him; likewise by his mother; likewise by Steerforth, who, even while still living, is remembered as though he were 'a cherished friend, who was dead' (ch. 32: 388); likewise by Little Em'ly – even though she turns out to be alive. Both David the character and, implicitly, his author, with David the narrator's commendation, blur the line between the adult and the child, preserving 'the power of observation' characteristic of the very young (ch. 2: 11). But David also blurs the line between the dead and the living, sometimes seeming to be incapable of telling them apart.

The sense of insecurity expressed in the novel's first sentence suggests that David may be an unusually nondescript character, especially for an eponymous 'hero', but he is also, in some ways, all too gifted. He has to find a place for himself, both conceptually and physically, geographically, in the world. And he is sensitive to this kind of issue in others; in Steerforth, for example, who defines himself through egotism, and declares that the way forward is to tell a story about yourself that locks others out, or makes them insignificant; to be a world to yourself instead of losing yourself in a generalised world that is all too extensive. When he hears that Barkis is at death's door, he responds: 'It's a bad job [. . .] but the sun sets every day, and people die every minute, and we mustn't be scared by the common lot. If we failed to hold our own, because that equal foot at all men's doors was heard knocking somewhere, every object in this world would slip from us' (ch. 28: 364). As George Eliot would later observe, having 'a keen vision and feeling of all ordinary human life', hearing 'that roar which lies on the other side of silence', would be fatal; and Dickens's novel, too, is full of characters who are 'well wadded', not with 'stupidity' as we normally understand that term, but with a constitutional incapacity to play the same game as those around them and thus be part of a shared and mappable world (Eliot 1986, ch. 20: 189). Wherever Steerforth is, he makes that place into his own territory; so, in very different ways, with a greater or lesser degree of success, do such different (in fact, profoundly antagonistic) characters as Mr Micawber and Uriah Heep.[3]

It would be illogical to take one of these characters as a role model, even if it seemed morally attractive to do so: they are defined by their

---

[3]   Another way of looking at this would be to emphasise the theatricality of these characters' personalities. Conceptualising oneself as an actor, and everyone else as audience, is another way of carrying on as though one's own little world were the one that mattered, not the bigger one depicted in the atlas. See Juliet John on Steerforth and 'the world as a stage' (177).

exclusiveness. And the novel as a whole hardly endorses a self-centredness equivalent and parallel to theirs. On the other hand, there are currents in the novel that imply: Who can blame them? To make a figure in the world legitimately, to one's own satisfaction and the benefit and admiration of others, is not easy. It is a chance that can easily be lost, or that proves to have been illusory all along, as at least one youthful prodigy finds out:

> Time has stolen on unobserved, for Adams is not the head-boy in the days that are come now, nor has he been this many and many a day. Adams has left the school so long, that when he comes back, on a visit to Doctor Strong, there are not many there, besides myself, who know him. Adams is going to be called to the bar almost directly, and is to be an advocate, and to wear a wig. I am surprised to find him a meeker man than I had thought, and less imposing in appearance. He has not staggered the world yet, either; for it goes on (as well as I can make out) pretty much the same as if he had never joined it. (Dickens 1981, ch. 18: 229)

To conform is to disappear. The head boy's small tragedy is that he goes out into the world, out of the world-in-itself of the school, and, without the egotistical wadding of a Steerforth, Micawber or Heep, loses himself in a head-count of millions. Through cases such as these, as well as David's own experiences and self-conception, the ideal of *Bildung* that this novel might appear to stand for comes consistently and credibly under threat.

In the light of this, the first sentence of the novel may contain even more ambiguity than is generally attributed to it. 'Whether I shall turn out to be the hero of my own life, or whether that station will be held by anybody else, these pages must show' (ch. 1: 1). David may mean that readers will have the chance to decide, in due course, whether the events about to be narrated show him to *have been* somehow at the centre of, in command of, or chiefly responsible for, the ways in which his life has developed. Or he may mean that the written narrative itself, conceived as the work of a character who grows up (if that phrase is not begging the question) to be a writer, is what may make that life, in the end, after all, heroic (so that is David who turns out to be the real 'head boy' – not the first man, Adams). Or he may be seen as hinting that some other specific individual will turn out to have been the hero of his (David's) life. (Thus, as re-readers of the novel, we may reasonably think that he is preparing the way for Steerforth – or Agnes.) But the sentence also raises the possibility that there is not *anybody* who will turn out to be, or to have been, the hero of David's life. What is more, the question can even be read as expressing uncertainty about whether anybody ever holds the 'station' (as though it were a publicly recognised title or rank, to which one might aspire) of being 'the hero my own life', in the sense of being the hero of *one's* 'own life'.

All of this is complicated further by the familiar notion that DC is CD: that this is the novel that tells us the most about Dickens as he saw himself; that it is the authorial 'I' (Dickens) who turns out to be the hero of the intradiegetic 'I''s (David's) life. Or does he? Or is that 'station' actually held by a character who is significantly someone other than his creator? Such a nit-picking assault could be prolonged indefinitely, and probably with diminishing returns. But what it boils down to is this: a scepticism about the significance and fullness of self (the character's; the author's; anybody's); and about the status and claims of the individual in relation to the world – whether of events, lives, experiences, texts, or all of these – in which that individual is placed.

The vulnerability of personal placement, in *David Copperfield*, is linked to an idea of travel as a threat. This is perhaps most obvious in the trauma of Little Em'ly's flight from what had seemed the most secure and stable of all possible homes: the ship that paradoxically stays put, the vessel that has already been turned upside down, has weathered the storm, and is still there, just like the various emotionally shipwrecked souls that it contains. But we can see this theme being introduced right at the start of the novel, when the 'old lady with a hand-basket' buys David's caul to protect herself from drowning – although she has no intention of going anywhere near water – and illogically inveighs against the 'meandering' that makes international commerce possible, providing her with tea (ch. 1: 2). Although ostensibly framed, just like the idea of seeing 'ghosts and spirits', as ridiculous, these prejudices receive support very shortly afterwards, when we hear what came of the meanderings of Betsey Trotwood's adventurous husband: 'according to a wild legend in our family, he was once seen riding on an elephant, in company with a Baboon; but I think it must have been a Baboo – or a Begum. Anyhow, from India tidings of his death reached home, within ten years' (ch. 1: 3). The sense of the foreign as farcical, here, should be seen in the context of a withdrawal from the world that Betsey eventually regrets: Baboons, Baboos and Begums have been like donkeys that, for Betsey, did not belong in the post-traumatic

garden of her life; and David, as narrator, may be seen as echoing her
wounded point of view, fleetingly and just for fun. But David speaks from
a more independent position, closer to what we might regard as his core as
a narrator, when he subsequently echoes the old lady with the caul, admit-
ting that his own reflections on the child-like adult could be construed as
'meandering' (ch. 2: 11). This view comes from the grown-up David, the
mind that has been formed, we are to understand, by everything described
in these pages. The echo points to a connection in the novel between, on
the one hand, questions of personal identity or ontology – Is David weak
(or perhaps 'undisciplined') to slip away from narrating events, towards
meta-narratorial reflections? Is he weak to obfuscate the distinctions
between being a grown-up or not? – and, on the other, the matter of the
scale, accessibility and navigability of the world as a whole: is it foolish or
dangerous to go physically out and about?[4]

David the character still harbours the idea that travel is ridiculous in
his early manhood, while he is suitor of the homely (in all but looks and
domestic skills) Dora – someone who is absolutely defined by her reluctance to stray, someone for whom China shrinks to the very emblem of
home as comfort, a pagoda for her spaniel (whose name, Jip, perhaps also
tames the unsettling notion of the gypsy). David is abetted in his courtship
by the fanciful Miss Mills. But then her father takes her abroad:

> Mr. Mills, who was always doing something or other to annoy me – or I
> felt as if he were, which was the same thing – had brought his conduct
> to a climax, by taking it into his head that he would go to India. Why
> should he go to India, except to harass me? To be sure he had noth-
> ing to do with any other part of the world, and had a good deal to do
> with that part; being entirely in the India trade, whatever that was (I
> had floating dreams myself concerning golden shawls and elephant's
> teeth); having been at Calcutta in his youth; and designing now to go
> out there again, in the capacity of resident partner. But this was noth-
> ing to me. (ch. 41: 504)

Had all Englishmen been like the young David, it seems, there would not
have been much of an Empire. He does travel later, when he spends three
years wandering on the Continent after Dora's death, but this has to do

---

[4] Contrast this with Robert L. Patten's more positive – and, in its own way,
very persuasive – reading of David's 'meandering' as a discovery of what it takes
to be a writer (1979: 286).

with processing what has happened at home rather than discovering the possibilities of the foreign – and, despite seeing that it works for others, David rejects the solution of emigration.

We can bring David's misgivings about geographical displacement into focus by turning to some of Dickens's non-fiction prose from this period; for example, his 1848 review of Capt. William Allen's *Narrative of the Expedition Sent by Her Majesty's Government to the River Niger in 1841*. The book in question vividly recounts a project combining commercial, religious and philanthropic ambitions, sponsored by the Society for the Extinction of the Slave Trade and for the Civilisation of Africa – a project that ended in chaos and the death, through disease, of most of its participants. Dickens's review was praised by Humphrey House, writing in the blood-streaked sunset of Empire, for 'its vigour, eloquence, and even, in places, enlightenment' (88), and it is true that Dickens does not think that bringing improvement to Africa is intrinsically wrong; what worries him is the scale involved, both in time and space:

> No amount of philanthropy has a right to waste such valuable life as was squandered here, in the teeth of all experience and feasible pretence of hope. Between the civilized European and the barbarous African there is a great gulf set. [. . .] To change the customs even of civilized and educated men, and impress them with new ideas, is – we have good need to know it – a most difficult and slow proceeding; but to do this by ignorant and savage races, is a work which, like the progressive changes of the globe itself, requires a stretch of years that dazzles in the looking at. It is not, we conceive, within the likely providence of God, that Christianity shall start on the banks of the Niger, until it shall have overflowed all intervening space. The stone that is dropped into the ocean of ignorance at Exeter Hall, must make its widening circles, one beyond another, until they reach the negro's country in their natural expansion. There is a broad, dark sea between the Strand in London, and the Niger, where those rings are not yet shining; and through all that space they must appear, before the last one breaks upon the shore of Africa. Gently and imperceptibly the widening circle of enlightenment must stretch and stretch, from man to man, from people on to people, until there is a girdle round the earth; but no convulsive effort, or far-off aim, can make the last great outer circle first, and then come home at leisure to trace out the inner one. (Dickens 1994–2000, II: 125)

Dickens continues in the same vein, making the same point with slight variations in the imagery, several times. This imagery is picked up in a recent book on 'mapping the world' in *Household Words*, by Sabine Clemm, who has this to say about Dickens's 1853 article on 'The Noble Savage':

> It is obvious throughout his article that Dickens wants to see 'savages' firmly at the outer edge of the concentric circles that surround the metropolitan centre. Yet their position in this model is precisely what is at stake in this article. What irks Dickens most and provokes him into writing this article in the first place is the 'drawing of any comparison of advantage between the blemishes of civilisation and the tenor of [the savage's] swinish life'. The suggestion that 'savage' life may be equal or even superior in some respects to 'civilisation' forces together the core and furthest periphery of the concentric circles that structure *Household Words*' view of the world, and threatens to unhinge this order completely. (161)

However, one of the most interesting paradoxes about Dickens is that this process of excluding the 'savage', which Clemm is no doubt right in detecting, is subverted by his very strong tendency to unveil the savage (foreign, disorderly, uncivilised, anarchic) 'at home', both through defamiliarisation of the physical land- and cityscape (in the anthropomorphisation of buildings and machines, for example) and through his presentation of sociopathic characters like Heep, Fagin or Orlick; or morally opaque ones like Tulkinghorn or Silas Wegg; or seemingly impervious hypocrites like Chester or Pecksniff; or demonically angry characters like Rosa Dartle or Bradley Headstone; or even 'straight', basically civilised and amiable characters, like David, who have 'a broad, dark sea' somewhere within them.

Dickens's exposure of the savage 'at home' is like his exploration of the things that cannot be processed and assimilated in an individual consciousness or selfhood, and opens up frightening prospects. As Clemm says, the orderly structuring of the world around England (or an Englishman), in *Household Words*, 'is not natural . . . but has to be maintained by a sustained conscious effort, as its individual components all have the potential to subvert and undermine it. *Household Words*' failure to offer a positive definition of Englishness opens the door to the possibility that the term may not actually mean anything' (162). This is like David Copperfield, trying to be the hero of his own life – and only achieving this, if at all, through the structure imposed by writing.

The fact of being in a particular place in the world (instead of being somewhere else) often struck Dickens as funny. He makes much, for example, of the drama involved in getting across the disruptive and dangerous obstacle of the English Channel, only to find oneself in another country that is, in important respects, much like one's own. The Channel is arbitrary, unnecessary: a kind of joke.[5] In *David Copperfield*, having a connection to a particular spot, even in England, often seems to make David laugh. This is his attitude to Traddles's patient attachment to Sophy, who is not only 'a curate's daughter' and 'the dearest girl', but, more idiosyncratically, 'one of ten, down in Devonshire'. This phrase is repeated four times,[6] the repetition insisting that it is somehow a joke, in the way that a comedian's banal catchphrase eventually becomes pathetic, touching and funny, because – at the end of the day – that's all they've got. It is as though David finds humour in the idea of being *someone specific*, with a clearly defined geographical and familial context. It is ostensibly Traddles himself who keeps characterising Sophy in these formulaic terms, but it is David who notices this as Traddles's verbal tic, and that in turn becomes linked to David's temptation to think of Traddles's romance as an essentially comic one – beneath his own ideal, timeless, universal attachment to the perfect Dora. The five subsequent occurrences of 'Devonshire', towards the end of the novel – with 'David' ventriloquising a self that is close to the 'David' who we are to understand has finally committed this narrative to print – are progressively less formulaic.[7] But similar points could be made about the impersonal narrator's fixation, in *Bleak House*, with Vholes's references to his father 'in the Vale of Taunton'.[8] Not to suggest that Vholes is like Traddles. Vholes could be said to be an innocently wicked lawyer (morally dessicated as he is, he really seems to know not what he doth), while Traddles is an innocently good one (never dreaming of what a deserving soul he is); but there is this naivety about place, in both of them, that expresses itself with similar comic results.

The opposite in *David Copperfield* to being comically attached to one particular spot on earth, no better or worse than millions of others, is to be fixated on the vision of an ideal place, which may ultimately equate with death. We see a version of this when David meets Ham and Mr

[5] See Rainsford 2002: 67.
[6] Dickens 1981, ch. 27: 346; ch. 28: 366; ch. 34: 420 (with a minor variation in the word-order); and ch. 41: 577.
[7] Dickens 1981, ch. 59: 705, 707, 709 and 710; and ch. 61: 724.
[8] Dickens 1977, ch. 37: 470, ch. 39: 482, 483 and 484; ch. 45: 541; and ch. 51: 608.

Peggotty on the beach, on the morning after Em'ly's defection: 'they were both as grave and steady as the sea itself: then lying beneath a dark sky, waveless – yet with a heavy roll upon it, as if it breathed in its rest – and touched, on the horizon, with a strip of silvery light from the unseen sun' (Dickens 1981, ch. 32: 389). Ham is still looking at the 'strip of silvery light' much later in the narrative (ch. 51: 631), the last time David sees him before his heroic death / wilful self-destruction. Later, David notices a similar fixation in the eyes of Rosa Dartle and Mrs Steerforth, who seem to be mesmerised by the same conjunction of time and space as Ham – the double death, the mutual cancelling out of tragic antagonists, leaving nothing behind – although for them, of course, with their arrogant and idolatrous family structure, it is only Steerforth's death that counts: 'As I moved away from them along the terrace, I could not help observing how steadily they both sat gazing on the prospect, and how it thickened and closed around them' (ch. 46: 575). And then David himself seems about to fall into a similar gaze-of-no-return, fixated on death conceived of as geographical location, the 'frozen region yet unseen' that he senses as Dora's end approaches (ch. 48: 597).

So, Dickens, through David, seems to express a certain alienation from *both* the acceptance of a simple, ordinary spot on Earth *and* gazing out, telescopically, towards some distant absolute. It is not that he is systematic about this. On the contrary, *David Copperfield* seems to dramatise unresolved misgivings about what to believe in, and where to invest our hopes.[9] Sometimes, salvation seems to lie in a redeeming singularity; not just one in ten (like the 'dearest girl' of Traddles's modest expectations), but one in 'a thousand', as in the spectacle of Mr Dick, walking back and forth with Dr Strong, 'by the hour', in a physical space apparently limited to one side of a courtyard: 'one of the pleasantest things, in a quiet way, that I have ever seen. I feel as if they might go walking to and fro for ever, and the world might somehow be the better for it – as if a thousand things it makes a noise about, were not one-half so good for it, or me' (ch. 17: 216). Dick's and Strong's confined rhythmical movement, here, is like a clock ticking, or a heart beating: as though they were managing time, or sustaining life, for the rest of us. The further a character travels from this sort of simple equilibrium, the more danger there will be. Betsey Trotwood

---

[9]   Malcolm Andrews is particularly good on David's failure to resolve himself through autobiography (1994: 169–71).

'would trust herself [. . .] in no such place' as a Court of Law, regarding them 'as a sort of powder-mills that might blow up at any time' (ch. 23: 300); and Em'ly takes us as far as Dickens felt able to go into the destruction of body and mind that awaits anybody who strays – physically as well as morally – too far.

Em'ly is more or less saved, in the end. But many are not, especially in the real world acknowledged in Dickens's essays: 'We would fain hope', he writes, that the achievements of Drs McWilliam and Stanger, heroes of the Niger expedition, 'would live . . . when the desperate and cruel of whole generations of the world shall have fallen into oblivion' (1994–2000, II: 123). These men are, in their own way, in extreme circumstances, like Mr Dick: redeeming instances of survival with decency intact, while so many others fall 'into oblivion'. There are 'the desperate and cruel' in the form of unredeemed 'savages' in Africa, not yet ready for the ripples from Exeter Hall to irrigate their souls, but there are also 'the desperate and cruel' at home, the Heeps and Murdstones, who are beyond reach, and must be escaped, circumvented or locked up: not real people but more like masked figures, driven by generic lusts, although they walk among us and may try to pass themselves off as being our friends (Heep) or as knowing better than we do (Murdstone) what we need.

Dickens can see the same types, wherever in the world he directs his attention. He can see the 'simple fellow' in his most sophisticated characters and quasi-authorial narrators, as well as in a comic type like Kit Nubbles,[10] and he can see the personified negation of all that he implicitly hopes for, both on a distant continent and immediately here and now. This is related to the power of Dickens's metaphors, breeching normal categories and boundaries. It is the mixture of radical openness and extremely strong views that makes Dickens what he is.

As John Jordan and others have noted, sympathy for Dickensian narratives of self-realisation is intercontinental.[11] Developing-world interest in Dickens can take the form of profound identification, as in these words of a young man in Burma: 'I am living in a Dickens atmosphere. Our country is at least one or two centuries behind the Western world. My neighborhood – bleak, poor, with small domestic industries, children

---

10   Dickens 1997, ch. 61: 470. See Rainsford 2012.
11   Jordan 1999 and 2009. See also Vegh.

playing in the street, the parents are fighting with each other, some are
with great debt, everyone is dirty. That is Dickens.'[12] But this can lead
to strange inversions of telescopic philanthropy – with the supposition,
not that the big problems only exist abroad (as per Mrs Jellyby), but that,
now, they only exist *here*: 'In the great cities of the West, the standard
of living is too high, public life too rationalized [. . .]. Modernity and the
welfare state did away with the naked sympathies and tragic destines of
the late-nineteenth-century novel' (Packer 2010: 3). More subtly, 'global
Dickens' can be seen as part of a vital reconfiguration of balance, scale
and discursive power between different parts of the present-day world.[13]

But Dickens needs to be used with caution. He was interested in the
facts of geography and the processes of travel, but less so in the specific
structures of international politics. All places are one for him, to the extent
that all characters have their own internal geography – or sometimes anti-
geography, as in the grieving David's displaced, out-of-his-skin experience of 'the void which somewhere seemed to be about me' (Dickens
1981, ch. 44: 552).[14] Later, when David thinks of his travels in Europe,
he sees himself 'passing on among the novelties of foreign towns, palaces,
cathedrals, temples, pictures, castles, tombs, fantastic streets – the old
abiding places of History and Fancy – as a dreamer might; bearing my
painful load through all, and hardly conscious of the objects as they fade
before me' (ch. 58: 697). Left behind with the dead (his mother, Dora,
Steerforth, Ham), thinking he has lost the possibility of being with Agnes,
he is stuck in 'the shifting quicksands of my mind' (ch. 58: 701). Africa is
now and England.[15]

Dickens can be read, at times, as an upholder of certain ideas of Englishness, of civilisation, of an orderly self constructed through pain and

[12]   Quoted in Packer 2010, 1. The young man calls himself 'Somerset', after
another of his favourite English writers.
[13]   See, for example, Cheadle, Cordery, the editor's introduction to Jacobson
(1-11), and Chennells 2010.
[14]   Compare poor Mrs Gradgrind, with her pain 'somewhere in the room'
(Dickens 2001, book 2, ch. 9: 151).
[15]   See Jennifer Gribble's discussion of the moral and psychological similarities
between Mrs Jellyby and John Jarndyce, and the relationship between Jarndyce's
own Bleak House and the one in which he installs Esther and Woodcourt: 'The
apparent pastoral of the happy ending shows the new world founded on the
unacknowledged and irresolvable feelings of the old' (98). It is as though Jarndyce
commits the errors and crimes of colonialism *within England*.

endurance, and these ideas can be turned upside-down so as to restore the balance or do justice to the other. Dickens can also be read as radically undermining complacency about the immediate English Victorian world, in a way that might make one want to throw in one's lot with the Micawbers and Mr. Peggotty, and flee. But the strongest impression that his texts provide is perhaps that fleeing would be as futile for any of us as for Milton's Satan, who carries his hell within him. Any place in the Dickensian world can reveal itself to be a provisional and vulnerable structure. As Jordan remarks, Dickens makes himself felt in the 'Anglophone diaspora of the former British Empire' as 'at once a sign of conventional Englishness and a source of its potential deconstruction' (1999: 239, 242). Or, as Bodenheimer puts it, Dickens 'was deeply suspicious of other cultures, but he expressed his racism through the fear of being duped' (209): in other words, there is always an intimate connection between the experience of foreignness and other conflicts and difficulties that can crop up anywhere, not least at home.[16] Dickens is not unique in this respect – indeed a highly flexible mapping of home and away, centre and periphery, safety and risk may be essential to the workings of the western capitalist economy – but that just makes Dickens's embodiment of these concerns all the more important.[17]

One of the young David Copperfield's most memorable experiences, among all of the familial and domestic turmoil, is one of geographical and topographical astonishment – through which the inner world of emotion and self-perception nevertheless shines through:

> We made so many deviations [. . .] that I was quite tired, and very glad, when we saw Yarmouth. It looked rather spongy and soppy, I thought, as I carried my eye over the great dull waste that lay across the river; and I could not help wondering, if the world were really as round as my geography-book said, how any part of it came to be so flat. But I reflected that Yarmouth might be situated at one of the poles; which would account for it.
> As we drew a little nearer, and saw the whole adjacent prospect lying a straight low line under the sky, I hinted to Peggotty that a mound or so might have improved it; and also that if the land had been a little more separated from the sea, and the town and tide had not been quite

---

[16]   See also Buzard, on 'travelling' and 'dwelling' in Dickens (116).
[17]   See Soja 157, and Freedgood 169.

so much mixed up, like toast-and-water, it would have been nicer. But Peggotty said, with greater emphasis than usual, that we must take things as we found them, and that, for her part, she was proud to call herself a Yarmouth Bloater. (Dickens 1981, ch. 3: 24)

Yarmouth really does seem to have struck Dickens as exceptional, 'the strangest place in the wide world', as he remarks to Forster in January 1849 (Dickens 1965–2002, V: 474). Grown-up Dickens, like David the narrator (rueful but loving chronicler of his younger self) knows that Yarmouth is not 'at one of the poles' in an objective, scientific sense; but they also know that each individual's world has its own axis, its own tilt, its own flatlands and pinnacles. Along with his 'crocodile book' (characteristically embodying both the fearfully outlandish and the comfortingly familiar – like Traddles's skeletons) and the lifetime projects of Dr Strong (the Dictionary) and Mr Dick (the Memorial), little David's geography book is both a vehicle and symbol of self-location, to be set alongside the novel itself – conceived as David's work or Dickens's. It is not that we should refrain from making analyses and judgements of Dickens's relationships with the real geo-politics of his time (or ours); on the contrary, his sustained popularity over nearly two centuries makes him internationally significant not just as a writer but also as a commodity and even a weapon (in the sense of an instrument of 'soft power'). But I would argue that the best studies of Dickens's real-world reach will be shadowed by his dissections of personal geography; and the best studies of his ideas of nationhood and race by his depictions of individual self-construction and placement, wherever it occurs. Peggotty's 'Yarmouth Bloater' is an extreme version of the absurdity – as David/Dickens seems to see it – of settling for a specific place, and, with it, a role, an identity, a destiny. And David is indeed both hero and 'simple fellow'; both 'Yarmouth Bloater' and type of the world-bestriding artist.

Works cited

Andrews, Malcolm, 1994. *Dickens and the Grown-up Child*. Basingstoke: Macmillan.

Bodenheimer, Rosemarie, 2007. *Knowing Dickens*. Ithaca: Cornell University Press.

Buzard, James, 1999. '"Anywhere's Nowhere": Dickens on the Move', in *Dickens, Europe and the New Worlds*, ed. Anny Sadrin. Basingstoke: Macmillan, pp. 113–27.

Cheadle, Brian, 1999. 'Despatched to the Periphery: The Changing Play of Centre and Periphery in Dickens's Work', in *Dickens, Europe and the New Worlds*, ed. Anny Sadrin. Basingstoke: Macmillan, pp. 100–12.

Chennells, Anthony, 2010. 'Savages and Settlers in Dickens: Reading Multiple Centres', in *Dickens and the Children of Empire*, ed. Wendy Jacobson. Basingstoke: Palgrave, pp. 153–72.

Clemm, Sabine, 2009. *Dickens, Journalism, and Nationhood: Mapping the World in 'Household Words'*. New York: Routledge.

Cordery, Lindsey, 2005. 'Dickens in Latin America: Borioboola-Gha Revisited', *Dickens Studies Annual*, 36: 355–61.

Dickens, Charles, 1965–2002. *The Letters of Charles Dickens*, ed. Madeline House *et al.* The Pilgrim Edition. 12 vols. Oxford: Clarendon.

Dickens, Charles, 1977. *Bleak House*, ed. George Ford and Sylvère Monod. Norton Critical Edition. New York: Norton.

Dickens, Charles, 1981. *David Copperfield*, ed. Nina Burgis. The Clarendon Dickens. Oxford: Clarendon.

Dickens, Charles, 1994–2000. *Dickens' Journalism*, ed. Michael Slater. 4 vols. London: Dent.

Dickens, Charles, 1997. *Our Mutual Friend*, ed. Adrian Poole. Harmondsworth: Penguin.

Dickens, Charles, 2001. *Hard Times*, ed. Fred Kaplan and Sylvère Monod. Norton Critical Edition. 3rd edn. New York: Norton.

Eliot, George, 1986. *Middlemarch*, ed. David Carroll. The Clarendon Edition of the Novels of George Eliot. Oxford: Clarendon.

Freedgood, Elaine, 2000. *Victorian Writing about Risk: Imagining a Safe England in a Dangerous World*. Cambridge: Cambridge University Press.

House, Humphry, 1942. *The Dickens World*. 2nd edn. London: Oxford University Press.

Gribble, Jennifer, 1999. 'Borrioboola-Gha: Dickens, John Jarndyce and the Heart of Darkness', in *Dickens, Europe and the New Worlds*, ed. Anny Sadrin. Basingstoke: Macmillan, pp. 90–9.

Jacobson, Wendy S., ed., 2010. *Dickens and the Children of Empire*. Basingstoke: Palgrave.

John, Juliet, 2001. *Dickens's Villains: Melodrama, Character, Popular Culture*. Oxford: Oxford University Press.

Jordan, John O., 1999. 'Dickens and Diaspora', in *Dickens, Europe and the New Worlds*, ed. Anny Sadrin. Basingstoke: Macmillan, pp. 239–50.

Jordan, John O., 2009. 'Global Dickens'. *Literature Compass*, 6: 1211–23; <http://onlinelibrary.wiley.com/doi/10.1111/j.1741-4113.2009.00664.x/full>.

Moore, Grace, 2004. *Dickens and Empire: Discourses of Class, Race and Colonialism in the Works of Charles Dickens*. Aldershot: Ashgate.

Packer, George, 2010. 'Dickens in Lagos'. *Lapham's Quarterly* (Fall). <http://www.laphamsquarterly.org>.

Patten, Robert L., 1979. 'Autobiography into Autobiography: The Evolution of *David Copperfield*', in *Approaches to Victorian Autobiography*, ed. George P. Landow. Athens, OH: Ohio University Press, pp. 269–91.

Rainsford, Dominic, 2002. *Literature, Identity and the English Channel: Narrow Seas Expanded*. Basingstoke: Palgrave.

Rainsford, Dominic, 2010. 'Victorian Moral Philosophy and *Our Mutual Friend*', *Dickens Quarterly*, 27: 273–91.

Rainsford, Dominic, 2012. '"Sentimental": Since the Death of Little Nell', in *Dickens and the New Millennium*, ed. Nathalie Vanfasse *et al.*, *Cahiers Victoriens et Édouardiens*, pp. 131–43.

Sadrin, Anny, ed., 1999. *Dickens, Europe and the New Worlds*. Basingstoke: Macmillan.

Soja, Edward W., 1989. *Postmodern Geographies: The Reassertion of Space in Critical Social Theory*. London: Verso.

Vegh, Beatiz, 2005. 'Dickens in Latin America: Views from Montevideo', *Dickens Studies Annual*, 36: 265–71.

Afterword: The 2012 bicentenary

FLORIAN SCHWEIZER

'I am sure that a man, a hundred years hence, should [he] sit down to write the history of our time, would do wrong to put that great contemporary history of *Pickwick* aside as a frivolous work.' (W. M. Thackeray, *The Paris Sketch Book*, 1840)

'It seems to be a national benefit, and to every man or woman who reads it a personal kindness.' (W. M. Thackeray [on *A Christmas Carol*], 'A Box of Novels', *Fraser's Magazine*, February 1844)

'There is no writing against this. One hasn't an atom of chance.' (W. M. Thackeray on *Dombey and Son*, quoted in George Hodder, *Memories of My Time* (London, 1870), 277)

IN THE CONTEXT OF THE BICENTENNIAL CELEBRATIONS for the author of *The Pickwick Papers* and *A Christmas Carol*, William Makepeace Thackeray's immediate observations on the longevity and impact of Charles Dickens's stories take on a prophetic quality: Dickens's works are far from being considered frivolous, *A Christmas Carol* has proved to be an international benefit (not least in a commercial sense), and it would seem that no other Victorian writer was able to take on the challenge to 'write against' Boz.

Writing this essay in 2011 – the bicentenary year of Thackeray's birth – I should be astonished at the lack of public interest in the author of *Vanity Fair*, who, after all, is considered by some second only to Dickens among the great Victorian writers. There have been a number of events in his honour, but somehow this escaped the attention of the general public.

And yet, I am not astonished all. Among nineteenth-century authors (and, for that matter, actors, editors, philanthropists, social campaigners), it seems that only Charles Dickens has maintained, if not increased, his hold on the public imagination. It may be unkind to draw a direct comparison between these two authors (not least because their professional rivalry has been discussed ad infinitum), but it indicates the quantum leap in popularity that sets Dickens apart from his contemporaries, or even from most English writers of other eras: the tercentenary of Dr Samuel Johnson in 2009, for example, attracted a respectable amount of recognition, but it did not stimulate a comparable level of interest.

In the run up to the bicentenary of Dickens's birth we have witnessed the on-going – even increasing – mutation/transformation of his love affair with the public during his lifetime into a multi-faceted cultural – or cultic – engagement with his heritage. What exactly makes up and shapes this unique relationship between the author and his twenty-first-century audiences is as fascinating as it is complex, and the dynamics are constantly shifting – will the bicentenary be seen as a public relations bubble created by the media, a commercial cash cow for clever product developers, a legacy-building celebration of Dickens heritage or simply a reconnection of Dickens with his readers at all levels?

If commercialised celebratory elements were prevalent even during the 1912 centenary, how will the bicentenary in 2012 strike the balance between its not-for-profit heritage objectives and the financial requirements that arise from an ambitious global programme of activities? There is no way of foretelling what the impact of the campaign will be – would that Thackeray could tell us how, in a hundred years' time, people will look back on the 2012 bicentenary.

The assessment of impact requires a set of pre-defined targets and objectives, a methodology for measuring success. How many visitors will attend exhibitions? What learning outcomes have been met? Which new audiences have been reached? These are some of the queries put to all professionals in the Dickens heritage industry, and yet, I believe, these are the very questions Dickens himself would have considered Gradgrindian in nature and effect. If we have to deliver facts and achieve targets, how can art and heritage specialists create programmes inspired by Dickens without limiting the pure enjoyment of cultural activity? And are these queries not diverting attention from the question we should ask ourselves: why are we commemorating Dickens, what is our connection with this quintessentially Victorian writer, and what is it about Dickens that still appeals to people around the world?

Some of the issues raised in this introduction have been at the forefront of my mind since 2007 when I first started planning Dickens 2012 and embarked on a journey of discovery of the Dickens heritage and legacy in the early twenty-first century. Now it strikes me that in order to deliver the 2012 campaign I have had to challenge constantly the validity and value of celebrating Dickens. Whether in grant applications, discussions around new project partnerships or the commissioning of new works, thinking around the question 'Why Dickens?' has been paramount in the work I have been doing; and I am not the only one who has approached Dickens in this way. In this essay I outline how the bicentennial programme was 'curated' to be more than simply a year-long Dickens festival of activities. It reveals the drivers behind the public programmes as being rooted deeply in Dickens's own understanding of culture and social responsibility. And it will, in a rather un-Gradgrindian way, provide a tool for evaluating the bicentenary against the vision and intentions that motivated the heritage sector to stage Dickens 2012.

Vision

From the beginning of the campaign Dickens 2012 contained three key vision components: culture, learning and charity. Broadly speaking, these were Dickens's own drivers as a writer, campaigner and philanthropist, so developing a vision around these elements seemed the safe thing to do, especially for an author whose recorded attitude towards posthumous recognition has proved to be controversial.[1] The culture component is eminently suitable given Dickens's contribution to world literature, directly through his writing and acting as well as indirectly through the adaptations and his influence on other creative minds. The promotion of and access to learning were clearly embedded in Dickens's actions and thoughts, so placing education at the centre of Dickens 2012 seemed an appropriate approach to connect people with Dickens. Finally, the author's charitable work has created a legacy that is not widely acknowledged and yet benefits the lives of thousands of people every year; charities set up, supported and managed by Dickens continue to thrive, and his ideas and sense of social responsibility inspire many new initiatives. By combining these components, Dickens 2012 clearly identified areas of

---

[1]   At the time of writing this essay, there were plans for three statues or memorial to be erected in the bicentennial year, rekindling the discussion around the interpretations of Dickens's will. See also Juliet John's chapter in the present volume.

work and activity that informed our programming, focusing the creative agenda for the bicentenary year with a view to building and preserving his legacy.

Central to the Dickens 2012 project was a focus on the younger Dickens. Challenging the existing iconic and widely recognised image of the 'bearded Victorian', the ambition was not to replace notions but to enhance and enrich the idea of Dickens the author. The lead image of Dickens 2012 is an engraving of the Nickleby portrait by Daniel Maclise, owned by Tate Britain and on display at the National Portrait Gallery (Figure 10.1). Showing Dickens at the age of 27, it is to many people a new image which may, initially, confuse audiences owing to the unfamiliar appearance; the plan is, however, that the confusion will change to a greater understanding of Dickens the man and writer, who developed alongside his contemporaries from a late Regency dandified youth to the eminent and established figurehead of the age. One of the benefits of promoting a younger Dickens is his function as role model to younger writers and artists; considering that Dickens became the world's most famous writer before he turned thirty and wrote one of the most popular stories ever written at the age of thirty-one, there is clearly potential to inspire young people to pursue their creative writing ambitions.

Stimulating creative activity and generating new contents motivated by engagement with Dickens added another level to the mission of the project. The cross-platform inter-textuality of Dickens and other artists has a long tradition, ranging from the early stage adaptations to the influence of Dickens on later artists such as van Gogh or ground-breaking film directors such as David Lean. Taking inspiration from Dickens is a dynamic and stimulating process that can lead to fantastic new creations, continuing the dialogue with Dickens and the creative sector. Dickens 2012 is committed to promoting new art and working with the creative industries, opening new avenues for reaching new audiences and venues that had previously considered Dickens as 'old-fashioned', 'irrelevant' and 'too traditional'. Breaking through attitudinal barriers, and showing Dickens as a new and emerging artist in the 1830s, have shifted that perception and led to a more open dialogue with new partners, including the British Council and Arts Council England, who have rediscovered Dickens as one of Britain's central creative minds.

As a balancing influence to the promotion of new artistic content and the image of the young Dickens, Dickens heritage activities have increased

Figure 10.1 Daniel Maclise, *Nickleby* portrait of Dickens (1839)
© Charles Dickens Museum

significantly, with funding available to a number of projects, ranging from small-screen film heritage programmes to multi-million-pound redevelopments of heritage sites and archives as well as exhibition programmes based on Dickensian material culture that is kept in collections around the world. Sites in the built environment pertaining to Dickens's life and works were being connected through public trails and new apps, merging heritage with new technologies. The 2012 bicentenary provides curators and programmers with new opportunities to explore Dickens, animating his heritage in three-dimensional models and through user-focused approaches that were unheard of in the 1912 and 1970 centenaries. It is a strong indication of Dickens's standing as a national author that the Heritage Lottery Fund as well as other trusts and foundations have pledged large sums to the restoration and interpretation of the historic assets managed by museums, ensuring that they are secure and protected for the benefit of future generations. With the bicentenary as catalyst, the appreciation of and care for Dickens heritage received a significant boost, strengthening the sector and increasing capacity for the on-going work carried out in museums to make Dickens more accessible.

Using technologies available for the first time for a Dickens anniversary, a large number of projects designed to make museum and library collections more accessible create new opportunities for the academic and education sector. The scope of these projects is as wide as it is deep, generating both new scholarly research tools – such as *Dickens Journals Online* (<http://www.djo.org.uk>) and the digitised holdings of Dickens's manuscript material at the Berg Collection of the New York Public Library – and materials for general users, who can access video interviews with specialists on the world-wide web and a wide range of free online learning resources. And whilst there have been few actual 'breakthrough' discoveries in the research leading up to the bicentenary (in the absence of new evidence), recent research studies have been leading to a better understanding of Dickens's legacy, underpinning the goals of the bicentennial commemoration.

Framework

From its inception in 2007, Dickens 2012 had to plan its activities around a number of external developments that affect the heritage and arts sector, especially in the United Kingdom, but to a lesser extent also in other countries that contribute to the bicentenary. By default, we had to build 'new' concepts such as sustainability, legacy, impact and accessibility into our thinking. What made the planning both more challenging and interesting is the coincidental 'clash' of three major British events in 2012: the bicentenary, Queen Elizabeth's diamond jubilee and the London 2012 Olympic Games, awarded to the United Kingdom in 2005. Especially the latter has had an immense impact on the planning of any other activity based in Britain for the year 2012; not only has public funding been diverted to the 2012 games, it has also influenced the mind-set of people in the arts and heritage. As an event requiring preparations on an epic scale, the sector has been steered towards supporting the Olympics, creating an often narrow approach to culture in 2012: little before or after the four-week competition has been receiving much attention from cultural policy-makers, and even the government's Cultural Olympiad, a movement that was meant to support the arts from 2008 to 2012, was reduced to a short festival ahead of the games. On a slightly smaller scale, the Queen's diamond jubilee marks another international highlight in British history, drawing attention to London only months after the February celebrations of Dickens. The culture sector, and in particular the Dickens 2012 organisations in and around London, has been undecided whether this clash will create more opportunities or problems, but there has been agreement that Dickens 2012 adds to the buzz of 2012 and will stand its ground, staking a claim as a key cultural highlight in the first quarter of the year. One fact is, however, already confirmed: the 2012 celebration of Dickens has been the most carefully engineered centenary, having to work with, around and perhaps even against the historical events taking place in and around London in 2012. In order to achieve this, we have strategic partnerships with the mayor of London for inclusion of Dickens 2012 in the mayoral cultural strategy for London, as well as partnerships with other local-government organisations, such as Portsmouth City Council and Kent County Council, to develop a recognised campaign that has full support at political and planning level.

Planning Dickens 2012

Set up in 2007 by the management committee of the Dickens Fellowship and the board of trustees of the Charles Dickens Museum, Dickens 2012 started as an initiative to build relationships with partner organisations across arts platforms. The bicentenary committee asked me to oversee and coordinate the development of the initiative, a process that started in Genoa at the international Dickens conference at which representatives of some of the core Dickens groups – the Dickens Fellowship, Dickens Society, the Dickens Project and Charles Dickens Museum – met formally for the first time to discuss a coordinated approach to the bicentennial calendar of events, and to plant the first seeds for a scholarly event that would become the most ambitious Dickens conference of 2012, a 'Tale of Four Cities'. Aiming for international recognition and exposure of Dickens 2012, the development of a website and digital strategy was crucial; this was aided by the grant award of the Museum Computer Network in the United States, which invited Dickens 2012 to attend their 2007 conference on digital projects in Chicago, at which the foundation was laid for bicentennial partnerships with the British Library and where the online strategy for the campaign was conceived with a focus on social media, rich digital content and information-sharing between project partners. This was soon implemented with the support of an early 2012 partner, the Worcester Polytechnic Institute, Massachussetts, which researched, designed and developed the first beta site of the <http://www.dickens2012.org> website in early 2008.

Forming and maintaining partnerships can be a challenge, especially if the subject of such partnerships is considered irrelevant and 'unproductive' as a current cultural influence. Early responses to approaches for partnerships were – from a Dickensian perspective – surprisingly negative; organisations such as the British Council, the BBC and the Arts Council, whose remit focuses on contemporary arts, were reluctant to commit any programmes to an author who had been dead for more than 130 years, while institutions such as the Victoria and Albert Museum and the British Library found it difficult to think about Dickens as the 2012 Games started to absorb the attention of national institutions. Consequently, a grass-roots approach was adopted, and partnerships were formed based on Dickens-related connections. One of the most important connections was to come from within the Fellowship: Adrian Wootton, chief executive of FilmLondon and a keen Dickens Fellowship member, expressed an interest in getting involved in the Dickens 2012 campaign with a vision to host a Dickens film retrospective at the British Film Institute and committing his organisation to promote Dickens on film, television and radio through his network. Taking on the media side of Dickens 2012, the Charles Dickens Museum and FilmLondon merged resources to form a more wide-reaching and powerful network that soon attracted partners such as the Museum of Modern Art in New York, the Museum of London and the BBC, as well as funders such as the Heritage Lottery Fund. Through the Fellowship's network Dickens 2012 recruited partners in France, the United States and Australia, spreading the bicentennial spirit further afield.

With the idea of the Dickens bicentenary campaign spreading more widely and quickly, an increasing number of organisations approached Dickens 2012 from 2008 onwards to sign up as stakeholders with projects either confirmed or under development: eligibility factors remained the same as at the beginning, with culture, education and charity at the heart of the campaign, and a not-for-profit policy only. As a result of a careful screening and selection process, Dickens 2012 continued to grow in scope and diversity while brokering new relationships as well as starting up new ones, providing forums for exchange at meetings and briefings. General stakeholder meetings at the British Library (2009) and the British Council (2011) were well attended and encouraged further growth. A joint Dickens logo and brand guidelines were introduced in January 2011, just in time for a public launch of Dickens 2012 on 7 February 2011 at the British Film Institute, Southbank. To improve ease of information flow from Dickens 2012 to the public, activities were divided into four categories: film, television and radio; literature and education; exhibitions and special events; and performance. A short introduction into each of these categories will conclude this essay.

Film, television and radio

Following the announcement that Andrew Davies's adaptation of *Dombey and Son* had been cancelled despite the success of *Bleak House* (2005) and *Little Dorrit* (2008), it seemed that the BBC was going to avoid Dickens drama during the bicentennial year until, early in 2011 and in recognition of an increased demand for Dickens, a whole Dickens season on the BBC was announced as a contribution to the bicentenary. New adaptations of *Great Expectations* and *The Mystery of Edwin Drood* were announced as part of BBC Books Season as well as an adaptation of *The Invisible Woman* for BBC Film. Dickens 2012's Adrian Wootton co-produced a BBC Arena documentary *Dickens on Screen*, while BBC Radio recorded a five-piece adaptation of *Sketches by Boz*, adapted by Michael Eaton, and BBC worldwide commissioned a radio play of *Martin Chuzzlewit* in Mumbai from Indian writer Ayeesha Menon.

But despite a seemingly late start from the BBC, film enthusiasts were never going to be disappointed in 2012: co-curated by Adrian Wootton and Michael Eaton, the British Film Institute, Southbank, put together the most comprehensive season of Dickens on film, television and radio in history, showing some of the earliest adaptations as well as current productions such as the BBC Arena, new film commissions and short films. Elements of the retrospective will be travelling both across the United Kingdom in 2012 as well as to other major film venues such as the Museum of Modern Art, Cinemateque Française in Paris and the Toronto Film Festival. In addition, the British Council will be sending a specially curated film programme around the world. Fostering talent and developing skills were part of Dickens 2012's vision for a sustainable bicentenary, and the work around film led to some extraordinary new schemes to inspire young directors to rediscover Dickens for a new generation. FilmLondon, for example, invited directors for a London-wide initiative to film contemporary Dickensian London in their boroughs; the two winning entries received start-up funding and their films will be premiered at the British Film Institute, Southbank, and form part of the British Council world-tour. In November 2011, Kent County Council submitted an application to the Heritage Lottery Fund to promote film education in schools, using Charles Dickens as a local hero and inspirational figure. In preparation for 2012 are productions from the opposite end of the film-making spectrum with blockbuster productions based on and inspired by Dickens: David Nicholls' adaption of *Great Expectations* (directed by Stephen Wooley) and a film version of *The Invisible Woman* (BBC Films). Both feature films will feature a new face on the Dickens scene – Ralph Fiennes, who is set to play Magwitch, Dickens himself in *The Invisible Woman* as well as possibly narrator for a Dickens documentary.

With such a plethora of recording activity ahead of the bicentenary the reception of Dickens on film will be boosted in an unprecedented concentration of new material, providing both the Dickens heritage sector and academic community with opportunities to assess how Dickens is re-invented and presented to twenty-first-century audiences.

Literature and education

At the very heart of Dickens 2012 is the appreciation of and access to Dickens's works, both fiction and non-fiction. The vast scope of what 'can be done' with his literature is as exciting as it is intimidating: adaptations, workshops, reading groups, reinterpretations, graphic novels, digital formats, readathons, performances, storytelling, apps – Dickens is being re-invented in ways that make him even more accessible than ever before. The grass-roots approach adopted early on in the campaign led to a focus on ensuring that readers of all ages and backgrounds would have access to Dickens, so increasing opportunities to teach Dickens in schools has been a significant component of Dickens 2012's remit: professional development events for teachers, new online learning resources for the classroom, new facilities at museums and heritage sites, and special awards for learning initiatives support the campaign at primary and secondary education stages, enabling teachers to teach Dickens in new and contemporary ways relevant to students. Learning activities have been built into many literary campaigns, such as the City Read events in Portsmouth and London, which use a specially commissioned Dickens 2012 edition of *Oliver Twist* as a set text for reading activities in libraries, book shops and public venues.

In the lead-up to 2012, Dickens has been rediscovered for the learning sector and is increasingly recognised for the wide range of writing he produced beside his novels: his journalism, speeches, reading adaptations and letters are more readily available in print and online. Dickens institutions have responded to this: the British Library, for example, funded the role of a Dickens Learning Programmes Manager at the Charles Dickens Museum for the first time, while the Heritage Lottery Fund is providing resources to the Museum and Portsmouth City Council to deliver more activities for learners. The English Association, one of the earliest Dickens 2012 partners, has organised many events around the bicentenary for teachers, and the Prince's Teaching Institute is hosting a one-day seminar on Dickens in June 2012. Internationally, the British Council launched new online resources for using Dickens's works in formal education for English as foreign language learners through downloadable work sheets, videos and writing challenges that run across fifty countries. A conference in Berlin, featuring A. S. Byatt, David Nicholls and other writers, is one of the international highlight events in 2012. The North Raleigh Branch of the Dickens Fellowship has launched a nationwide reading campaign in the United States, inviting students to submit short video clips of readings from Dickens, excluding novels that are more widely read and thereby promoting Dickens's other works. As a legacy project, the Charles Dickens Museum will open a learning and visitor centre as part of its redevelopment programme 'Great Expectations'.

Literary activities range from privately organised reading groups to major global readathons, from World Book Night events with a Dickens theme to high-profile readings from major actors including Simon Callow, Ralph Fiennes, Miriam Margolyes and Sir Patrick Stewart. Dickens 2012 has partnered with publishers Penguin to support reading activities in widely available editions; in addition, 2011 has seen a significant increase of new editions from other publishers as well, introducing a new aesthetic of Dickens editions designed to appeal to different types of readers; notable is an edition of *Great Expectations* and *A Tale of Two Cities* produced by Penguin for the world's biggest book club run by Oprah Winfrey under the title

'A Date with Charles Dickens'. A number of major literary campaigns, such as the City Reads in London and Portsmouth, aim to introduce Dickens to new generations of readers while enhancing the reading experience of existing Dickens audiences through events and community activities in libraries, archives and other literary venues. A partnership between Booktrust and the Charles Dickens Museum will culminate in the London Reading Dickens campaign, which will run in the autumn of 2012, inviting the public to read Dickens and respond to Dickens's writing at sites of Dickensian interest. In recognition of Dickens's impact on world literature, contemporary writers in the United Kingdom and overseas are getting involved in events commemorating Dickens and are contributing articles on their 'relationship' with Dickens. The *Guardian* takes the lead on their 'Dickens at 200' website with contributions from Philip Pullman, D. J. Taylor, Philip Hensher and many others. New writing on Dickens includes an anthology of poems in Dickens's honour, sketches in Boz's style in a British Council-run global campaign as well as experimental writing from the new Portsmouth poet laureate and the Charles Dickens Museum's writer-in-residence.

Exhibitions

If the number of exhibitions commemorating Dickens and showing the extensive body of his material legacy is an indication of the strength of the Dickens heritage sector there clearly is no need to be concerned about the future of Dickens: in December 2011, at least fourteen exhibitions were either already open to the public or in the advanced planning stages. The first show under the 2012 banner to open its doors to the public was staged in the Pas de Calais at Condette, in the Chateau D'Hardelot; a display exploring both Dickens's life in general as well as his love of France and his weekends on the French coast with Ellen Ternan. Next in line was The Morgan Museum and Library in New York, which launched its 'Dickens at 200' show in September 2011, followed by displays on Dickens in the National Portrait Gallery, the Victoria and Albert Museum and, in early December 2011, the British Library. The main exhibition of 2012 was opened on 7 December 2011 at the Museum of London as 'Dickens and London'; the natural successor to the Victoria and Albert Museum exhibition in 1970, this display curated by Alex Werner combines traditional displays with audio-visuals and animations that set a new standard for the display of literary exhibitions. Displays in Zurich, Paris, Portsmouth,

Oxford, Lowell (Massachusetts), Belfast, at the Watts Gallery in Surrey, the Berg Collection as well as panel and document displays in many other cities are due to open in the course of 2012, opening up public and private collections on an unprecedented scale.

Controversially, the Charles Dickens Museum in London is set to be closed from April to December 2012, and will therefore miss the Jubilee and the 2012 Olympic Games. Due to the availability of project funding for the complete restoration and redevelopment of the Museum in 2012, the decision to close in the bicentenary year was made taking into account three considerations; firstly, the Museum is in need of the investment in the building and collections, and delay might have jeopardised the feasibility of the project; secondly, never before have visitors had such a wide range of Dickensian alternatives, which means that visitors will be able to experience Dickens in other venues throughout the year; and finally, the Museum will set up pop-up sites in south-east England and run outreach programmes, enabling the Museum to have a presence in 2012 outside its historic site.

Special events and performance

The vast range and diversity of Dickens events that fall outside the above categories is staggering: from puppet theatre in Sofia to 'flash mob perform-ance' on the streets of London, from royal receptions to Dickensian hip-hop happenings, the 2012 bicentenary inspires project programmers to truly innovative and thought-provoking concepts for the celebration of The Inimitable. Among the many hundreds of events and other developments are several that stand out and will add a sense of energy and ambition to 2012 to match that of the author himself. Two royal receptions will be held around the date of Dickens's birth, involving the Queen and the Prince of Wales in high-profile activities. On the day of Dickens's birth itself Westminster Abbey will hold a major wreath-laying service, organised by the Charles Dickens Museum, as a public highlight of the Dickens 2012 campaign; readers will include Ralph Fiennes, Claire Tomalin and Mark Dickens, head of the Dickens family, as well as the archbishop of Canterbury and, of course, the dean of Westminster. Later on in the day Southwark Cathedral's bellringers will be ringing a full peal to commemorate an author so closely connected with that borough; the evening will culminate with the official dinner at Mansion House, with readings by Sir Patrick Stewart and presentations of the Royal Mint special Dickens coin to all guests.

The birthday itself will be 'sandwiched' by one of the most ambitious academic conferences ever staged, with four venues en route from Paris to London. As one of the first bicentenary ideas developed in 2007, this conference will explore the meanings of 'Dickensian' as a concept, that seems more relevant in our time than it was in Dickens's. A specially commissioned new play will be performed at the Guildhall in the City of London in February 2012, with Sir Derek Jacobi as Dickens, produced by the Royal Theatrical Fund, a charity set up by Dickens in 1837. This is one of the many events in 2012 that will highlight the very real contribution that Dickens has made as a philanthropist and social campaigner – other charities who will recognise and honour his achievements include NewstrAid (known to Dickens as the Newsvendors' Benevolent and Provident Institution), the Authors' Licencing and Collecting Society, Great Ormond Street Hospital, Barnados, the Foundling Museum, the Royal Society of Arts and the Royal Society of Literature. Events organised by these and many other charities witness to how Dickens's non-literary efforts are now becoming increasingly acknowledged, and how his role in the public imagination has expanded from the novelist who was celebrated in previous centenaries to a man whose faults as a person are outweighed by his qualities as a literary genius, model citizen and eminently inspirational artist whose influence on world culture is celebrated in 2012.

As the concluding essay to a bicentenary volume on Dickens, this Afterword may also be seen as the Preface to the bicentenary year; it will stand as a record of the vision and ambitions for the bicentennial celebration of Charles Dickens. And perhaps it will give future researchers an opportunity to assess and evaluate the impact of the Dickens 2012 bicentenary. In the meantime, Dickens will continue to entertain his audiences.

DICKENS 2012

Index